IMAGES
of America

PERRY

On the cover: **GRANEY FAMILY, C. 1938.** The Graney family sits down to dinner. Standing at back are Florence Graney and her husband, James. James's father, Timothy James Graney (1870–1955), was the former police chief of Perry. The family has been in Perry since Patrick Graney (James's grandfather) emigrated from Ireland in 1855. (Courtesy of Hometown Perry, Iowa.)

IMAGES
of America

PERRY

Pamela J. Jenkins and Martha A. Tanner

ARCADIA
PUBLISHING

ISBN 978-0-7385-6166-0

Published by Arcadia Publishing
Charleston SC, Chicago IL, Portsmouth NH, San Francisco CA

Printed in the United States of America

Library of Congress Catalog Card Number: 2008926399

For all general information contact Arcadia Publishing at:
Telephone 843-853-2070
Fax 843-853-0044
E-mail sales@arcadiapublishing.com
For customer service and orders:
Toll-Free 1-888-313-2665

Visit us on the Internet at www.arcadiapublishing.com

Contents

Acknowledgments

The stories of people's lives are represented in these pages. With care, people told us their stories and lent us their photographs. We have caught only a glimpse of this intricate history, but we want to thank everyone who works to preserve Perry's history and continues to understand how the present is connected to the past.

Of the 15,000 photographs in the collection of Hometown Perry, Iowa, we chose those that told the story of hope and loss. We could not include all photographs or all events, but we hope this book provides a way for the conversation to continue.

All the photographs in this book are from the collection of Hometown Perry, Iowa, with support from the Fullhart-Carnegie Trust. Bill Clark, the former president of Hometown Perry, Iowa, gave us his support at every turn, as did Howard and Roberta Ahmanson, who saw the importance of the work.

This book would not have been possible without the staff that collected, processed, documented, and cared for the photographs. The authors would especially like to thank Linda Reis, who helped build the collection and provided invaluable research assistance for this book. Others whose work is reflected here include Kate Durbin, Katie Edmondson, Janice Fox, Megan Martin, Cherlyn Miner, Erin Trost, and Keith Yanner. We would also like to acknowledge the two previous written histories of Perry: Eugene Hastie's *History of Perry, Iowa* and Marge Patterson's *A Town Called Perry*. And we thank our editors at Arcadia, Ted Gerstle and John Pearson, for their thoughtful work.

INTRODUCTION

Perry's settlers, one of whom was Dutch Henry, homesteaded west of the Raccoon River in 1848. David Bonine, Francis Johnson, and Cornelius McKean also came to Dallas County around this time. John Moore arrived in the Buffalo Grove area in 1849. Seth Dayton and Peter Mowrer arrived about 1855. Jacob Mace arrived in the Buffalo Grove area in 1857.

In 1864, Judge Henry Thornburg and his wife constructed a 14-room house four miles south of Perry on the river. Before 1868, there was nothing to distinguish the present site of Perry from any other piece of prairie farmland. Across Frog Creek about a quarter mile to the west of the present town was the country store kept by D. J. Pattee, and about one and a half miles beyond to the northwest was the Alton post office. By 1867, Alton School opened. Prairie was all around, with an occasional patch of plowed ground and a farmhouse here and there.

In 1868, the Des Moines and Fort Dodge Railroad reached Perry. When the railroad's location was assured and the promise of a state obtained, John and Harvey Willis, who owned adjoining pieces of land, laid out the town in the winter of 1868–1869. In 1869, the first train arrived. The town was founded in the same year and named after Colonel Perry, an official with the Des Moines Valley Railway. The original plat contained about 220 acres, and 5 acres were given to the railway company for its depot grounds in addition to 20 lots south of Willis Avenue. By 1880, the population of Perry was 800.

One way to tell a story of a small town is to list historical events. Instead, this book provides a variety of photographs by theme. These photographs perhaps allow a deeper view of history through people and place. All the photographs in the book come from the collection of Hometown Perry, Iowa. For more than a decade, this museum and research center accumulated photographs in the process of collecting the life stories of the residents of this small town. When Hometown Perry researchers interviewed community residents, they asked if the museum could borrow photographs that were important in their lives. These photographs were scanned and ultimately formed a collection of more than 15,000 images. In these photographs, the larger events of the 19th and 20th centuries are depicted through the ordinary lives of the residents of Perry. There are pictures of events that have a national and international connection, including war, crops on the way to market, chautauqua events, revivals, railroads, meatpacking plants, and the development of schools.

Iowa became a state late in 1846. Perry was settled after the Civil War, and the war was a turning point in the settlement of the state. Many veterans were founders of small communities like Perry. After the Civil War, Perry was created nearly overnight when the railroad decided on its route. On one day, there was no town, but soon after, there was a store, a school, and a church. There were already people living in the area, but the coming of the railroad defined the community then and for many years to come. People came to Perry from everywhere. These plains welcomed them and, not without struggle, nurtured their lives and families for generations.

As author Lewis Atherton points out, the horse provided the day-to-day transportation from farm to town, around town, and sometimes on longer journeys. But it was the railroad that connected these communities to the larger world. The railroad brought goods and equipment, but most importantly, people and knowledge. The railroad took people away to Chicago for a ball game, to Des Moines for a concert, and off to war.

Like many other towns, Perry is defined by how people know each other. Residents of a community know each other's parents and grandparents and every piece of information about them. The residents in Perry that were interviewed had the self-effacing midwestern perspective on their community. One resident said, "We didn't even have a town square, we had a triangle." Perry lost the competition for county seat but still was seen as a thriving community.

Small towns are fragile in the early 21st century, but even in the late 19th century, towns appeared overnight and faded just as quickly. Perry has gone through enormous changes, most of which are glimpsed in these photographs.

In an essay called "Grandma's Backbone, Dougie's Ankles," Gary Comstock argues for the virtue of "little sense," or little stories rather than grand narratives: "We should not try to explain places of little sense. There is no General Theory of Little Places into which each particular Iowa county, farm community, or religious sect can be fit. How do we talk about such places? By telling stories about them, one by one." Here each photograph represents one of the many stories about small-town life.

These photographs do not tell a universal story: places like Perry are filled with the particular stories that cannot be found anywhere else. People came from Ireland, Germany, or England. They came to farm, work the railroad, build a church, and educate themselves and their children. Over generations, this town developed its own unique story that is glimpsed in these photographs. Small towns are made up of little stories that define a lifetime, a generation, and a community.

According to Atherton, small towns in the Midwest are dominated by churches, schools, and home. These institutions are reflected through the photographs in this book, and they still play an integral part in any small town in the Midwest. The variety of work that existed in any small town is also reflected in these photographs. Finally, the photographs show what people lost, including family members, farms, churches, and, in some ways, the community, as it was known. These five themes—family, work, education, faith, and loss—emerged from the community's stories and photographs, and they are the themes around which this book is organized. The photographs selected here represent a slice of midwestern life in Perry told through these themes. This story in pictures is about the people who made up this small town, how they made their lives, their families, and how they worshipped. These photographs tell the story of the town from its beginning until the late 20th century.

In many ways, Perry is like all midwestern towns founded in the 19th century. It is linked to the land surrounding the community. Many writers begin and end with the land as their touchstone in describing the Midwest. While these photographs show the land, it is the people that dominate the landscape.

One

FAMILY

This chapter shows the variety of families that lived in Perry over time. People from many different locations chose to make this community their home. Perry was founded by individuals who, for the most part, had come to the area from other parts of the country. Quickly, however, immigrants from other parts of the world were settling in and around this young community. The story of American immigration can be found in this small town; Germans, Irish, Italians, and central Europeans all came here looking for work and land. Also, Perry has been home to African American families from the beginning of the 20th century to the present day. Each brought with them their traditions and their desire to be part of the American experience.

Many of these families stayed, and now there are residents who represent the fifth generation in the same place. This rootedness is critical to how the community survived through the changes and conflicts of the last 150 years. A characteristic of this rootedness is that communities have a knowledge about families that often goes back for decades. A person meets another on the street of a small town and recognizes that person by their grandparents, parents, and residence.

These families were also connected by experience. Parents and children often went to the same school, even having the same teachers. The sharing of this lived experience over time helped to shape the community. Even when family members left home, they took with them this sense of place and belonging.

Yet these photographs and their interpretation are not just nostalgic or romantic about the past. When new people came to Perry, as they did continuously, there was conflict. Residents joked that they were "still newcomers because they had only lived in Perry 20 years." The most recent immigrants, Hispanics from more than nine countries in Central and Latin America, are working hard to keep their cultures and become part of this small town.

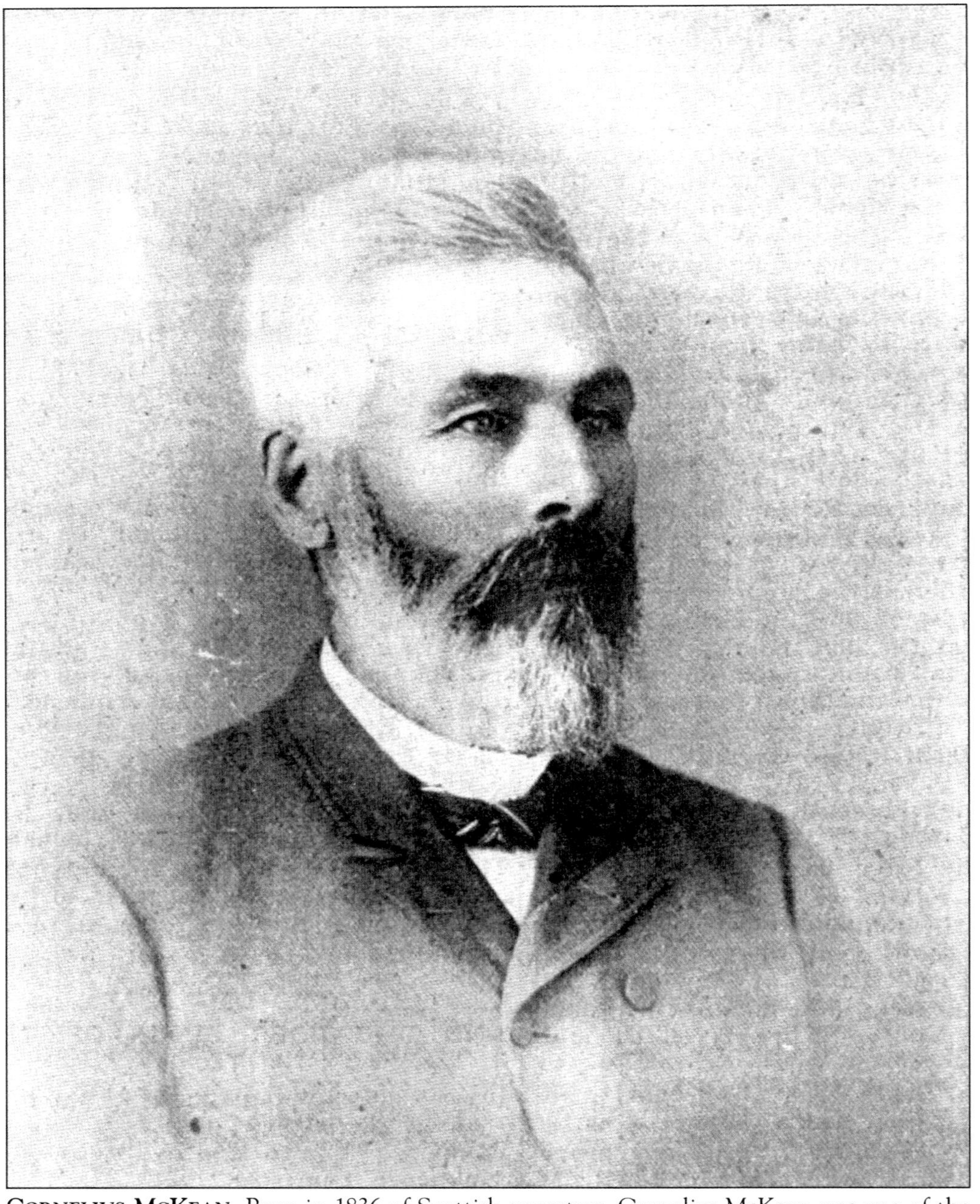

CORNELIUS MCKEAN. Born in 1836 of Scottish ancestors, Cornelius McKean was one of the earliest settlers in the Perry area, arriving in Dallas County from Missouri in 1852. He served as postmaster at Alton, which established its post office in 1857, and was also a justice of the peace, township clerk, and school director at various times. He was injured in a collision with a train in 1907 and died in 1911.

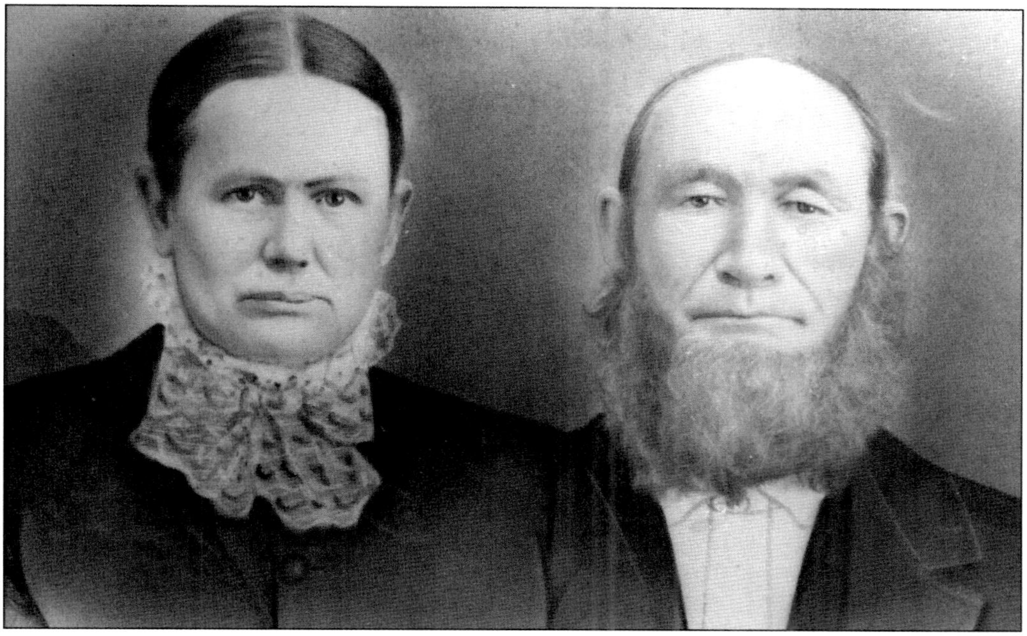

JOHN H. AND MARGARET ROBERTS. John H. Roberts also came to Dallas County before Perry became a town, arriving in 1854. He served in the Civil War and returned to Dallas County in 1865. The Robertses' frame house was situated on land south of Perry. The Spring Valley School was also located on their property.

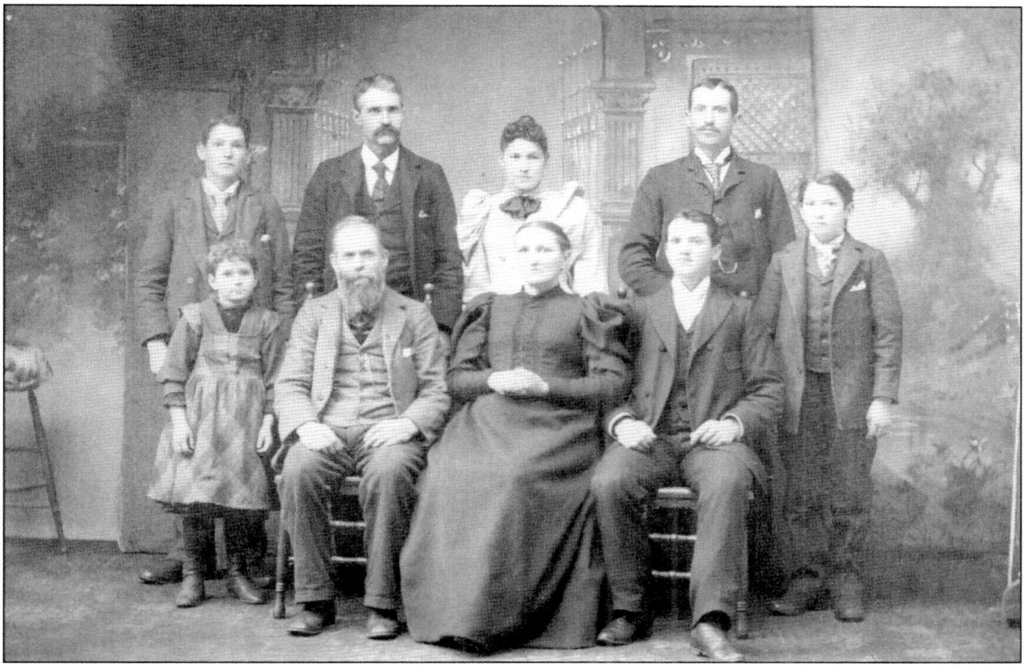

FAMILY OF LEVANT C. AND LUCY DORMAN. Levant C. Dorman, originally from Batavia, New York, came to Perry after serving in the Civil War, fighting in many battles in Virginia. He and his wife, Lucy, moved to the Perry area in 1869.

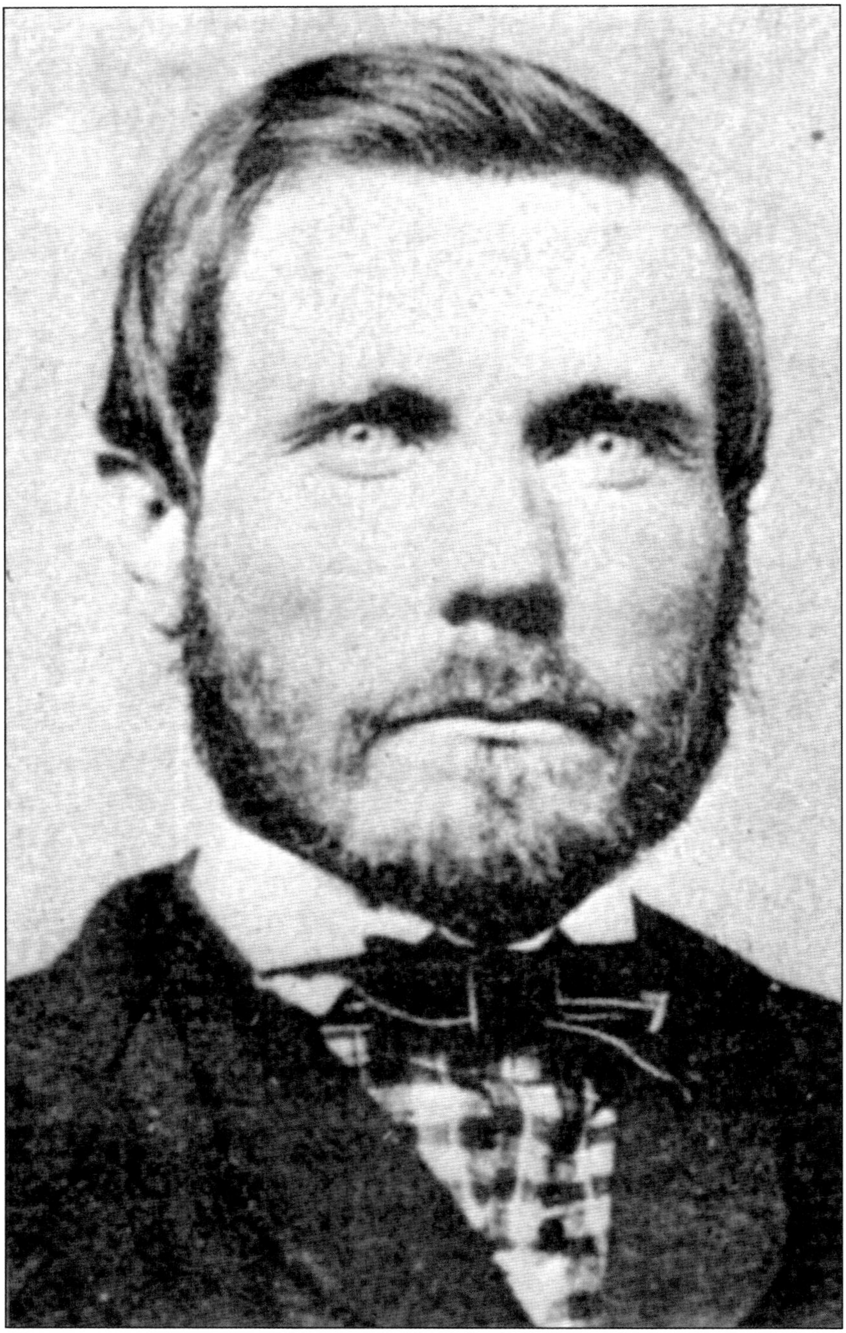

HARVEY WILLIS. A stock dealer born in Indiana, Harvey Willis came to Dallas County around 1859. He and his wife, Eliza, lived in a log cabin for their first 15 years. After buying 240 acres in Perry, Willis sold some of the land to the Des Moines and Fort Dodge Railroad for a right-of-way through town. At one time, Willis operated two sawmills south of Des Moines. One of the main streets in Perry is named for his family. Descendants of Willis called Perry home until the 1990s.

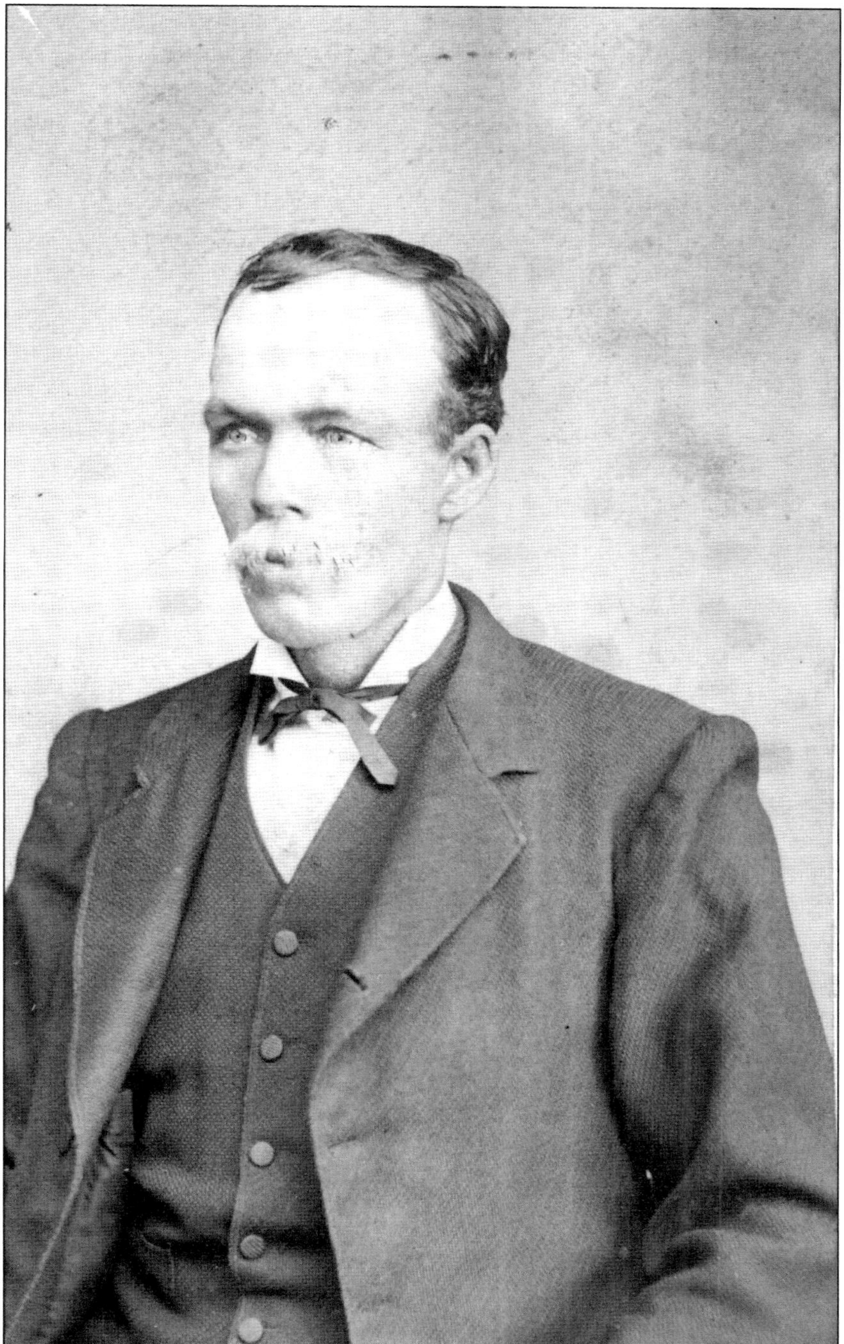

WALTER McTAGGERT. The McTaggert family initially settled in Ohio after emigrating from Scotland. About 1865, after her husband, John, died, Grace McTaggert (Walter's mother) came to settle in the Buffalo Grove area west of Perry. The family moved to land that John had purchased 10 years earlier. Walter, who lived from 1845 to 1925, was a community leader in Lincoln Township.

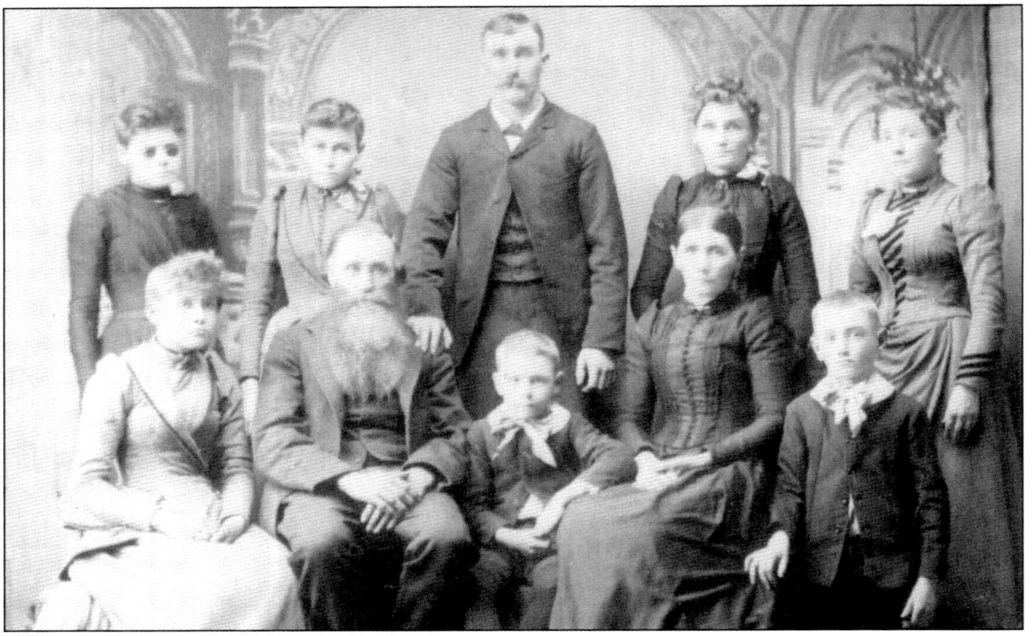

SETH DAYTON AND FAMILY. One of the region's earliest settlers, Seth Dayton moved to the Perry area in 1854. His first wife, Loraine Wilcott, died in 1859, leaving three children. He married Mary Gardiner in 1860 and they had six children. Dayton built a brick house that had a horse racetrack and also served as a stagecoach station. Legend has it that he lost the farm in a horse race.

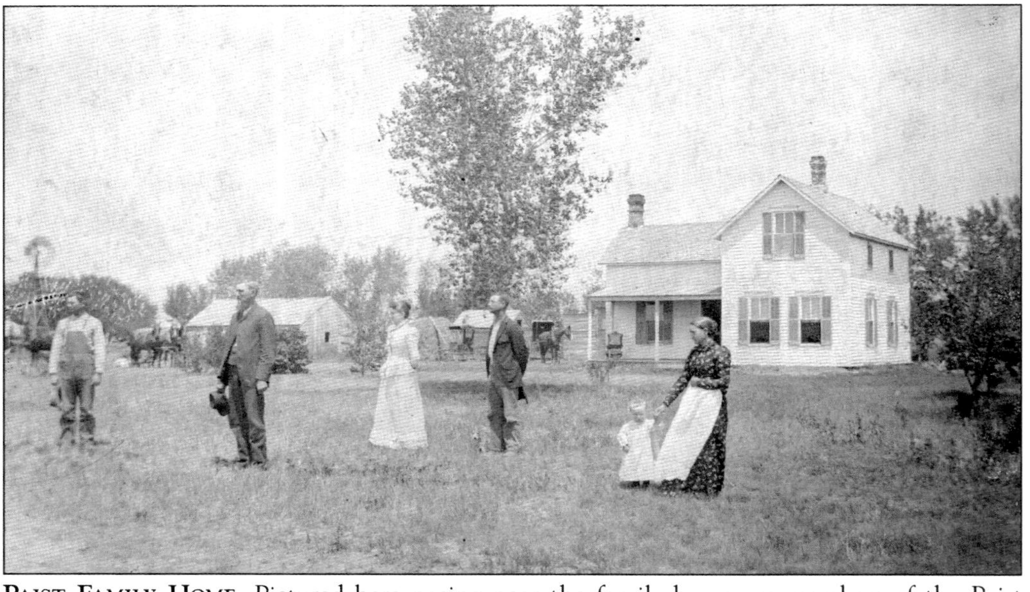

PAIST FAMILY HOME. Pictured here posing near the family home are members of the Paist family, including Louis E. Paist, Lydia Murphy Paist, Lee Paist, and the grandparents Murphy. Louis and Lydia's son Ray worked on the railroad and was killed in a train wreck in Perry in 1921. Although this home was located near Kearney, Nebraska, the family later made its home in Perry.

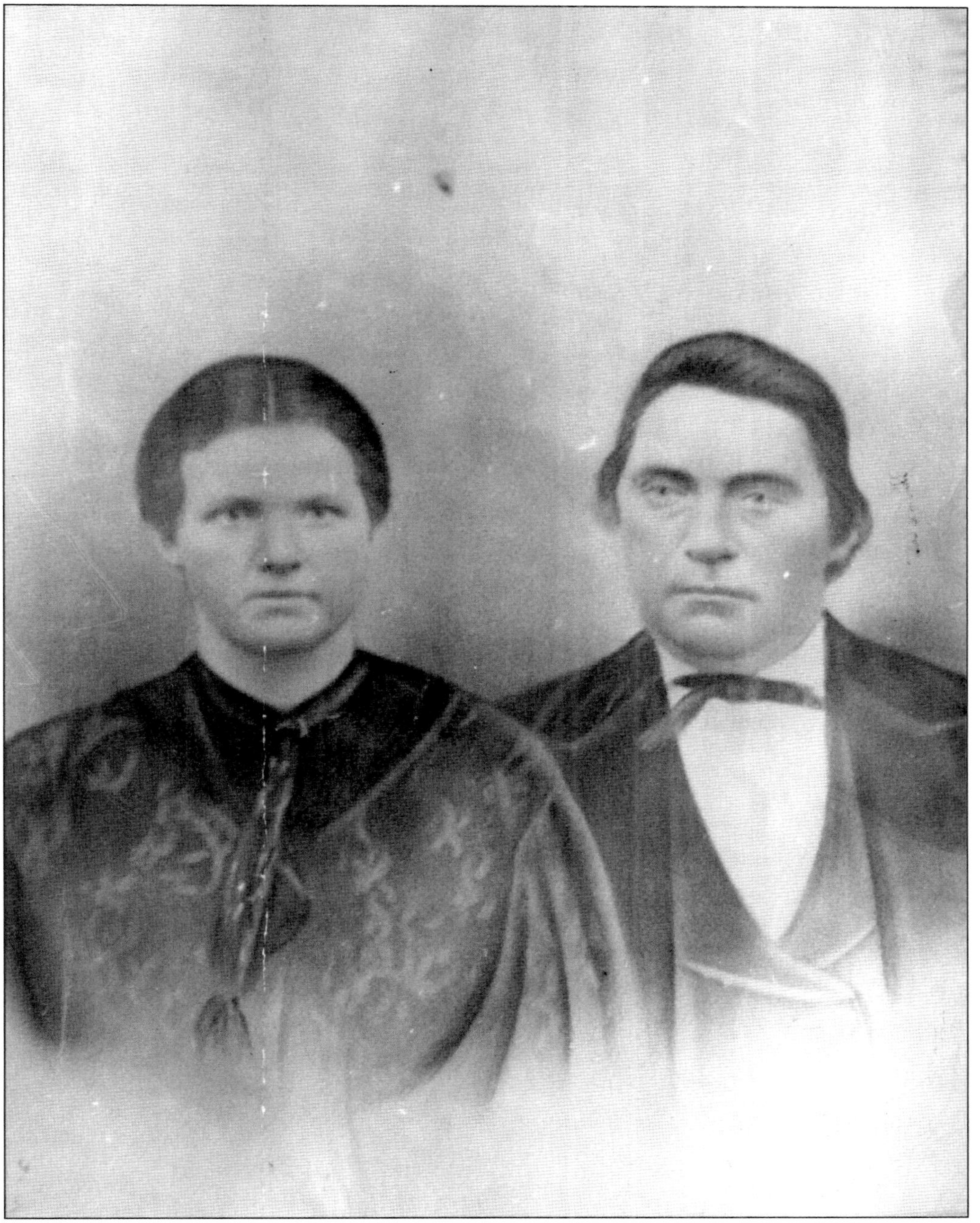

PATRICK D. AND ELIZABETH GREEN MCGOEYE. Patrick D. McGoeye (1859–1920) emigrated from Ireland to the United States in 1861 when he was just two years old. His wife was born in Illinois to Irish immigrant parents. McGoeye worked as a street commissioner then later managed a cement block company in Perry. In 1907, he was described as "high sheriff of the Superior Court in Perry." In 1910, he was employed as a marshal by the City of Perry and continued in that position until 1920. The McGoeyes lived most of their married lives at 1726 North Third Street in Perry.

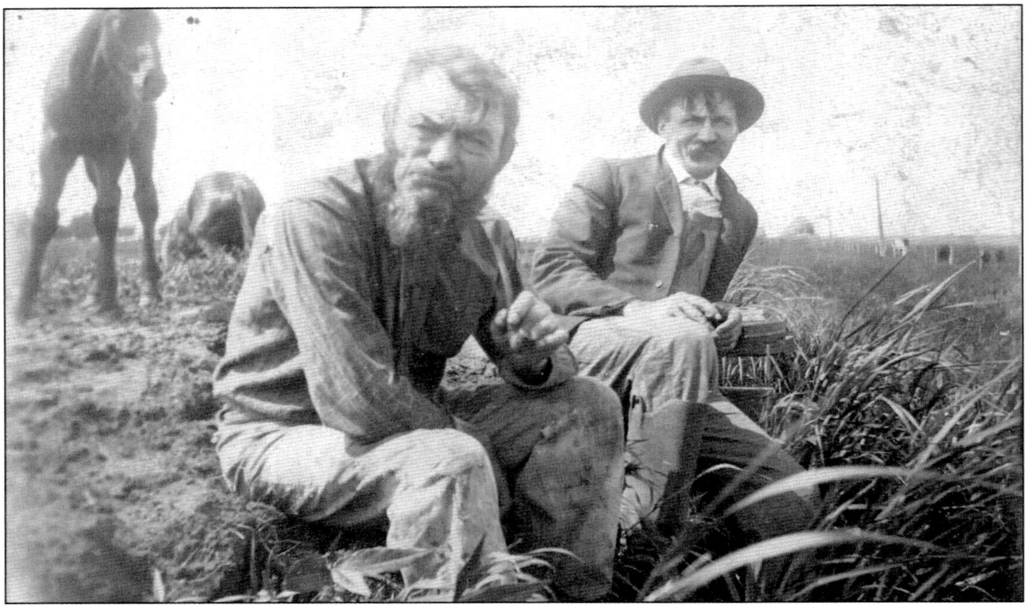

CHARLES AND JACOB HEINZ. As is often true for midwestern communities, Perry was a home for many German families. The Heinz family was among the German settlers in the Perry area. Charles Heinz was born in Saarbrucken, Germany, in 1873 and came to Dallas County with his family 10 years later. The Heinz family farm, south of Dawson, dates to 1881 and is now considered a century farm.

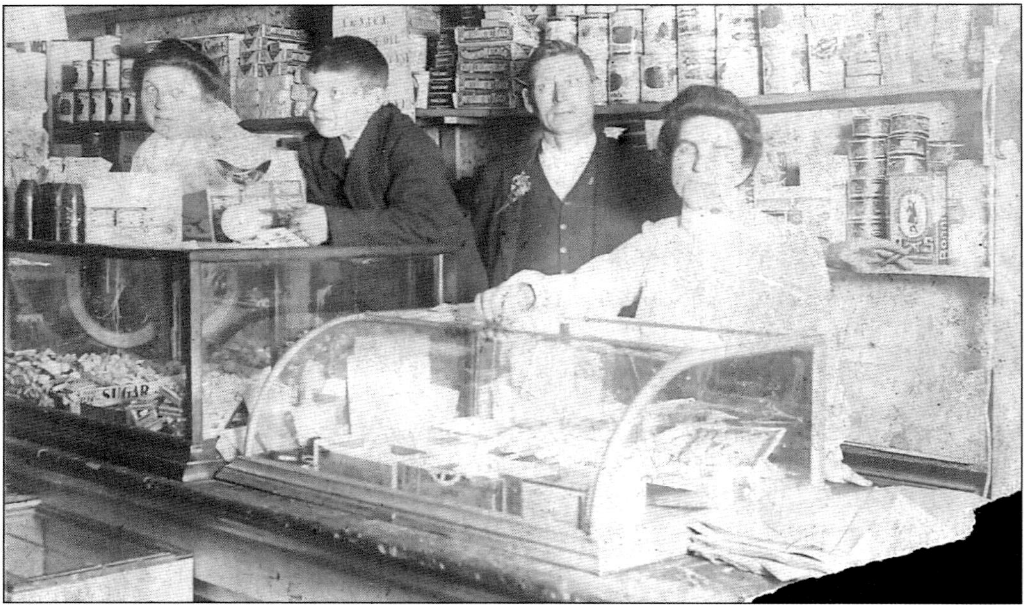

MUIR FAMILY. From left to right, Agnes, Albert, Alexander, and Retta Muir are pictured in their store in Perry. Alexander, born in Scotland in 1865, worked as a coal miner, farmer, and merchant. He and his wife, Retta, had two children. The Muir family owned a small grocery store on Second Street. Agnes went on to become a farm wife, and Albert worked on the railroad after serving in World War I.

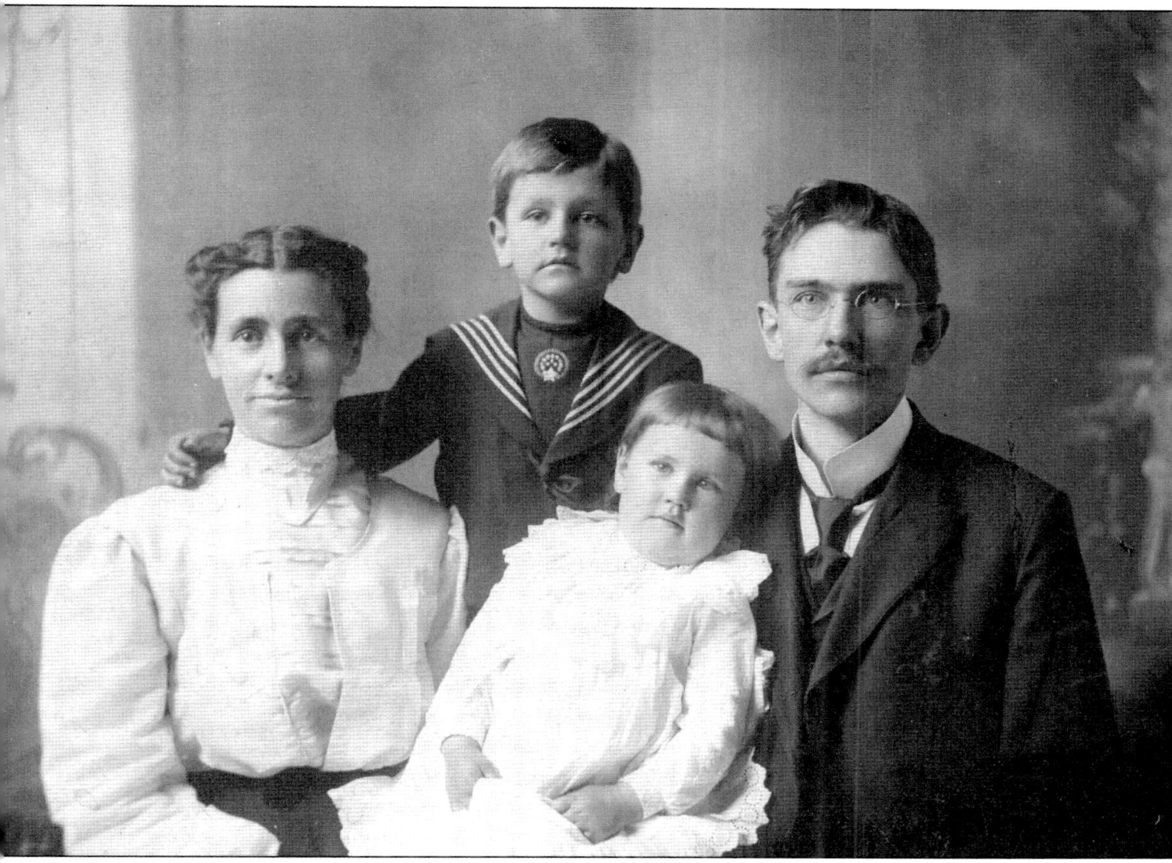

C. Durant Jones and Family. C. Durant Jones, pictured here with his wife, Ida, son Horton, and daughter Lois, arrived in Perry in 1904 and went on to play many roles in the town's history, including working as a newspaper publisher, writer, minister, politician, mayor, temperance worker, and public speaker. He owned Jones Business College, established a chautauqua traveling education program, operated a bus line, owned a construction company, and worked in real estate.

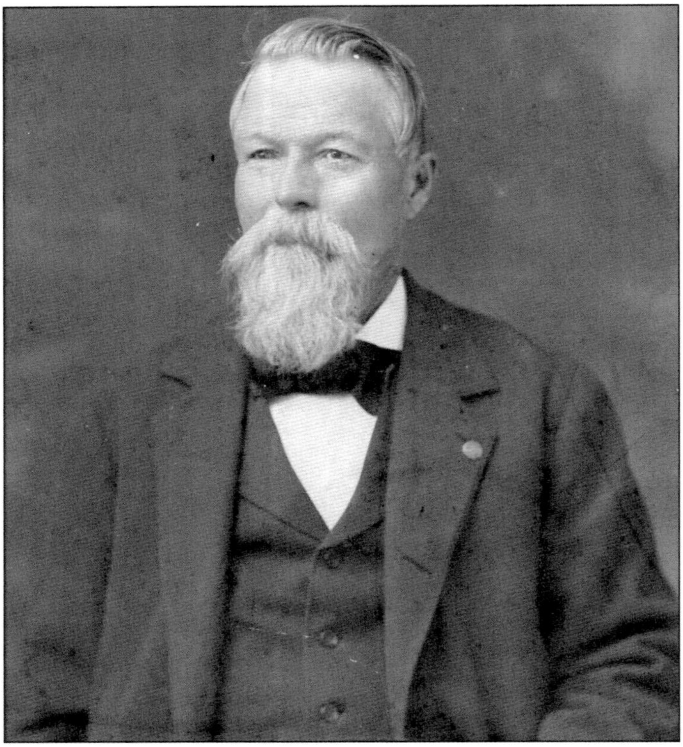

EDWARD FRANCES LEE. Born in 1834, Edward Frances Lee and his wife built a home near Dawson, west of Perry, after arriving in the area from Ohio in 1858. A Civil War veteran, Lee farmed and also served as a member of the school board. The family remains in Perry; Lee's grandson Eddie Lee was a longtime railroader and mayor of Perry.

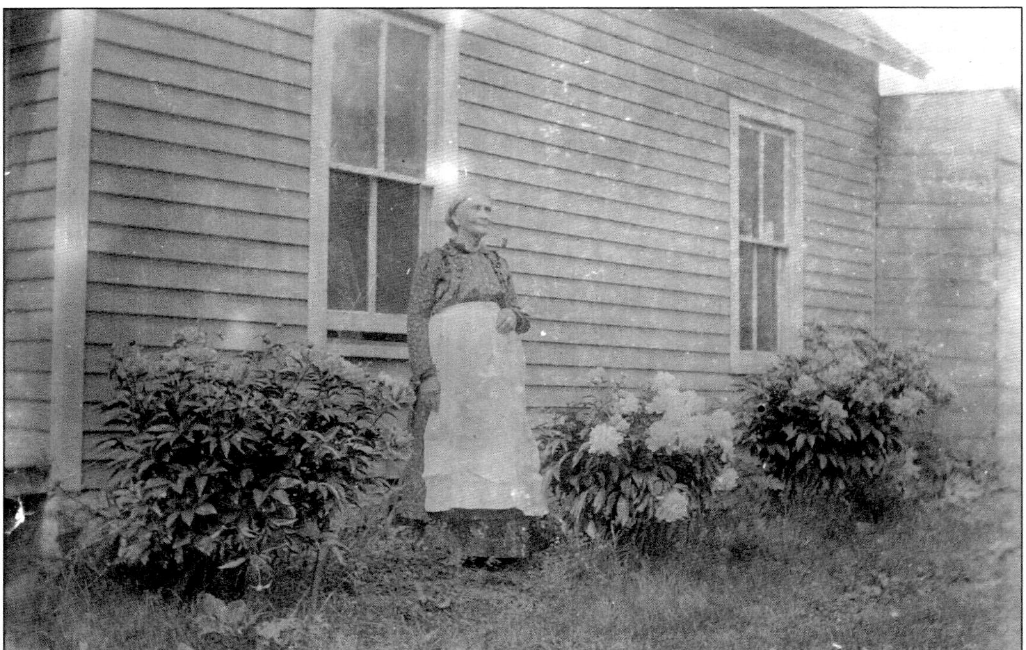

SUSAN ELIZABETH ELDER HART. Susan Elizabeth Elder Hart, a weaver, lost her husband in the Civil War. Her great-great-grandson Harley Weyer grew up in Perry and went on to become a NASA engineer.

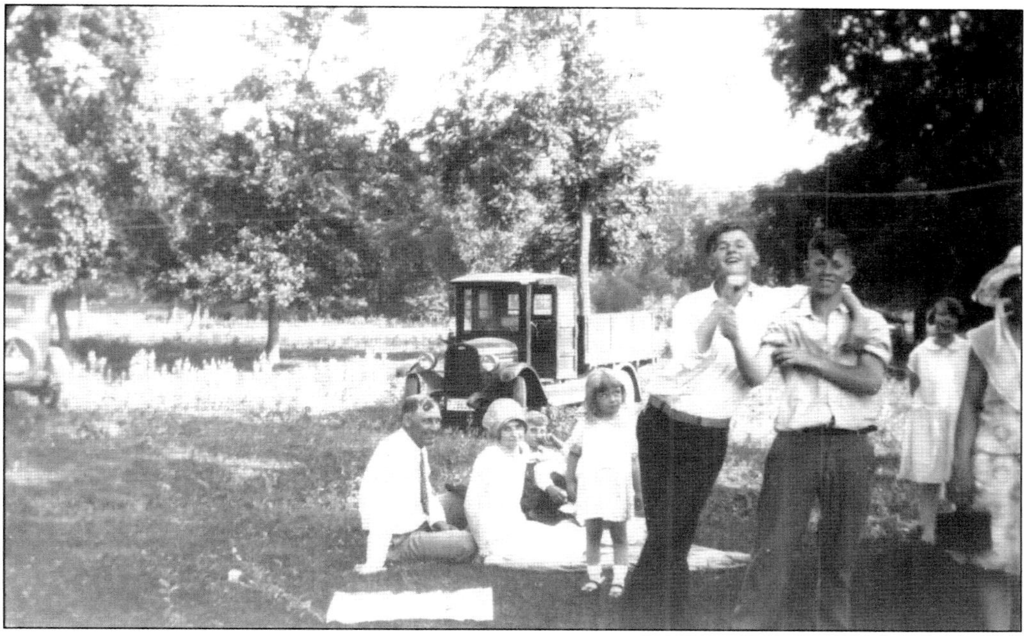

IVA CREWS TOLLE ON A PICNIC. Iva Crews Tolle's husband, E. M. Tolle, worked at the Perry Post Office and operated Tolle's New and Used Furniture at 1025 Railroad Street in Perry. The couple had six children: Veva, Juanita, Halcyon, Ronald, Rex, and LeRoy. Descendants of the Tolle family still live in Perry.

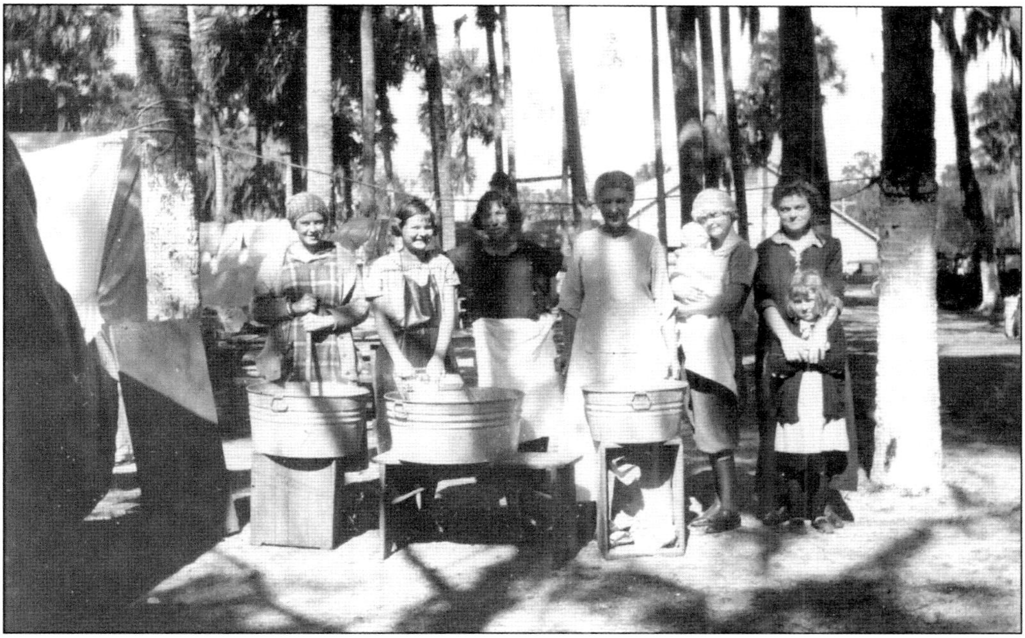

FRIEDRICHSEN FAMILY VACATION. Automobiles made it possible for Perry families to travel around the country. The Friedrichsen family is washing clothes at a campsite in Daytona, Florida, in the early decades of the 20th century. The family farmed near Bouton east of Perry. Descendants of the Friedrichsen family are part of the Bouton community to this day.

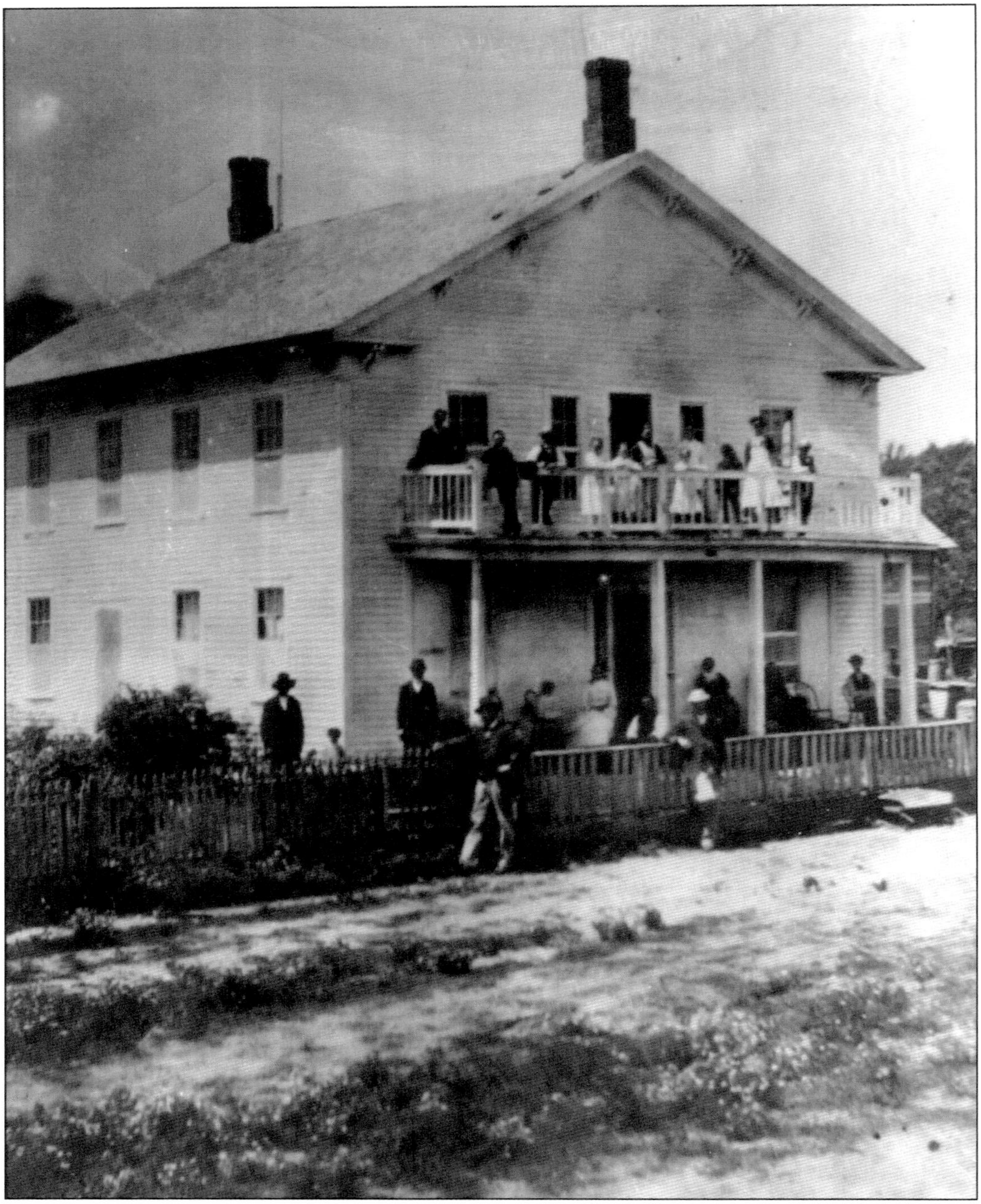

JUDGE HENRY THORNBURG HOME. Another early settler, Henry Thornburg, was a Dallas County judge from 1851 to 1861 and served a term as senator in the state legislature. Thornburg also owned and operated the only mill west of Keokuk, which was located on his land along the Raccoon River four miles south of Perry. On this property, Thornburg and his wife built a 14-room house that doubled as a stagecoach inn. In the home, the Thornburgs raised 22 children, 21 of whom were adopted. The house was torn down in 1954.

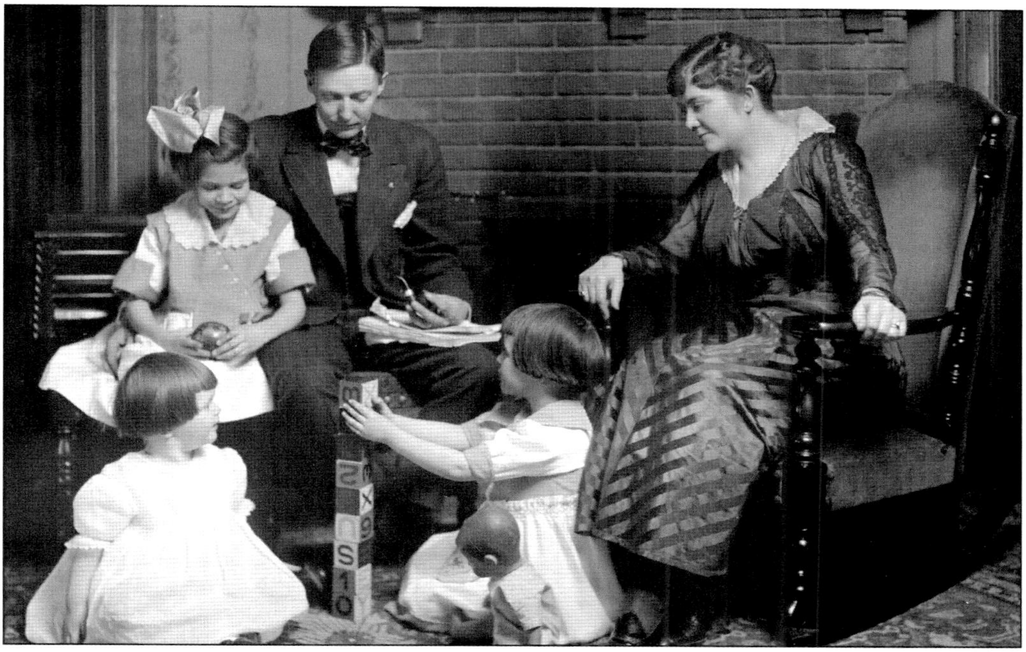

HARRY PATTEE AND FAMILY. The Pattee family has a long history in Perry. Harry Pattee was an officer at First National Bank, which was owned by his father, D. J. Pattee. In 1903, Harry was shot by an intruder at the family home at 1119 Fourth Street. He suffered from his wounds most of his life, as the bullet fragments were never fully removed. The family disposed of its interest in the bank in 1922 and moved to Texas.

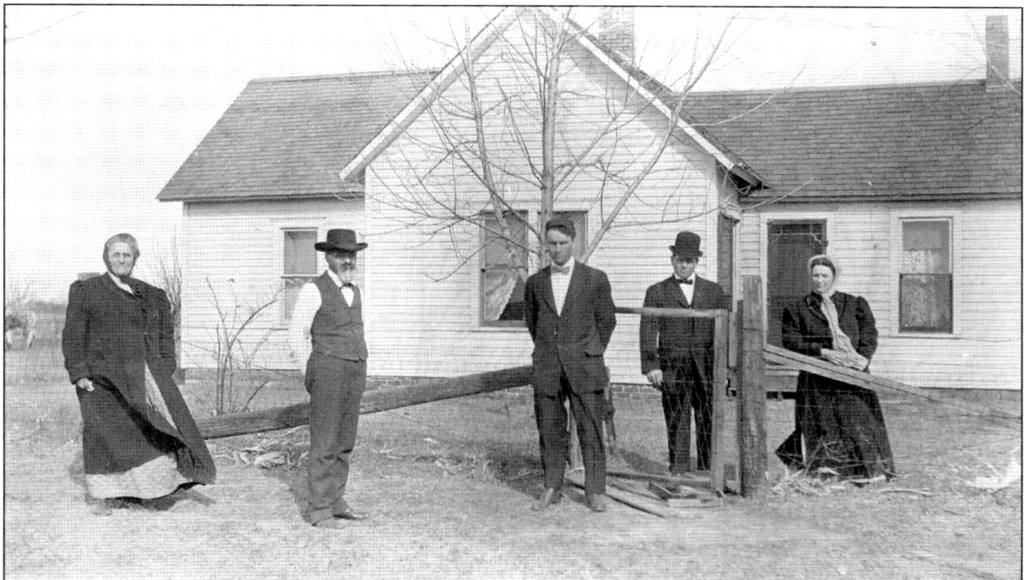

BERTHEL E. SCOTT AND FAMILY. The Scott family, pictured here around 1920, is one of many of Irish heritage who settled in the Perry area through the years. Berthel E. Scott's parents came through Ellis Island and settled in Minburn south of Perry. Bridget Scott worked as a maid at the Pattee Hotel after her husband was killed in an accident.

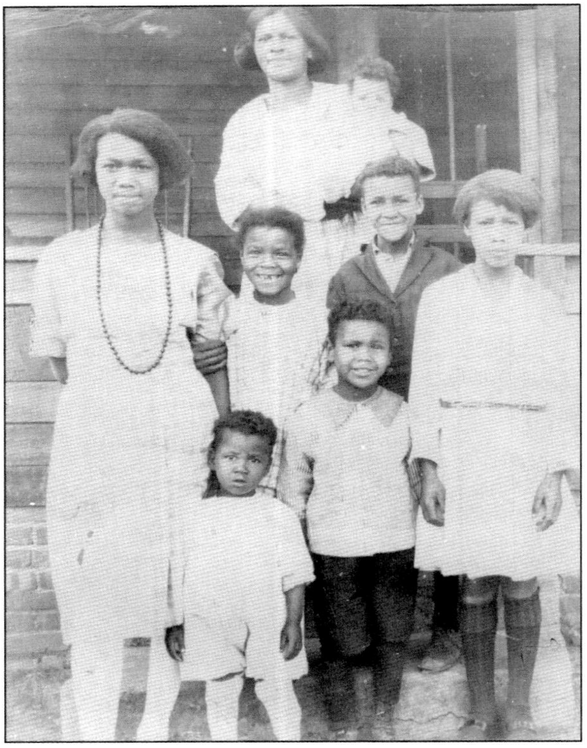

LALLIE WHITE AND HER CHILDREN. Lallie White, pictured here around 1924, was the mother of Sophie White Tate, a longtime Perry resident, and Roy Whyte, a well-known trumpeter and composer (he changed the spelling of his last name as he started to develop his music career). Lallie raised 10 children, 6 of whom are pictured here. From left to right are (first row) Kenneth, John, and Maude; (second row) Margaret, Vera, and Daniel; (third row) Lallie and baby Sophie.

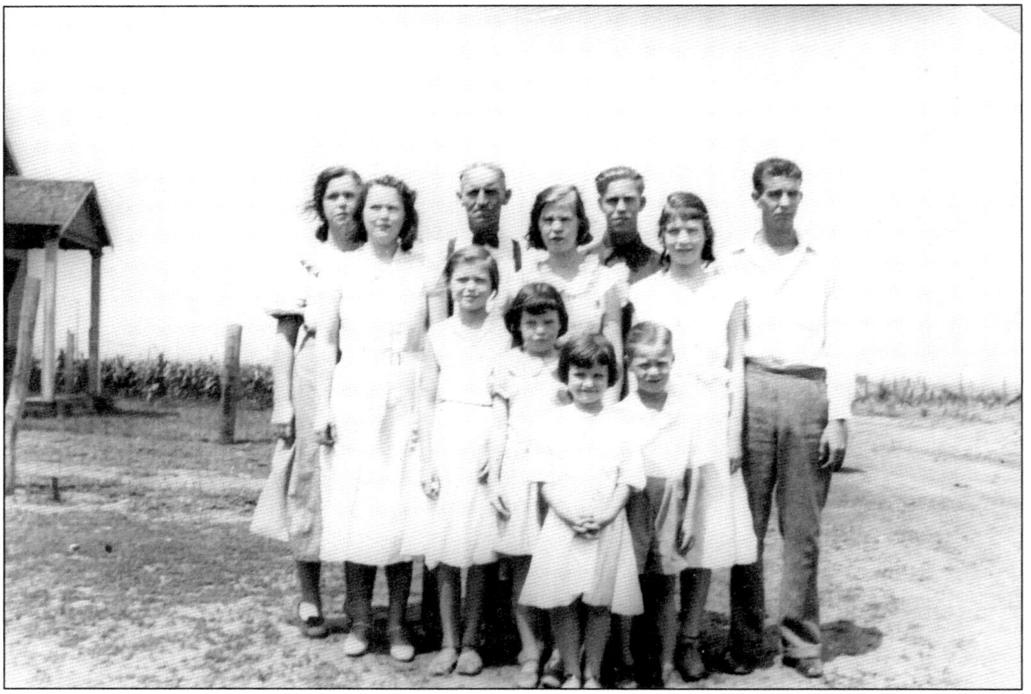

CARR FAMILY. Leo Carr's family, of English heritage, settled in Moran, a mining town east of Perry. His father worked as a coal miner until the mine was closed around 1940.

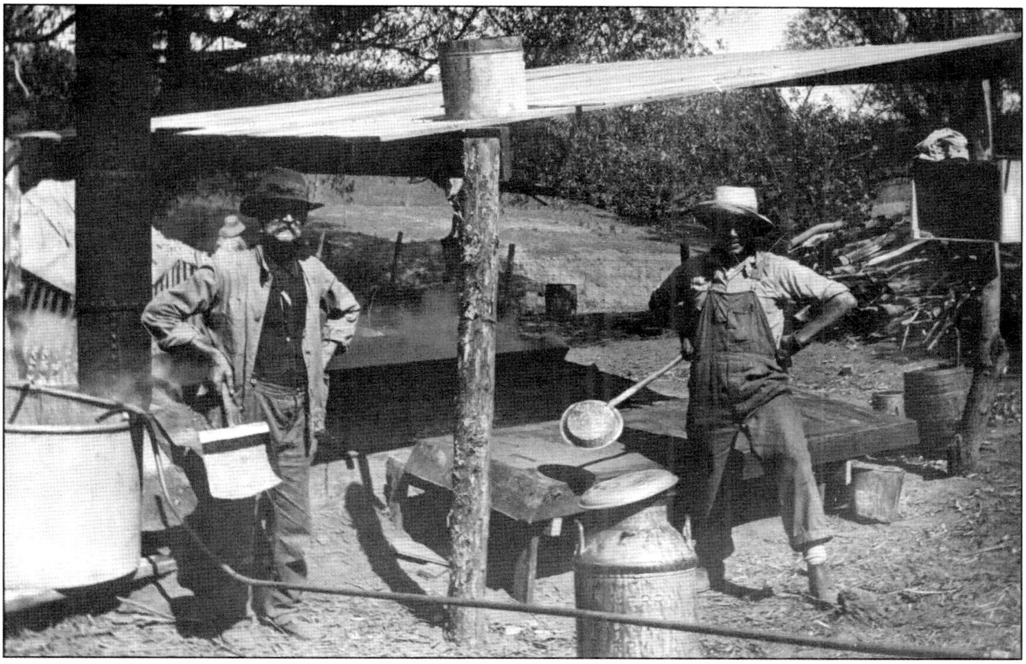

JIM YORK AND JOSEPH HAGER. Pictured here in the late 1920s, Jim York and Joseph Hager take a break from working at a sorghum mill. Hager's parents emigrated from Austria and the family settled on a farmstead near Perry.

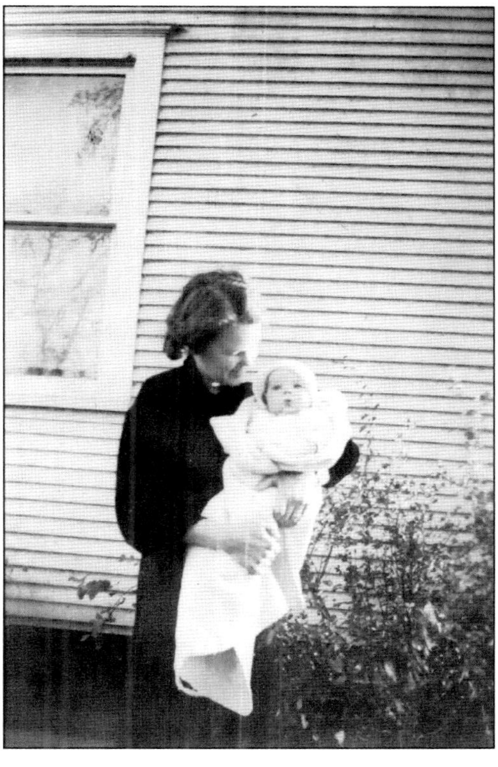

HELEN NELSON HOLDING DAUGHTER KAREN. Both sides of Karen Nelson Taylor's family came from Sweden, and, like Perry residents of many backgrounds, have continued to keep their heritage alive. Her mother's family settled near Boone and attended a Lutheran church in Ogden, where some of the services were in Swedish. Her father's family settled in Earlham west of Des Moines.

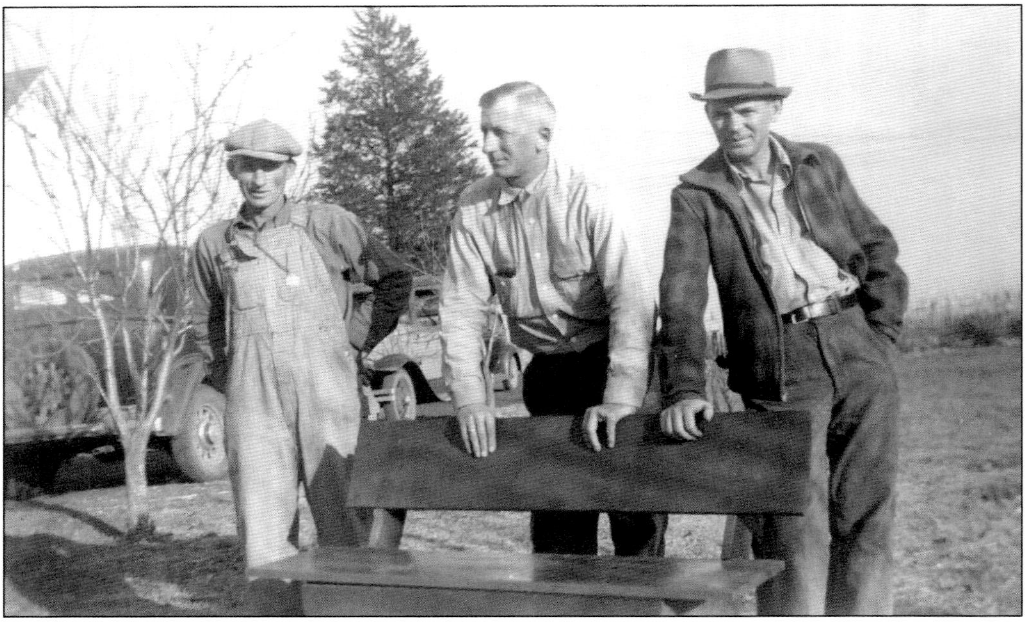

VODENIK BROTHERS. From left to right are John, Fred, and Carl Vodenik around 1939. Fred and his brother emigrated from Austria and worked on the railroad after settling in Perry. Fred's son also worked on the Chicago, Milwaukee and St. Paul Railroad (commonly known as the Milwaukee Road) his whole life, as a conductor on a freight train.

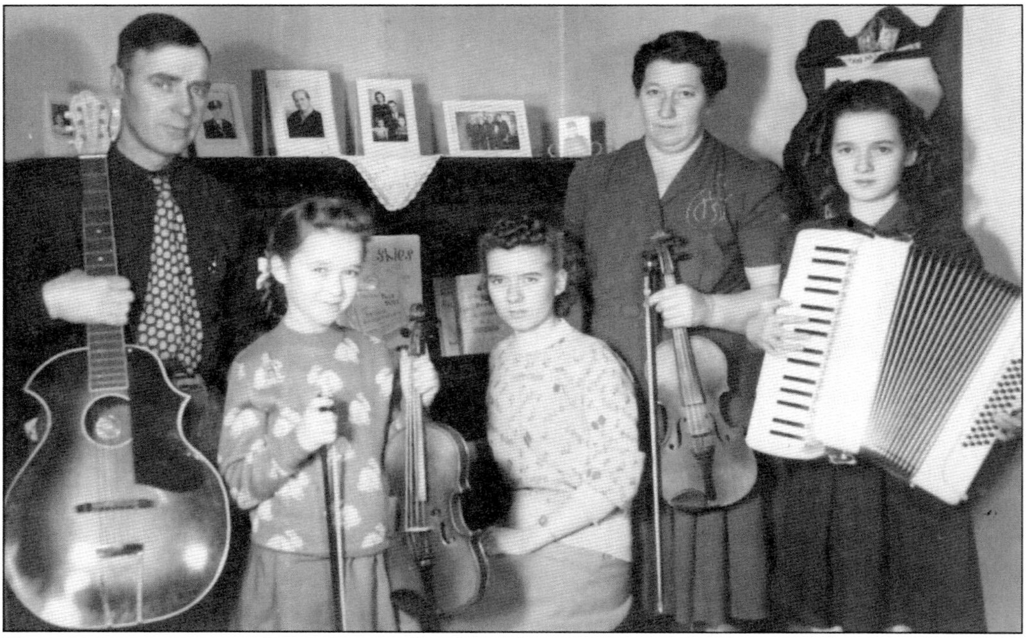

FAGEN FAMILY BAND. One of many families of Irish background in Perry, the Fagens formed a family band. From left to right in 1945 are Victor, Norma Sue, La Dora, Ruth, and Marvel. Marvel Fagen Clark took accordion lessons in Des Moines starting in high school and later taught accordion and formed an accordion band in Perry.

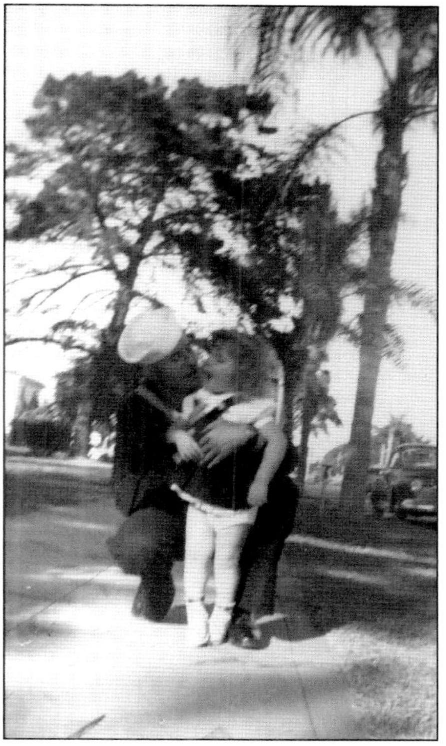

PERRY SOLDIERS. Many of the threads of world history run through Perry's story; even this small town in rural Iowa felt the effects of many world wars through the years. Many of its sons and daughters served in the armed forces from the Civil War to the present day. Below, Ivyl Garnes poses in his World War I uniform. Right, Clarence Peel leaves for Korea. Born in 1919, Peel worked for Perry Water Works for 27 years. He served in World War II and the Korean War.

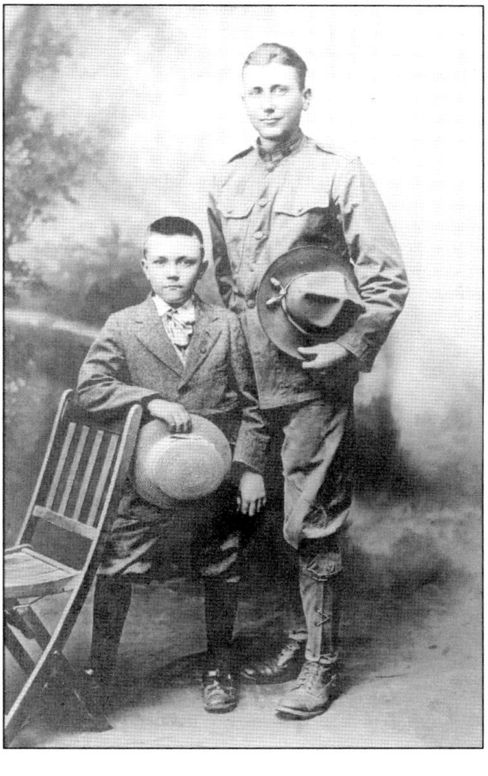

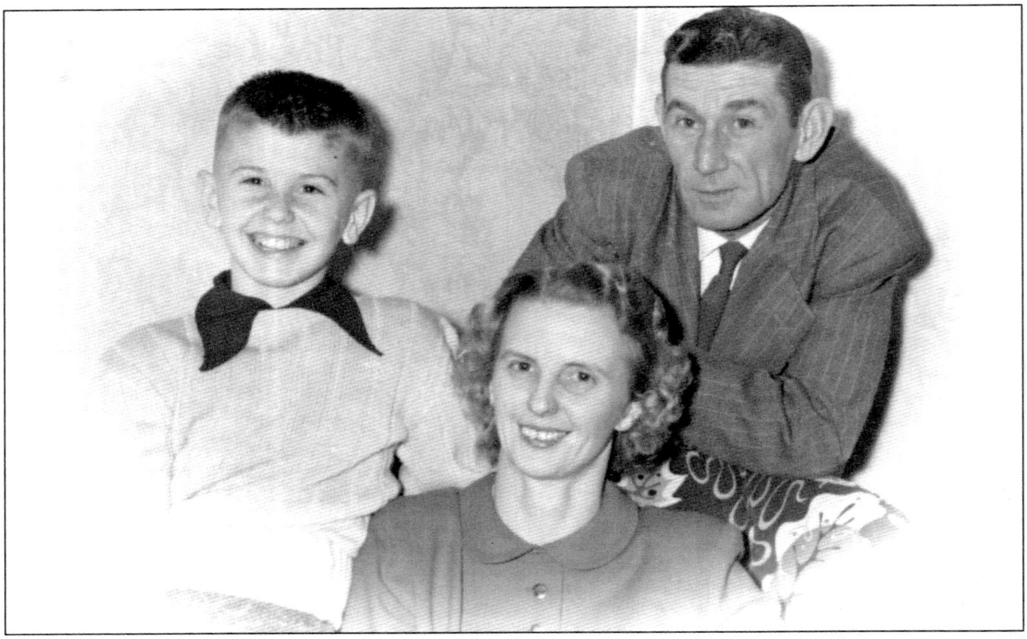

JOHN TURNER FAMILY PORTRAIT. John Turner, pictured here in 1950 with his son J. D. and wife, Edie, was a social studies teacher and coach in the Perry Community School District. He taught in the public schools for 44 years but also spent a few summers working in coal mines and on the railroad.

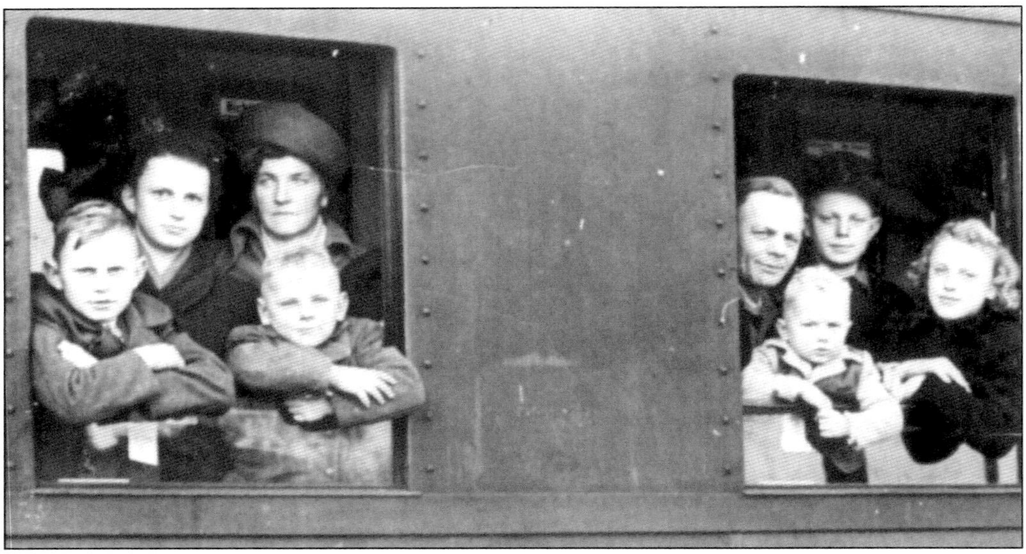

SEIFERT FAMILY LEAVING GERMANY. The Seiferts were one of many families of German heritage in Perry, but they came with a later wave of emigrants. Embarking from Germany are Maria Seifert, Martha Seifert (mother), Erich Seifert, Alfons Seifert Jr., Alfons Seifert Sr. (father), Josef Seifert, Elfriede Seifert, and Carl Heinz. In 1951, the family left Durr-kunzendorf, Germany, where they lived for generations. They came to the United States through the Catholic Relief Service after a time working as indentured servants to a Polish family in Germany that had taken over their farm. In Iowa, they settled on a farm near Dawson.

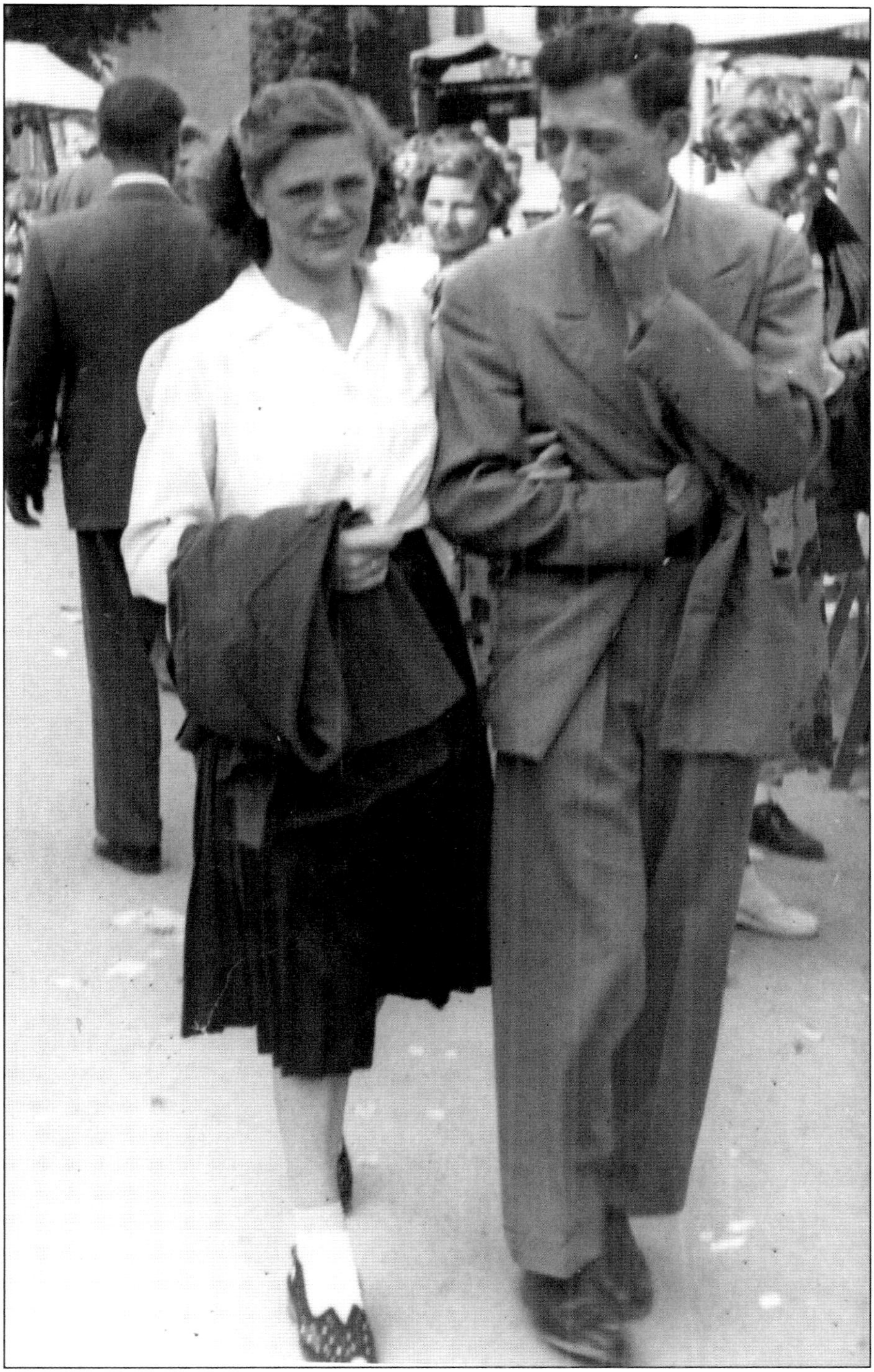

KATHERINE AND PETER GELBOWITZ. Katherine Gelbowitz grew up in Yugoslavia, but the family left for Austria by horse and wagon in 1944 after the Germans invaded. She and her husband, Peter, married in 1952 and later immigrated to Perry where his mother was already living.

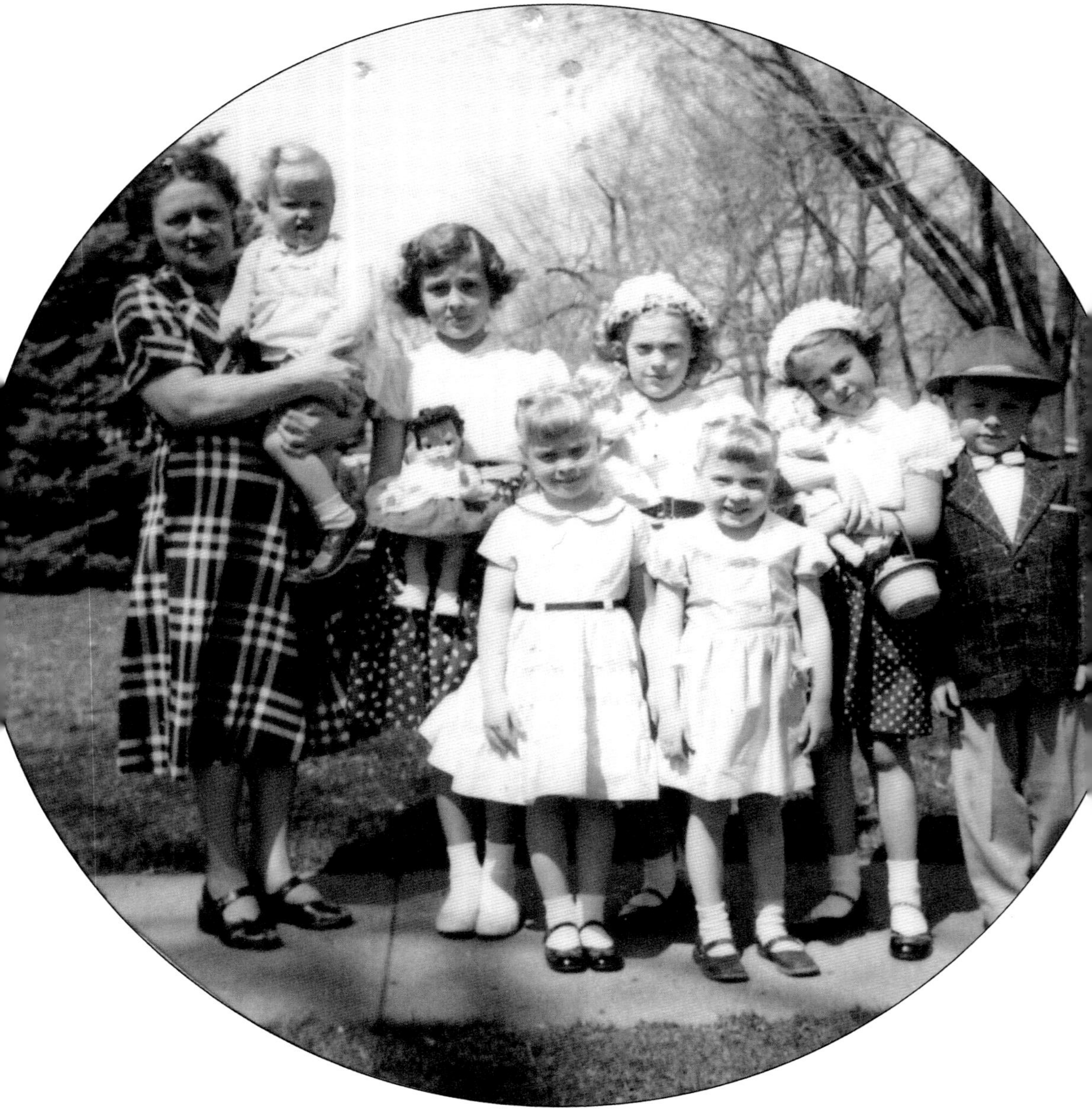

WIFVAT CHILDREN WITH THEIR GRANDMOTHER PEARL WIFVAT. Van and Ramona Wifvat met at the Ray B. Smith drugstore in Perry, where Ramona worked. Van's grandparents emigrated from Sweden, and his grandfather fought in the Civil War. Van's father, a lawyer, grew up on a farm near Perry. Ramona's great-grandparents emigrated from Westport, Ireland, in 1863 and settled near Bouton.

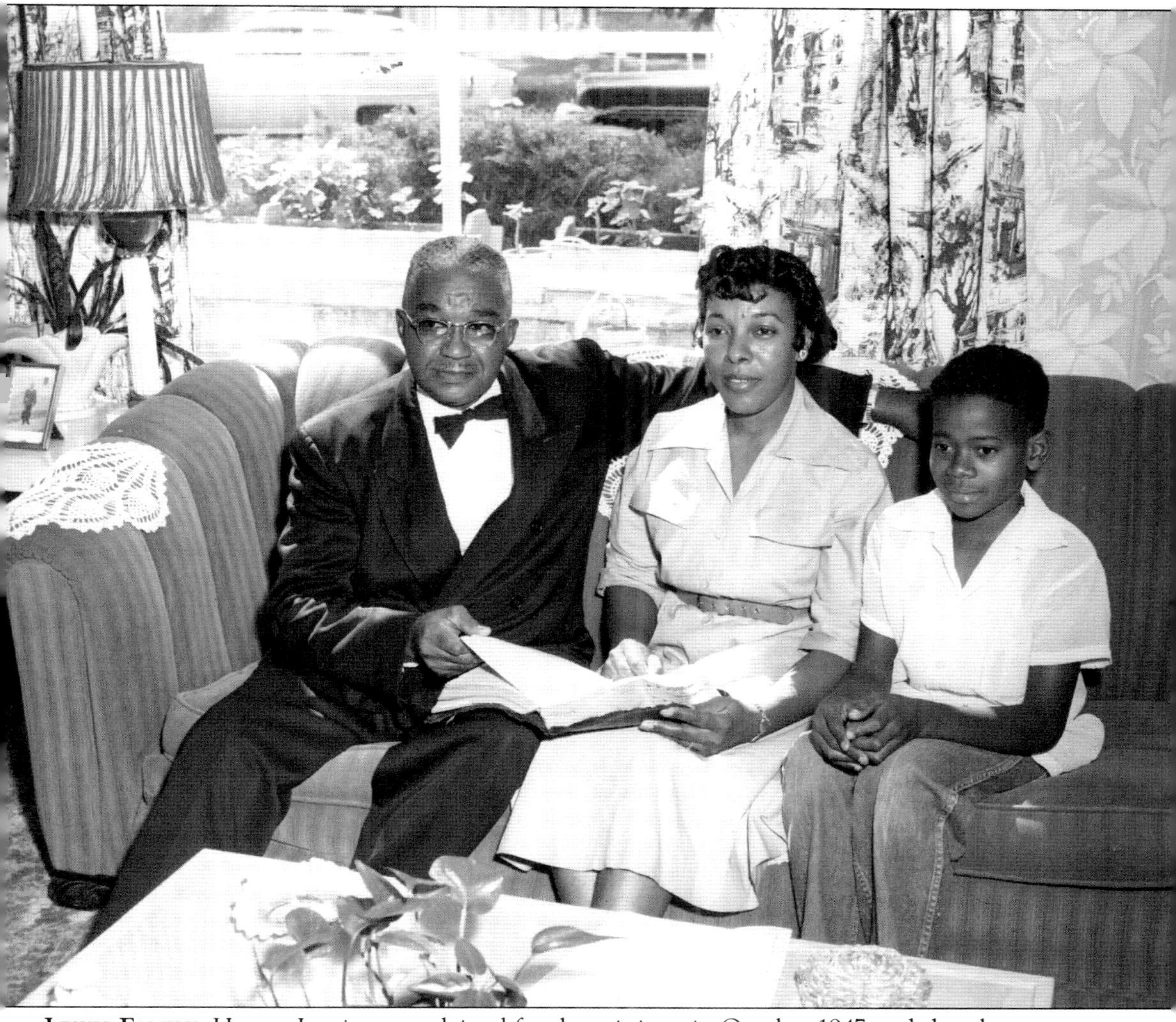

LEWIS FAMILY. Horace Lewis was ordained for the ministry in October 1947 and then became the pastor of Bethel Baptist Church in Perry, located at Seventh and Rawson Streets. Horace is pictured with his wife, Dora, and son James Henry. Horace also worked at the Dallas County Hospital. Dora owned a beauty salon in Perry and was known to remark, "He took care of souls, I took care of heads."

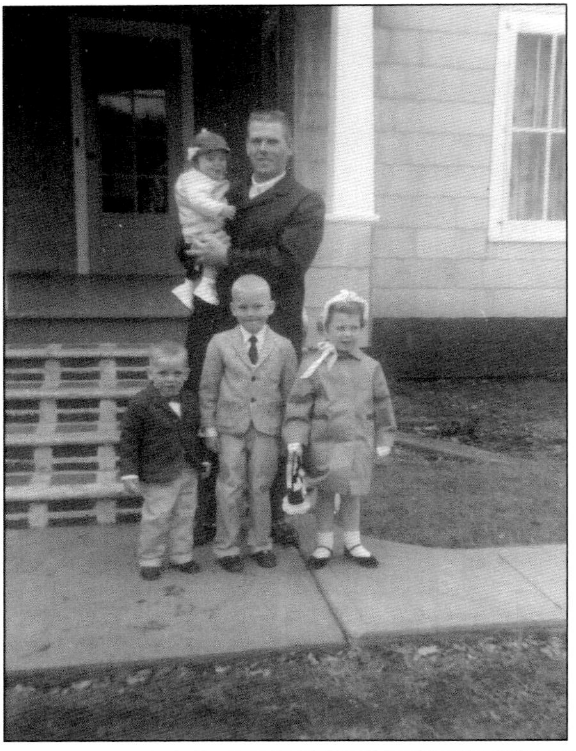

BILL BULLOCK AND CHILDREN. The Bullock family is pictured here. From left to right are (first row) Craig, Curt, and Debbie; (second row) Bill, holding Scott. In the 1950s and 1960s, Bill worked for a furniture store and also drove a truck on delivery routes. In 1976, the Bullocks bought a Maid-Rite restaurant, one of many family businesses in Perry. They had the business until 1998.

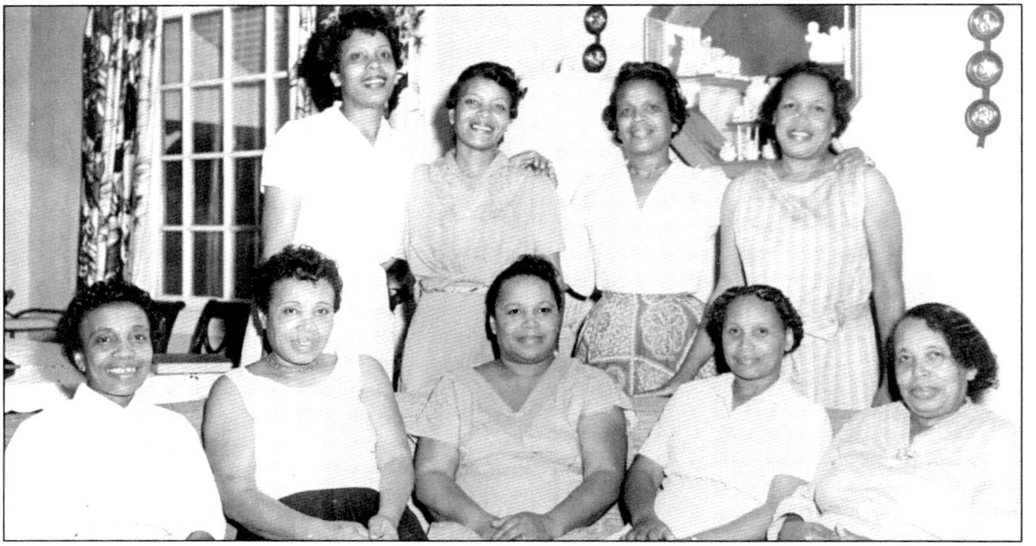

WEAVER FAMILY. Will and Mary Weaver had 12 children, 9 of whom are pictured here. From left to right are (first row) Florence, Thelma, Bill, Marjorie Terry, and Opal; (second row) Cleo, Peggy, Naleeu Neal, and Christine. Opal was instrumental in founding the Church of God in Christ in Perry. Her sons Everett and Phillip Tindrell were also church leaders. Everett became a bishop in the Church of God in Christ after moving to Des Moines. Phillip, a longtime teacher and administrator in the Des Moines Public Schools, also served as assistant pastor of Bethel Baptist Church in Perry.

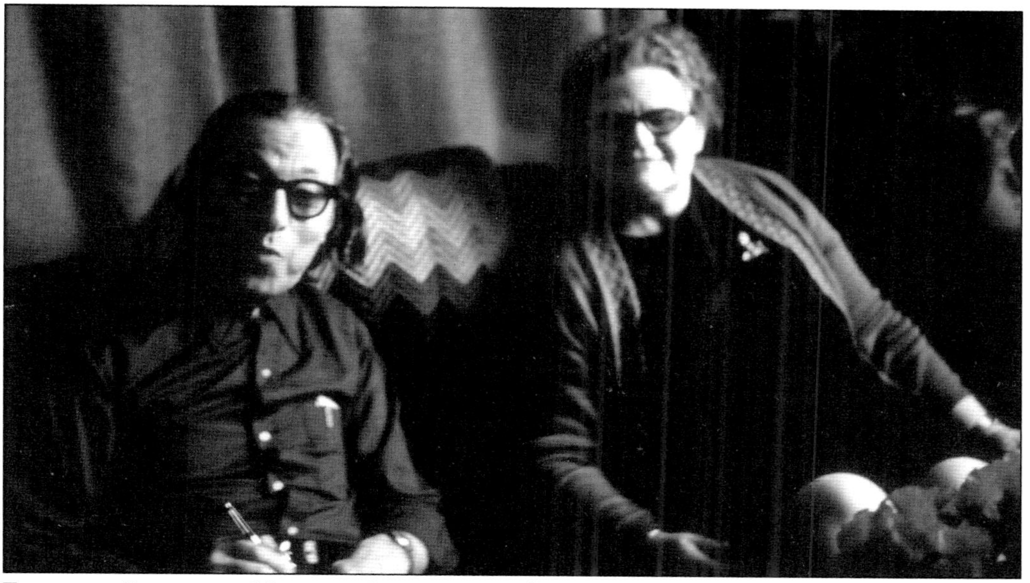

Emil and Lauraine Natalle. Lauraine Natalle's ancestors were early settlers in the Perry area. One, Lanford Mills, settled in the Buffalo Grove area around 1850. The Natalles' story shows how threads of world history weave their way through small-town life. Emil served as a combat surgical technician during World War II. His post-military career took him and his wife, Lauraine, to Japan, Russia, Newfoundland, and other places, where he worked for the federal government running schools on American military bases.

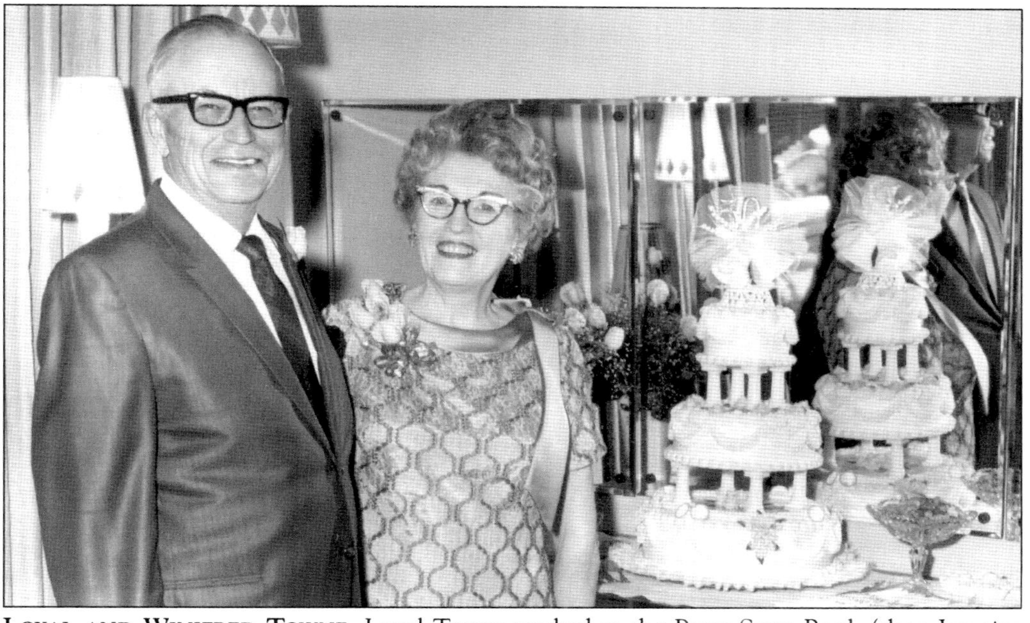

Loyal and Winifred Towne. Loyal Towne worked at the Perry State Bank (then Jamaica Savings Bank) and farmed near Jamaica in Dallas County. Towne's son Morris has fond memories of coming to Perry with farm wares on Saturdays. He says it was a time "when you couldn't walk down the street hardly on a Saturday evening because of the people congregated and visiting and shopping."

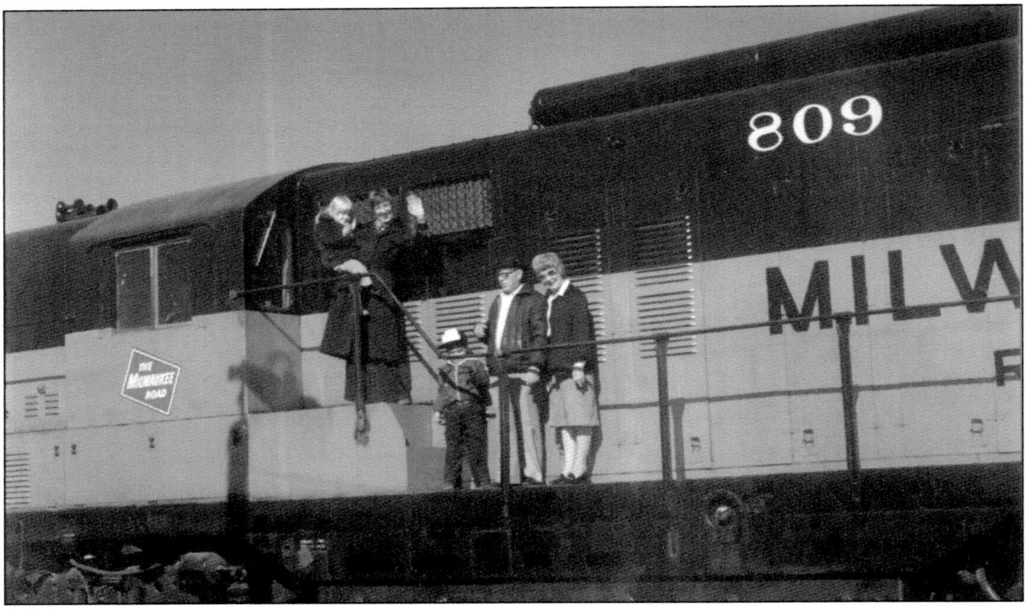

Wasson Family Standing on Milwaukee Engine. The Wassons were one of many railroad families in Perry. William H. "Sandy" Wasson, born in Perry in 1915, was the son of an engineer on the Milwaukee Road. He attended St. Patrick's Catholic School and then Perry High School, where he played baseball and football and wrestled. He worked as a mechanical foreman at the roundhouse in Perry.

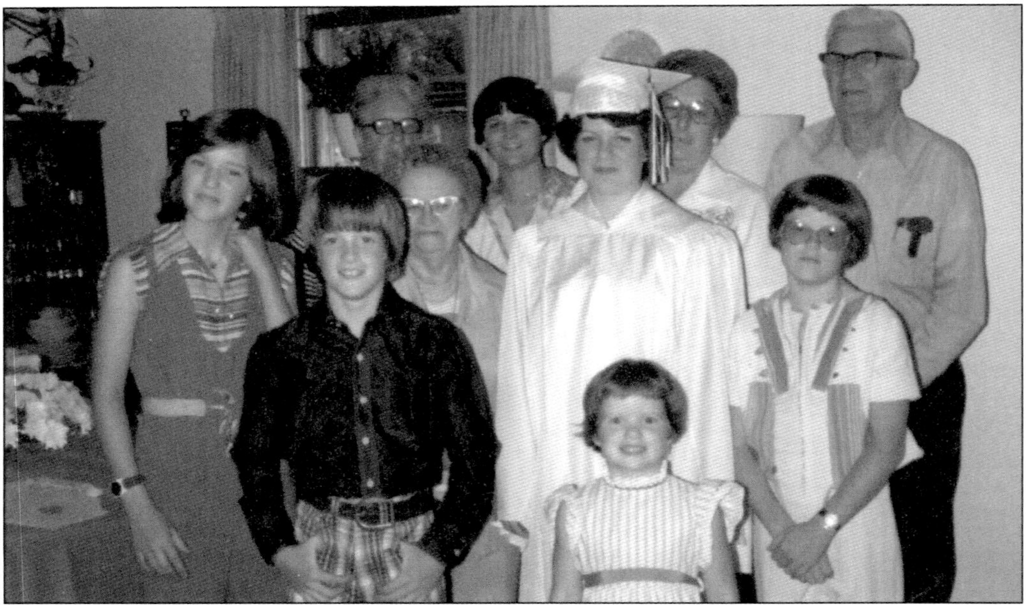

Galligan Family High School Graduation. Jim Galligan grew up in Wisconsin and served a tour of duty in the Korean War. After a stint at Rayovac Battery in Madison, Wisconsin, Galligan went to work for Oscar Mayer in the transportation department. Ten years later in 1966, his work in the packing industry brought him to Perry, as has been true for many others through the years.

Two

WORK

The labor of the Midwest is most often portrayed in relation to land and farming. Throughout this chapter, there are pictures of farmers and their tasks. Farming was once a collective activity where neighbors helped each other and a small farm with less than 200 acres could support a family. Much of the small-town life was defined in relation to the land. During the Depression, for example, when cash was scarce, farm wives supported their households with milk and egg money. Much of the rhythm of small-town life focuses on the farm—planting, growing, and harvesting. While farming was critical to the development of Iowa, the work of the community was much more diverse.

The rhythm of Perry was also formed by the railroad, which became as important as farming in the life of this community for more than 100 years. For railroaders, the family life of engineers, conductors, brakemen, and firemen was on a particular schedule. For many years, the men worked away from home for at least a night. There were railroad parades, picnics, and other local events for railroad families.

From the very beginning of the community, merchants of all sorts came to make a living. Grocery stores, drugstores, general stores, liveries, and music stores were all part of the landscape of the community. In the early years, there were neighborhood grocery stores on many corners. Today the influence of the newest immigrants shows on the main street with Hispanic grocery stores, clothing stores, and restaurants.

Manufacturers of all types made their appearance in Perry. Some manufacturers, such as an automobile and washing machine company, were unsuccessful, but two tillage companies and a foundry did find success in Perry.

The national and international economic trends continue to affect Perry. How the main street changes in the future, what businesses come to town, and how the town responds remains unclear.

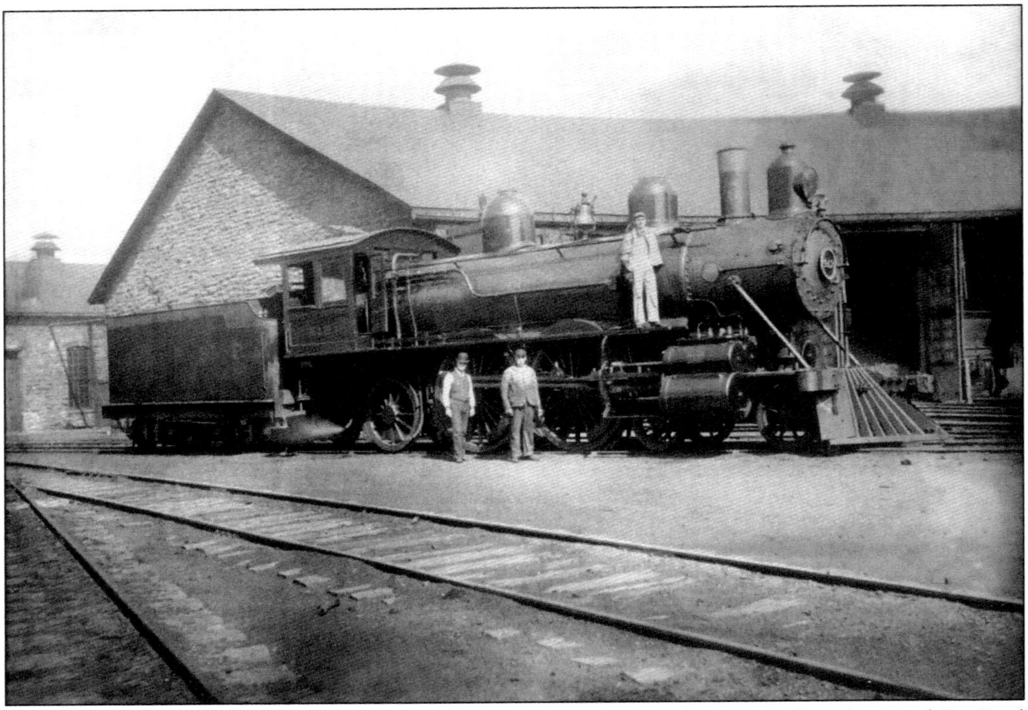

CHICAGO, MILWAUKEE AND ST. PAUL RAILROAD. The first Chicago, Milwaukee and St. Paul Railroad train, running from Chicago to Council Bluffs, came through Perry beginning in 1882, and the route continued until 1980. The first Chicago, Milwaukee and St. Paul roundhouse (above) in Perry was located between Seventh and Eighth Streets east of downtown. The roundhouse began operation in 1883, as did the depot (below).

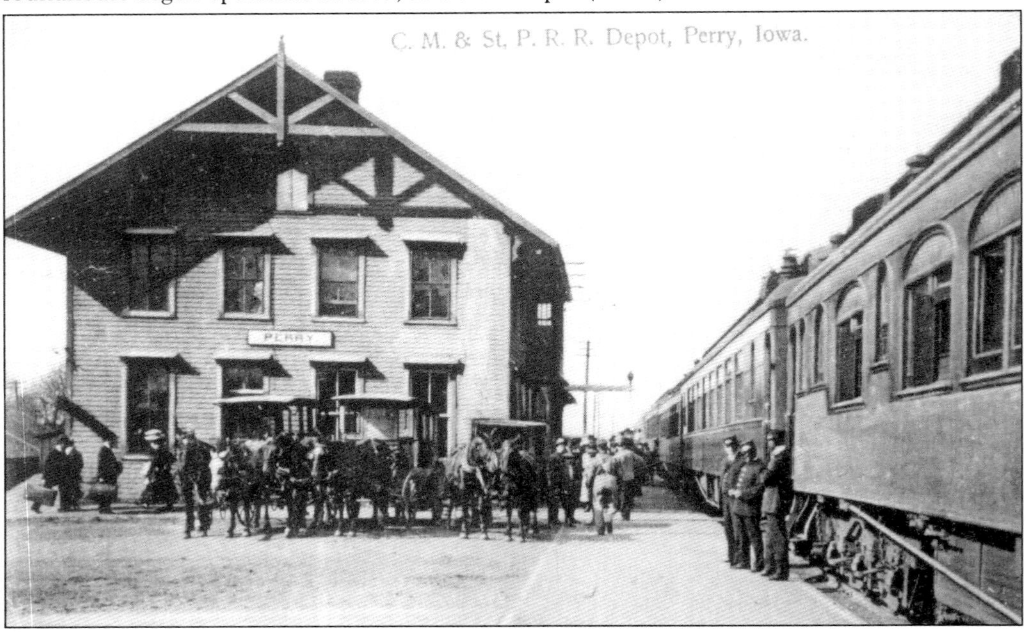

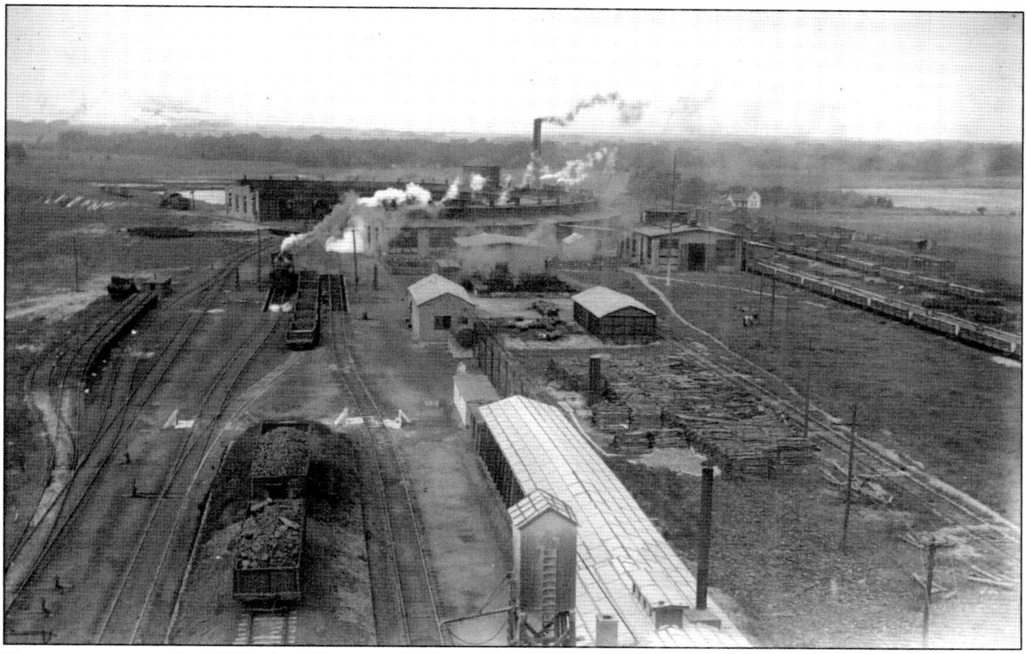

ROUNDHOUSE. By 1912, the Chicago, Milwaukee and St. Paul Railroad needed a new roundhouse in Perry. The railroad acquired two farms west of town to build it. The site included shops, a yard, and a yard office.

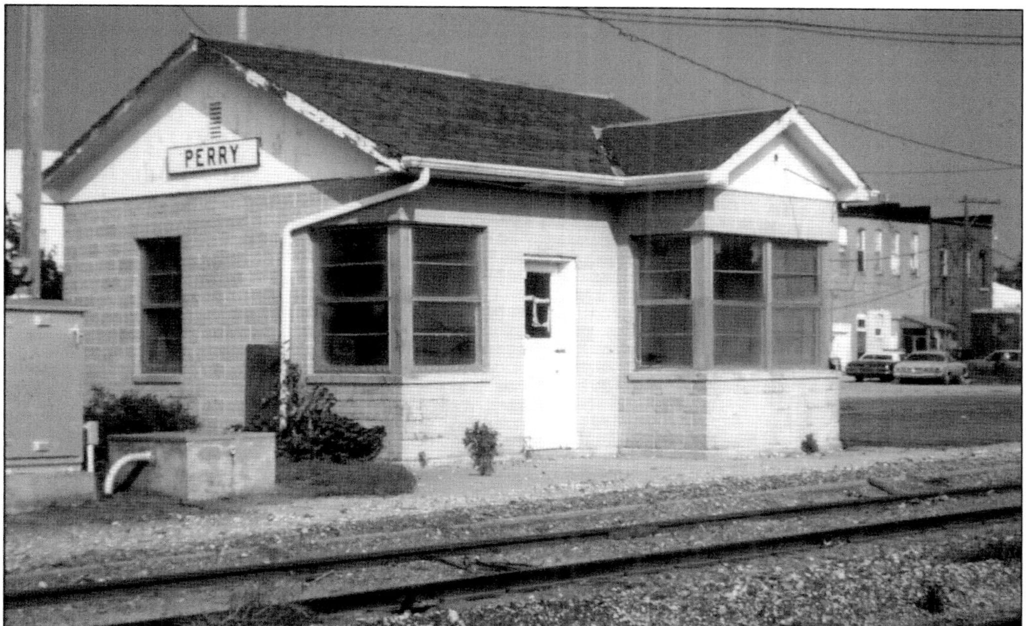

NEW MINNEAPOLIS AND ST. LOUIS DEPOT. The Minneapolis and St. Louis Railway originated in Minneapolis and merged with the Iowa Central Railway in 1901. It primarily transported freight but also offered some passenger service. The new Perry depot, which opened in 1950, was located at the corner of First Avenue and Willis Avenue. It now belongs to the City of Perry.

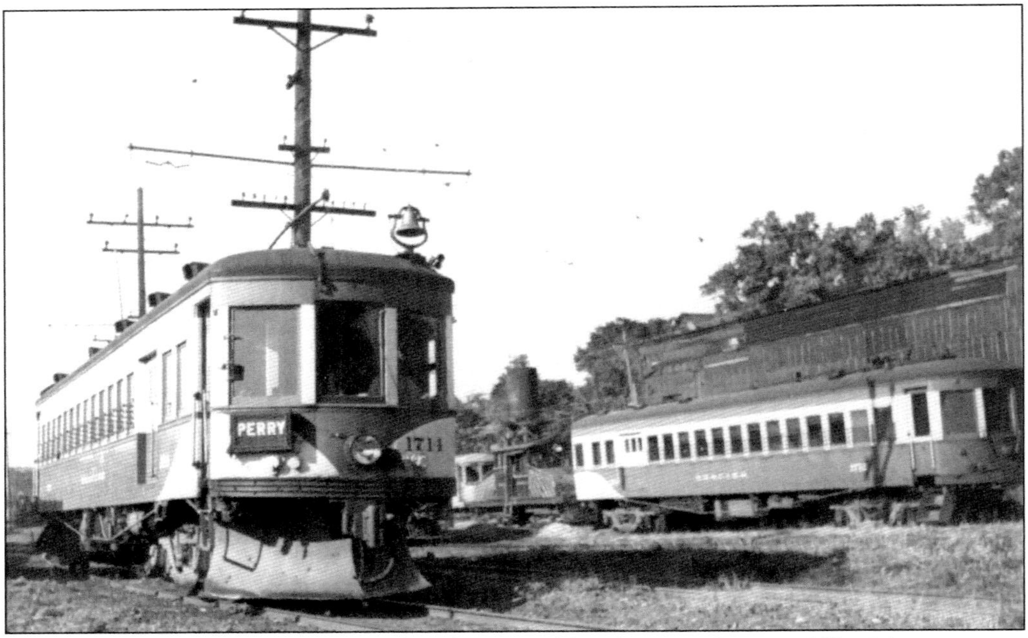

INTERURBAN DEPOT AND TRAIN. This electric rail line between Perry and Des Moines was in operation from 1906 to 1949. Cars traveled the route several times daily, making it possible to travel from Perry to Des Moines for shopping or work. The depot was on the corner of Willis Avenue and West Third Street.

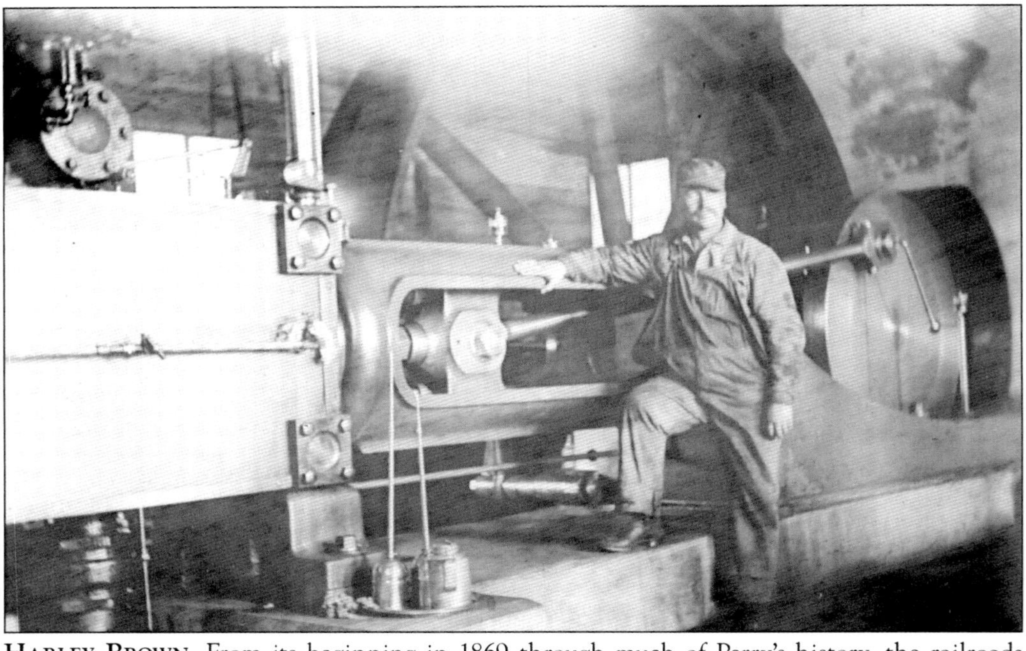

HARLEY BROWN. From its beginning in 1869 through much of Perry's history, the railroads were a mainstay of livelihood for the town's residents. They worked as conductors, engineers, mechanics, brakemen, firemen, and timekeepers. Harley Brown, pictured here, worked as a mechanic at the first roundhouse in Perry.

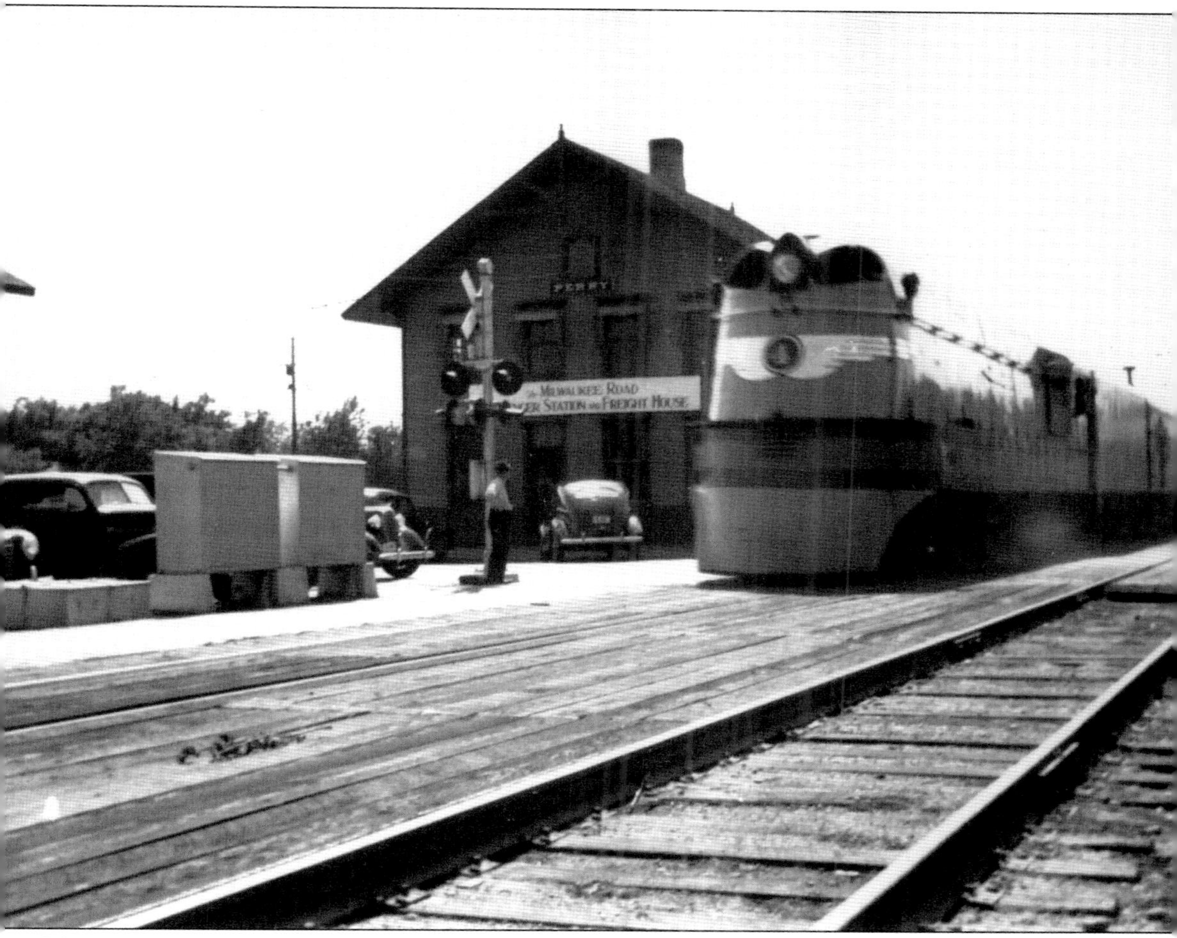

MILWAUKEE ROAD TRAIN AT PERRY STATION. In December 1940, the Chicago, Milwaukee, St. Paul and Pacific Railroad passenger train *Hiawatha* began its daily run through Perry on its way between Chicago and Omaha. It continued until 1955. These high-speed trains, pulled by steam locomotives, first appeared in 1935.

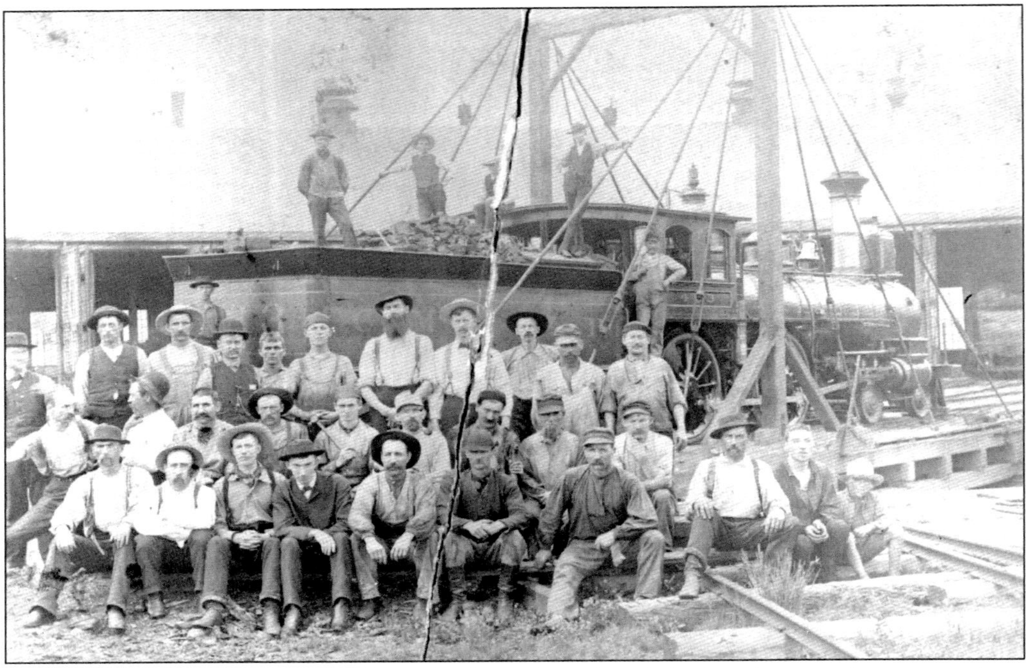

STEAM ENGINE. These men likely worked on the railroad during the era of steam engines, around 1890.

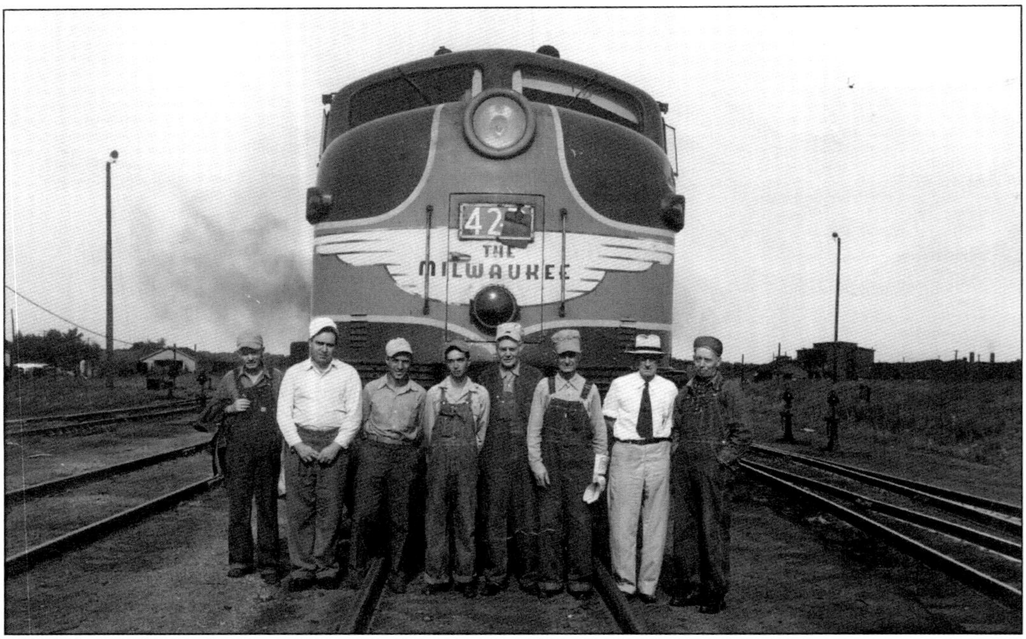

MILWAUKEE ENGINE AND RAILROAD WORKERS. From left to right are Carl Vodenik, Jack Snyder, Art Santee, Eddie Collins, Bill Barker, ? Santee, Bill Barker Sr., and Earl Holdridge. This train features the Milwaukee Road colors of orange and maroon. After 1955, when the Chicago, Milwaukee, St. Paul and Pacific Railroad assumed operation of Union Pacific Railroad trains over the line, the color scheme changed to Union Pacific's yellow, red, and gray.

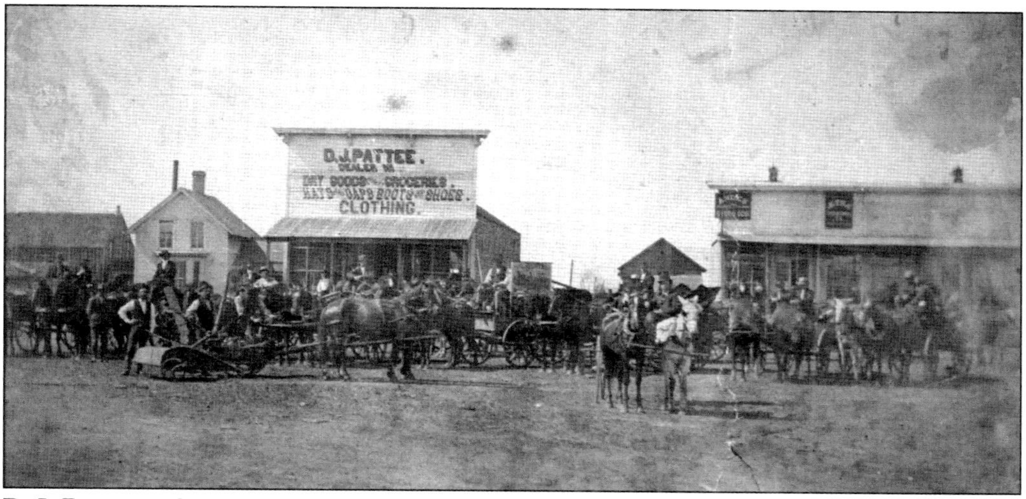

D. J. PATTEE'S ORIGINAL STORE BUILDING. The first business in Perry, D. J. Pattee's store, was built in 1867 on the west side of the railroad tracks. Its original name was Rawson and Pattee before Pattee bought out his partner. In 1884, the store moved to the south side of Warford Street between First Avenue and Second Street. In 1901, Pattee tore down the building and took the lumber to his farm to build an icehouse.

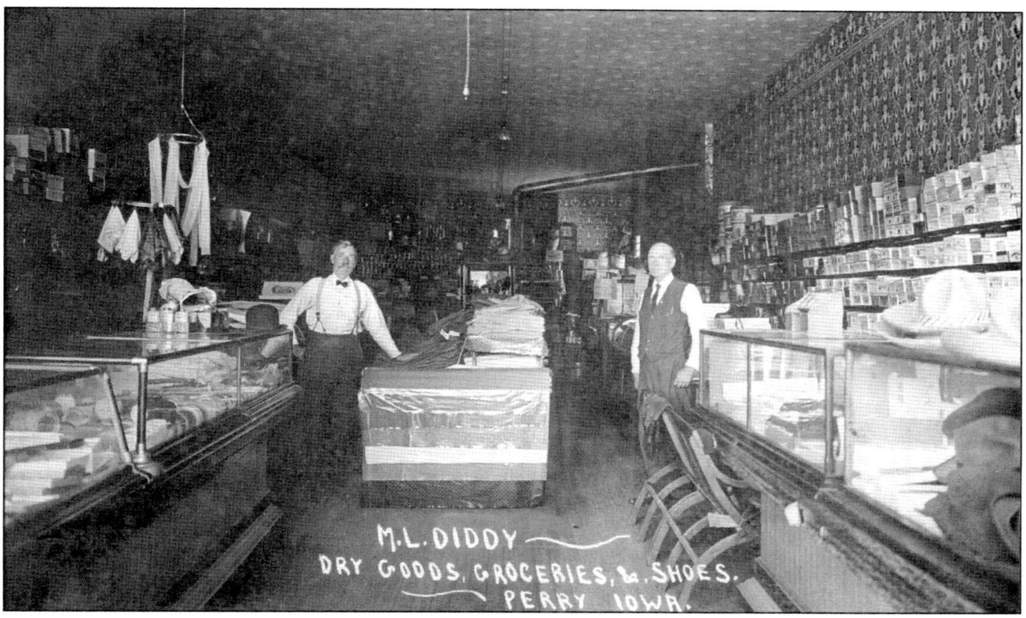

M. L. DIDDY DRY GOODS, GROCERIES, AND SHOES. M. L. Diddy opened his general store in 1882. The store, located at Third Street and Willis Avenue, was destroyed by fire in December 1914. This was one of many dry goods stores in Perry over the years.

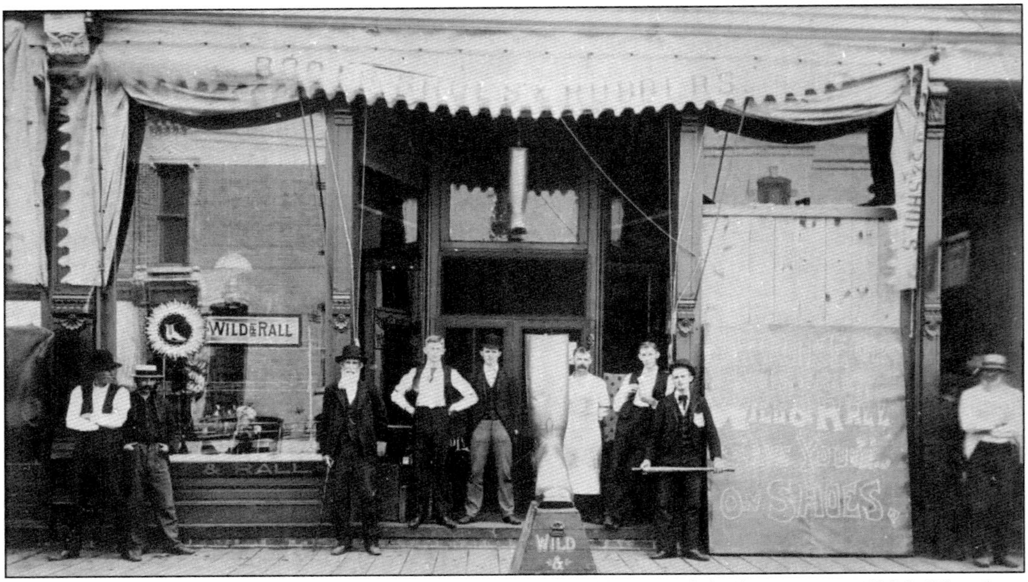

WILD AND RALL SHOE SHOP. The firm of Wild and Rall opened for business in 1886. The shoe shop was located in the Russell building at the corner of Second Street and Willis Avenue. Harry Marckres owned the business, then called Rall's, from 1919 to 1937. Marckres passed the business to his son John, who owned it from 1937 to 1944.

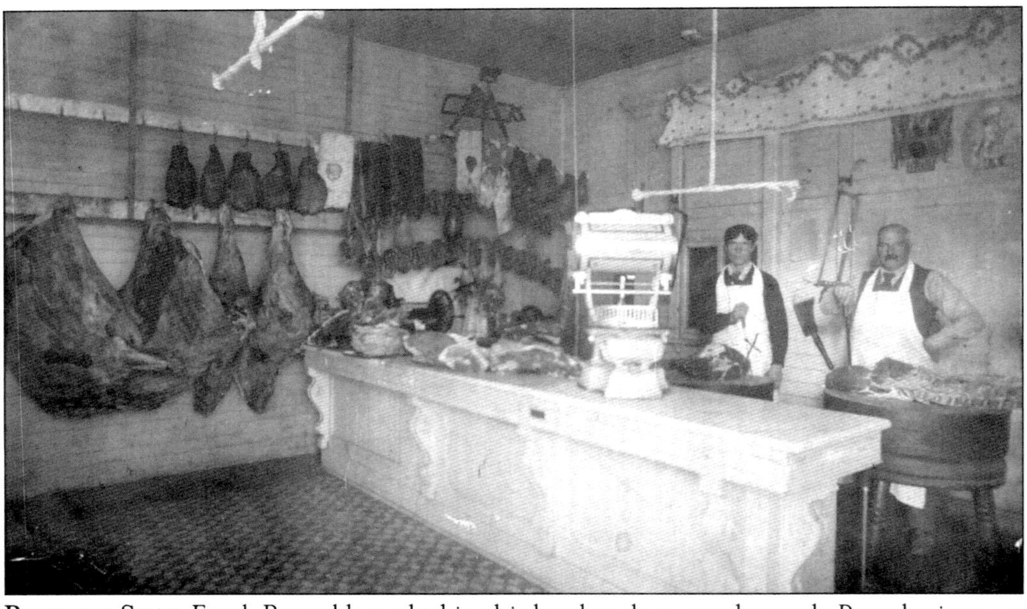

BUTCHER SHOP. Frank Reynolds worked in this butcher shop, another early Perry business, at the end of the 19th century. Its location is not clear, but it may have been north of what is now 1010 Second Street.

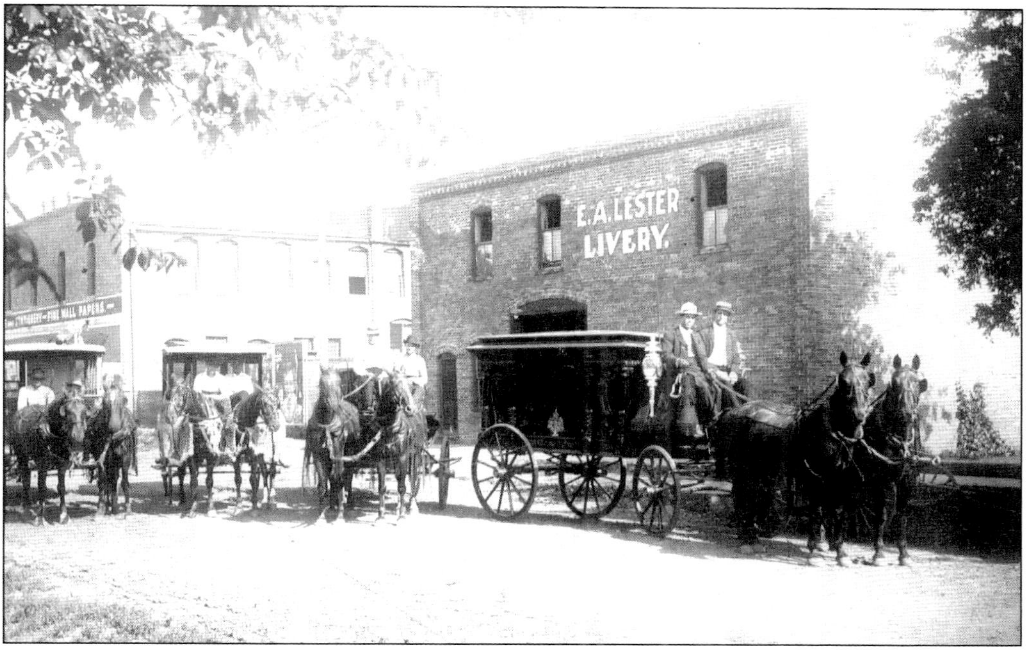

E. A. Lester Livery. Horses and buggies stand ready to deliver for the E. A. Lester Livery. Lester bought the Stewart House bus line in 1893 then added a livery barn to his business in 1901. Later he also acquired a hearse and ambulance.

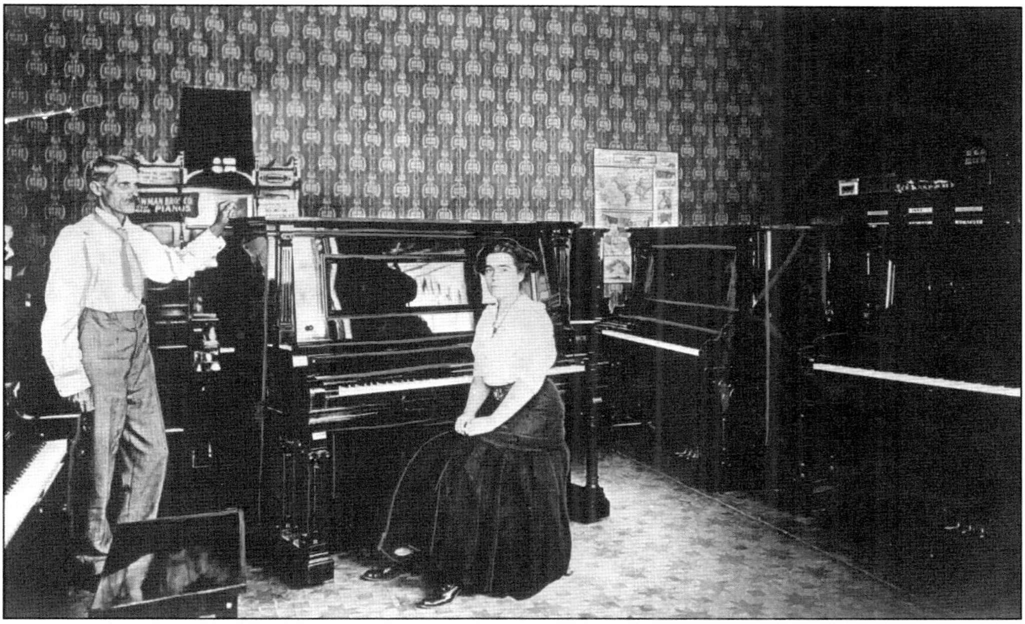

George W. and Viola Worth. George W. Worth sold new and used musical instruments from a location on the west side of Perry's downtown triangle. The store was destroyed when the Melick Block burned in September 1893. In December 1903, it moved from south of the opera house in Elizabeth Hughes's millinery store on Second Street. By 1911, Worth Music Store had moved to the Citizens Bank building. George W. Worth died in 1926, and Viola died in 1938.

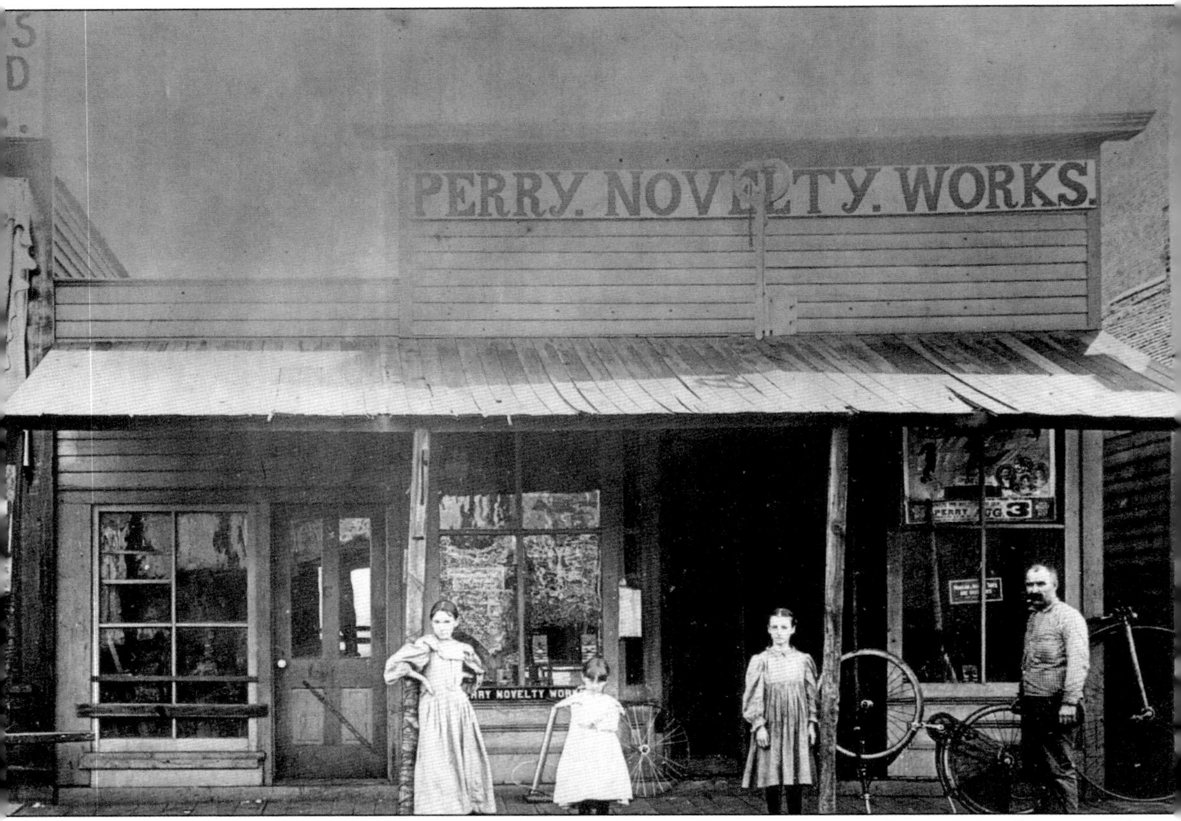

PERRY NOVELTY WORKS. In January 1894, J. W. Pefley came to Perry from Pennsylvania and opened a small shop. Allen Cox purchased the shop from Pefley in 1906.

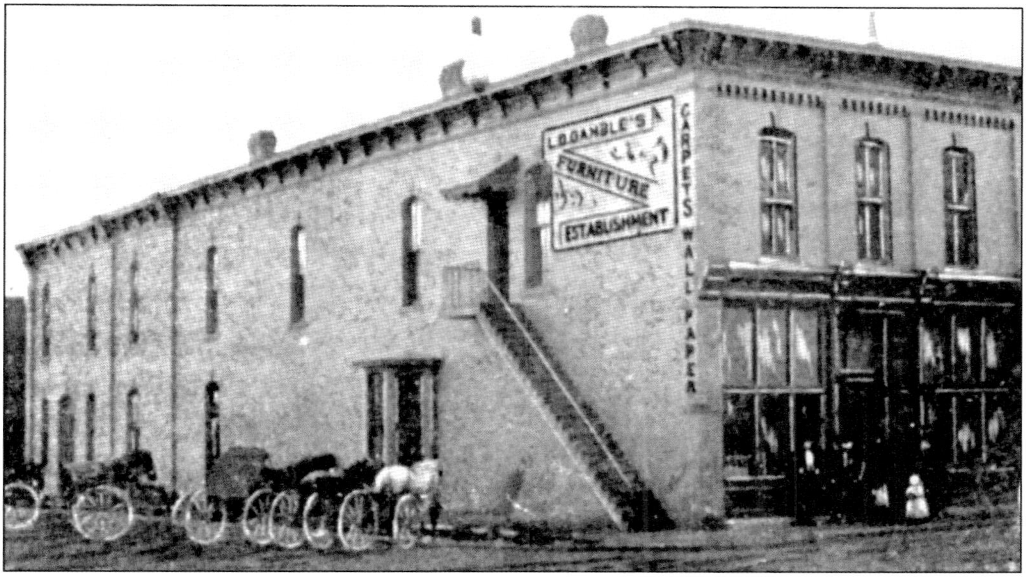

LEVI D. GAMBLE FURNITURE STORE. Levi D. Gamble, born on January 29, 1842, in Illinois, served in the Civil War and then came to Perry in 1869. After first opening a grocery store, in 1880, he established his furniture business on Perry's downtown triangle. In 1883, Gamble built the brick block on the northwest corner of Second and Warford Streets. After a fire in November 1898, Gamble rebuilt his store on the same lot. In June 1928, he sold the store to L. R. Burrington.

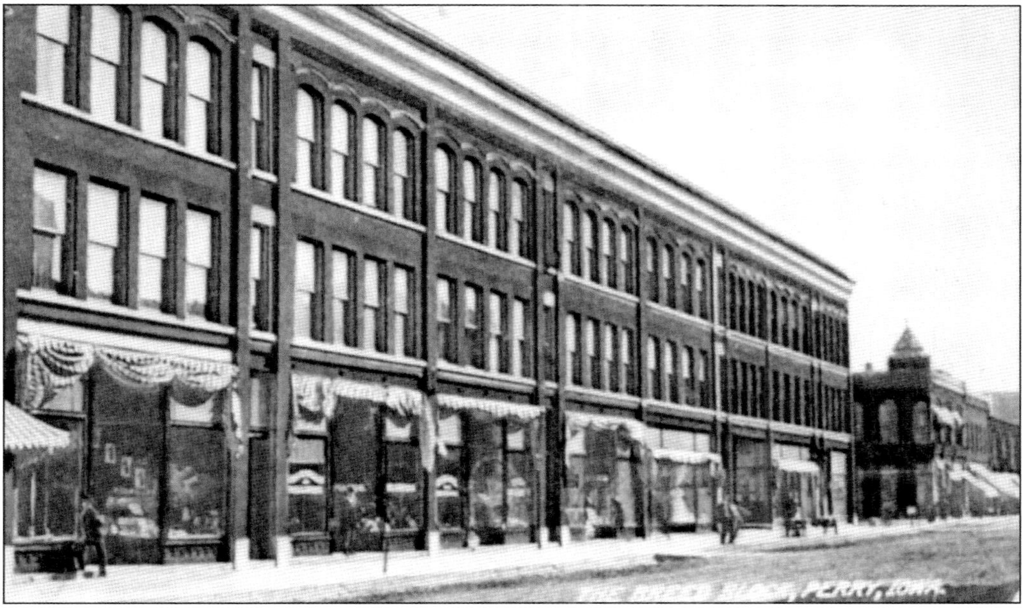

BREED BLOCK. The Breed Block was the name given to six new buildings on the east side of Second Street between Warford and Lucinda Streets. A fire destroyed the previous buildings in November 1898. Businesses in the block included a bank, W. H. McCammon Clothiers, Thomas J. Gilbert Hardware, H. and E. Ringheim Dry Goods, and Fenner and Edmondson Boots and Shoes.

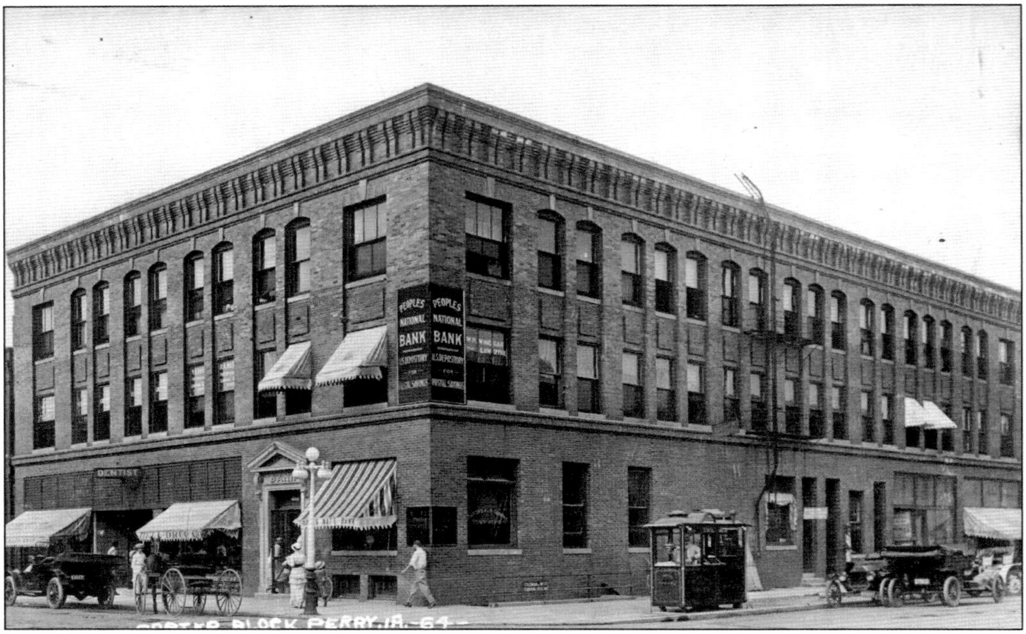

CARTER BLOCK. This block at the corner of Second Street and Willis Avenue, around 1913, housed Peoples National Bank, Bell Drug, Bulkley Brothers, and a popcorn stand (beside the building).

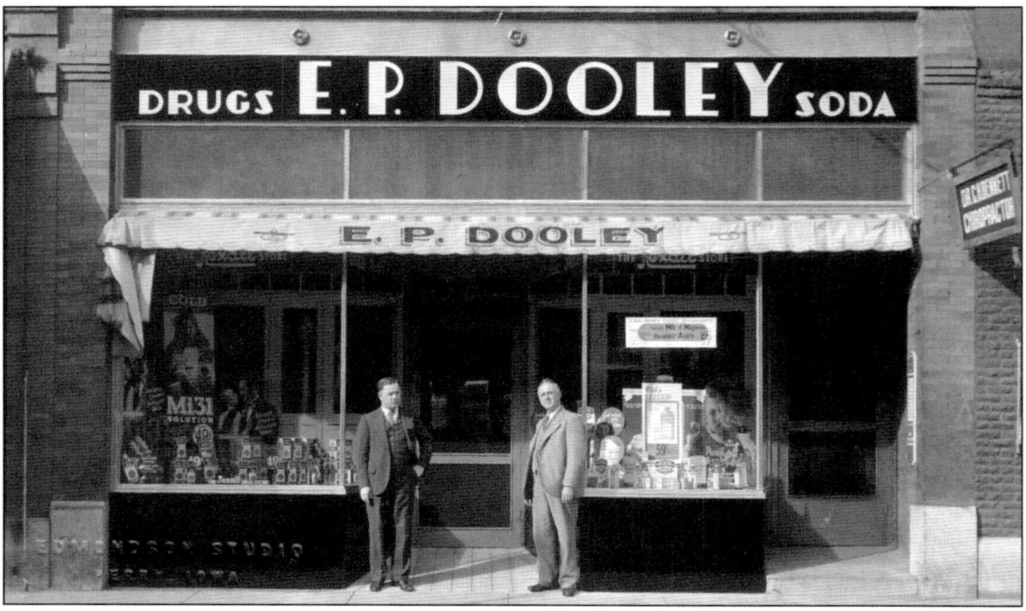

E. P. DOOLEY DRUG STORE. One of many drugstores in Perry, Dooley's was located at 1209 Second Street. Shown here are Fred Marker (left) and Edward Patrick (E. P.) Dooley. Dooley attended country school then Jones Business College in Perry and Highland Park College in Des Moines. In 1945, Dooley sold the store to Mr. and Mrs. Robert Stoner, who later sold to Lloyd Holcomb in February 1948.

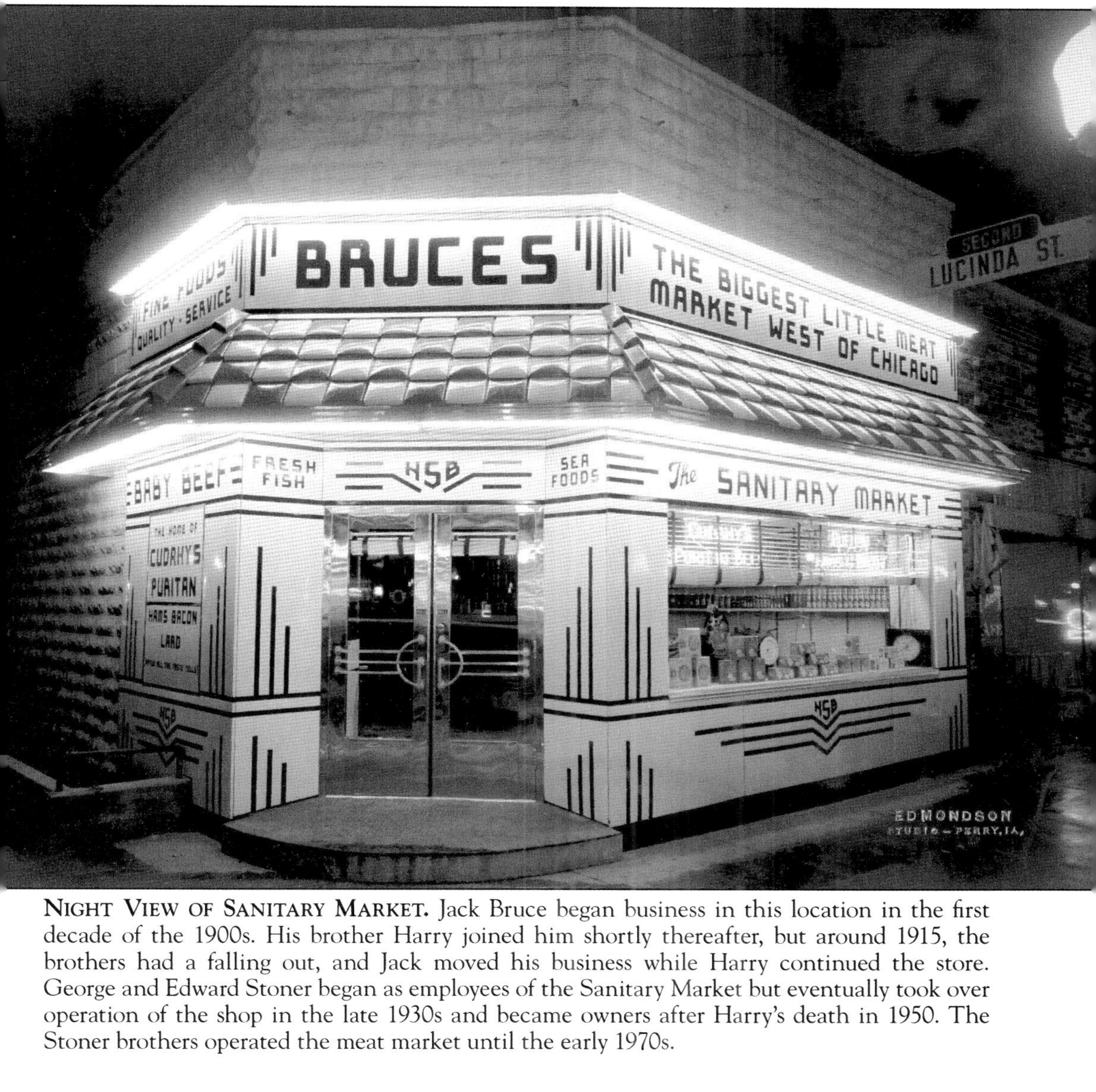

Night View of Sanitary Market. Jack Bruce began business in this location in the first decade of the 1900s. His brother Harry joined him shortly thereafter, but around 1915, the brothers had a falling out, and Jack moved his business while Harry continued the store. George and Edward Stoner began as employees of the Sanitary Market but eventually took over operation of the shop in the late 1930s and became owners after Harry's death in 1950. The Stoner brothers operated the meat market until the early 1970s.

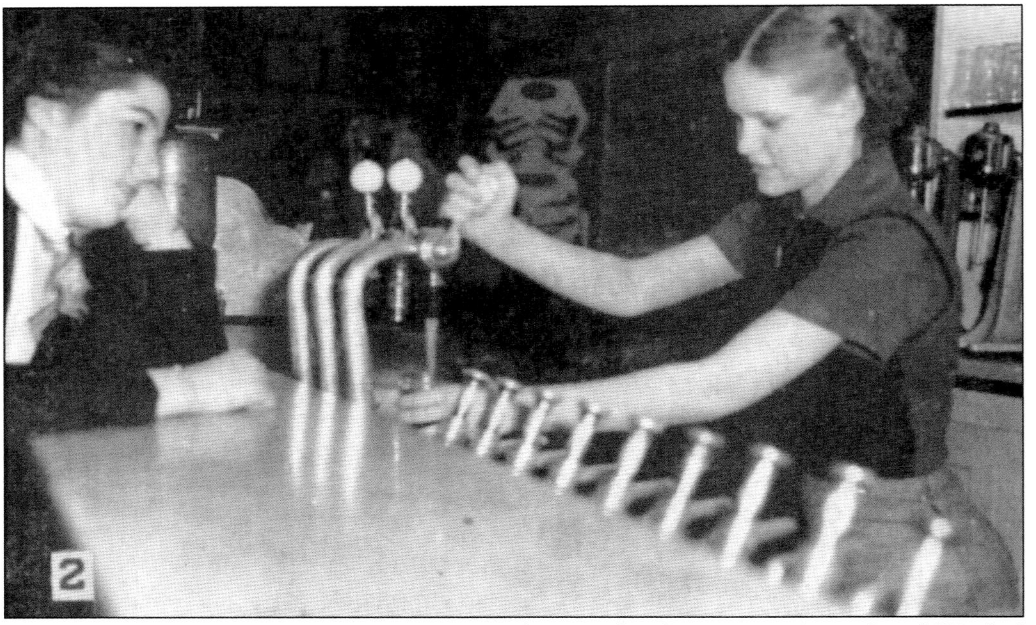

RAY B. SMITH SODA FOUNTAIN. Ray B. Smith opened a drugstore at Second and Warford Streets with his wife, Irene. Smith later built a second store on Willis Avenue. Otto Mau bought the Second Street drugstore in 1950 and named it Mau Pharmacy.

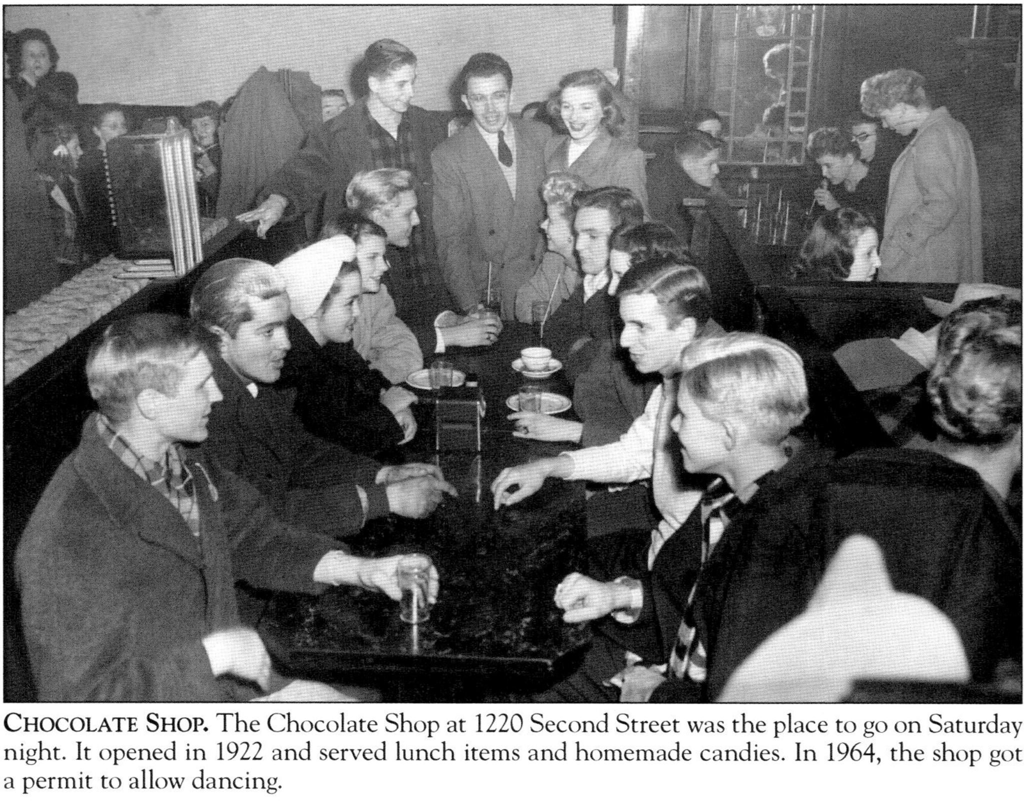

CHOCOLATE SHOP. The Chocolate Shop at 1220 Second Street was the place to go on Saturday night. It opened in 1922 and served lunch items and homemade candies. In 1964, the shop got a permit to allow dancing.

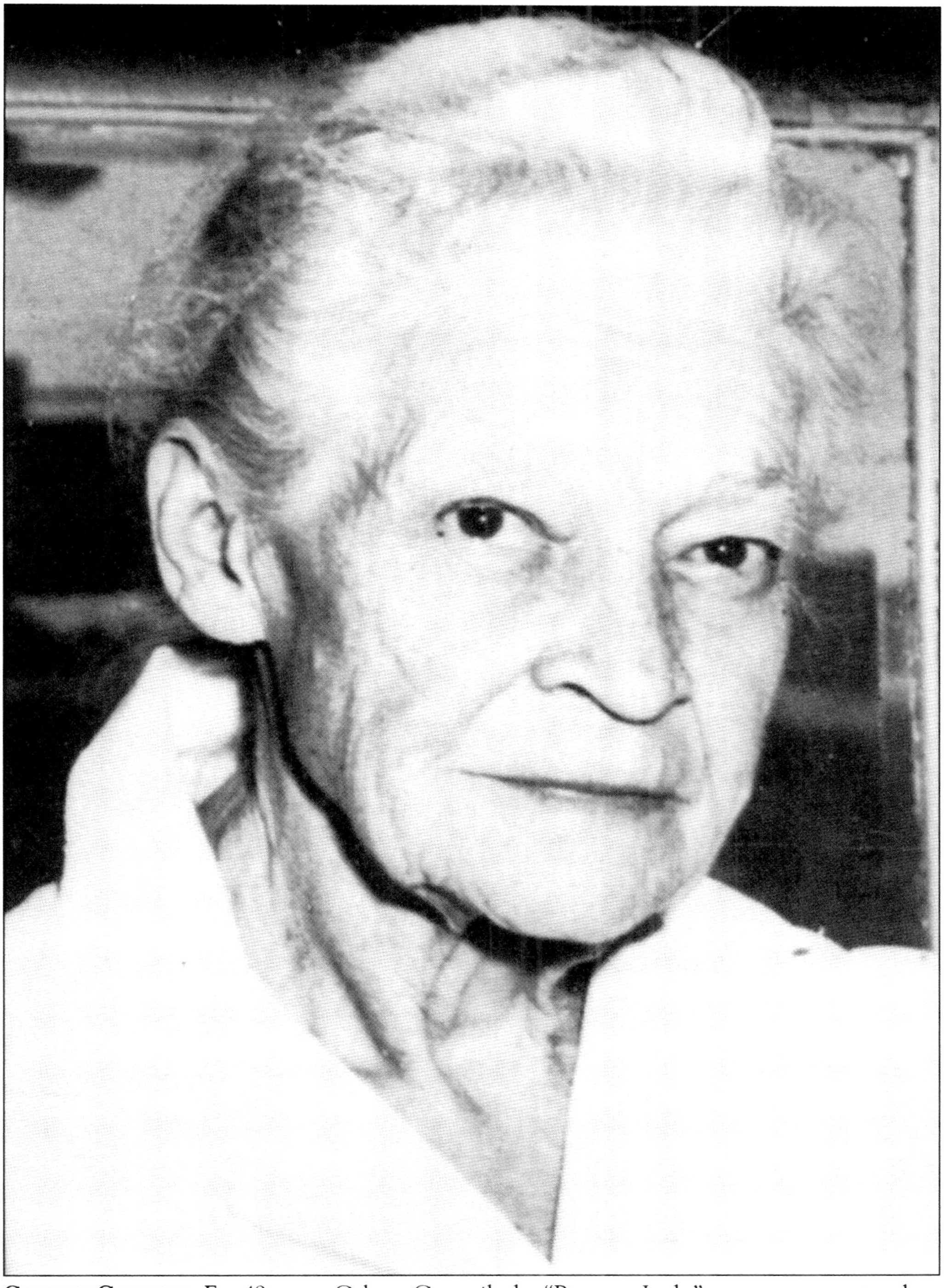

CELESTE COUNCIL. For 49 years, Celeste Council, the "Popcorn Lady," ran a popcorn stand on the corner of Second Street and Willis Avenue where she sold popcorn for 5¢ a bag. She was born in 1882 to an early settler family in Perry and died in 1969. On Saturday evenings, the lines for her popcorn were around the block.

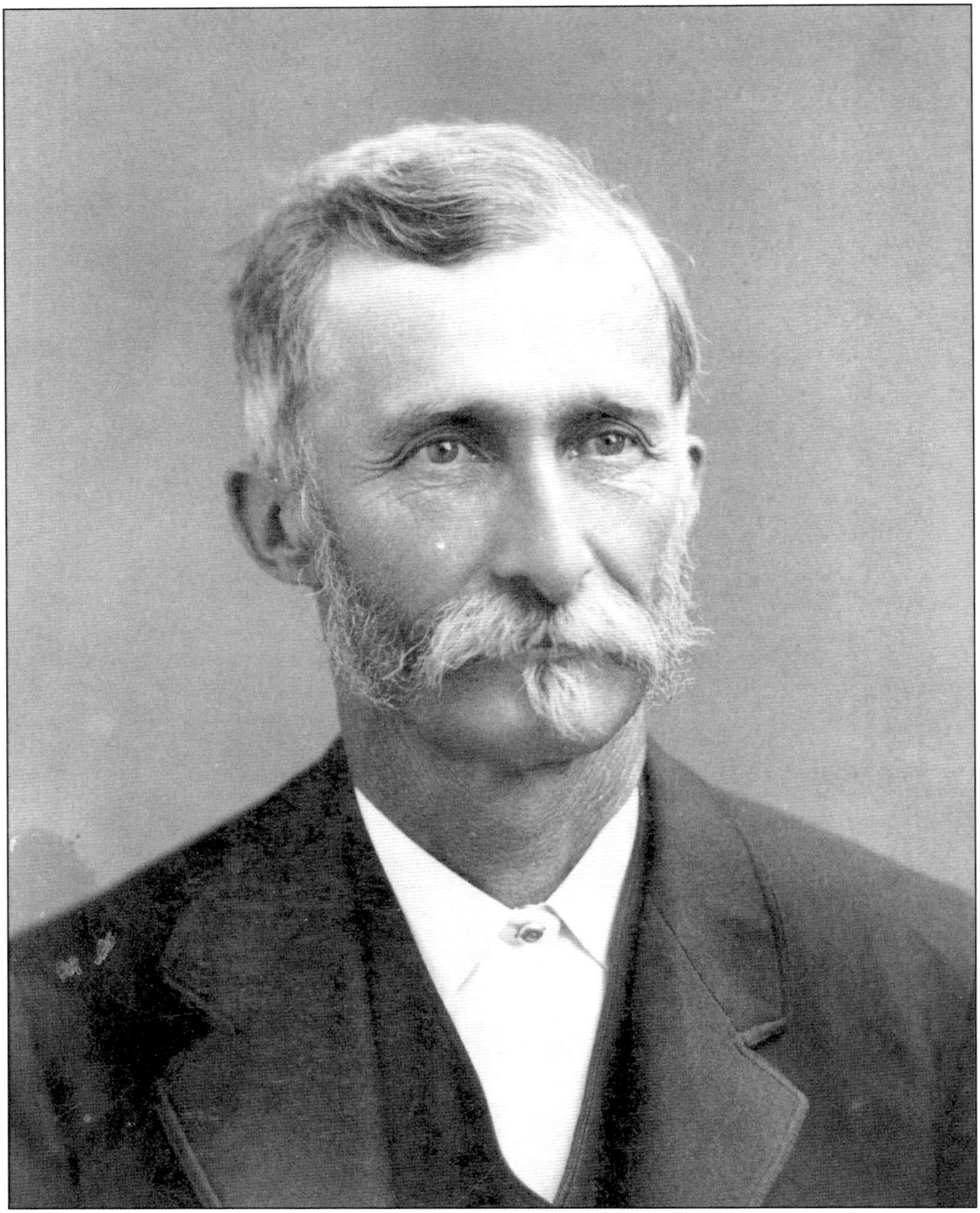

DR. PETER MOWRER. Dr. Peter Mowrer, who came to Perry in 1856, was the town's first doctor, though by 1884, there were nine doctors in Perry. Born in Pennsylvania in 1830, Mowrer was the oldest of eight children. After receiving his medical degree at the University of Pennsylvania, he set up a practice in East Vincent, Pennsylvania, before coming to Dallas County. He also resided briefly in Keokuk. Frog Creek School, a one-room school, was located on his farm one mile south of Perry. He died in 1909.

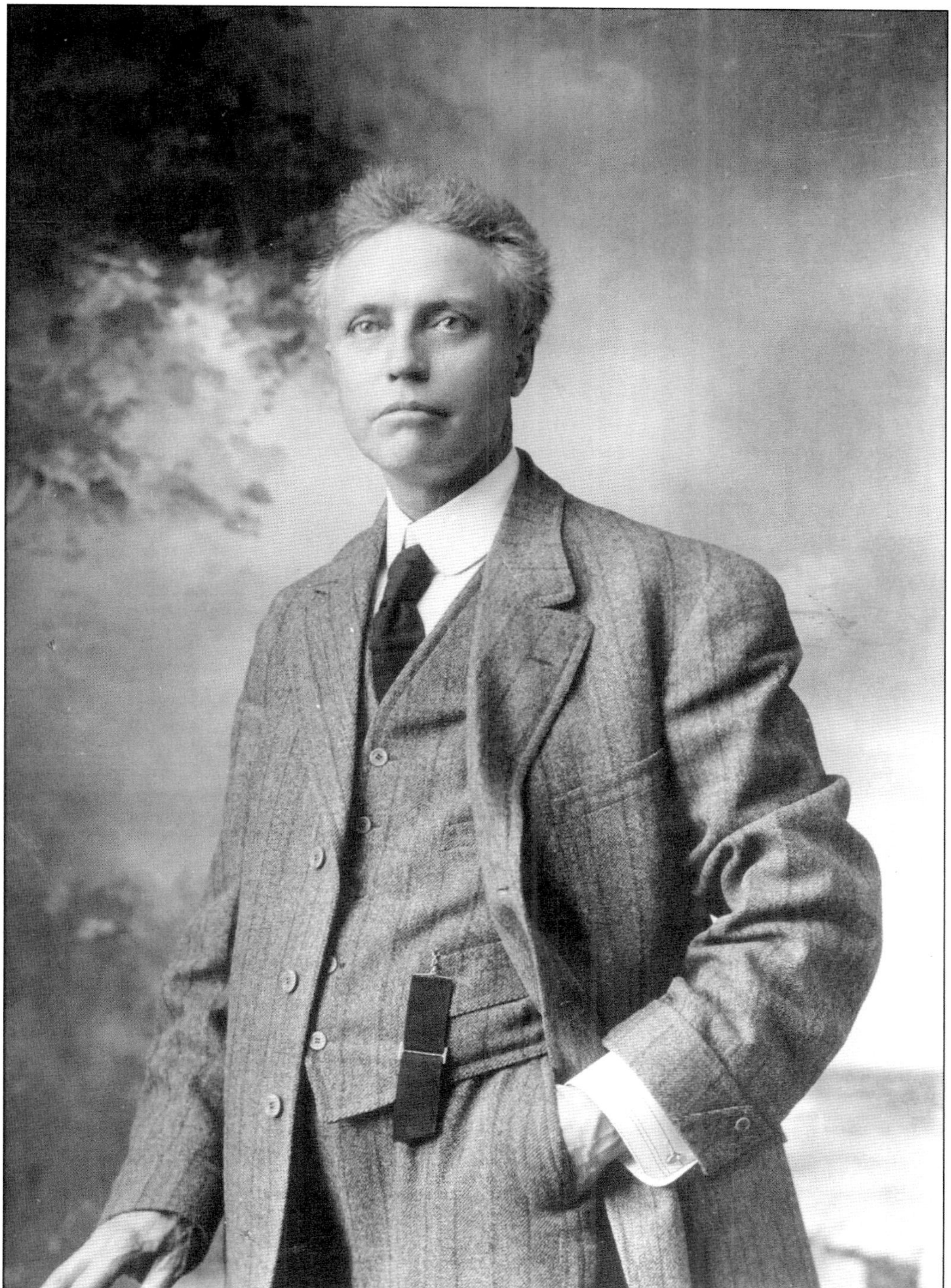

Dr. A. J. Ross. Dr. A. J. Ross served as a physician in Perry for more than 50 years. He married Mabel Leonard, daughter of another doctor. Ross had offices in Perry between Second and Third Streets as early as 1884.

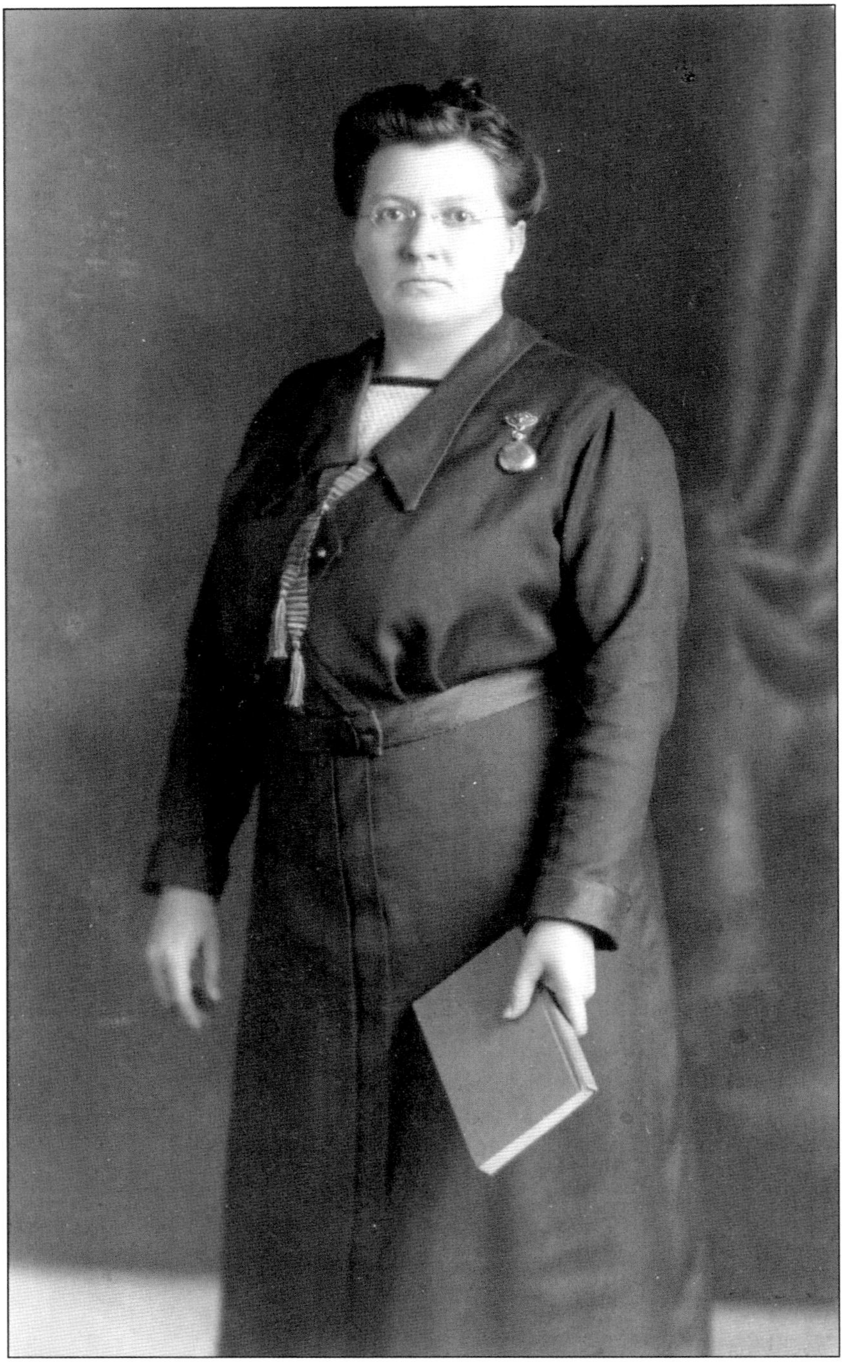

Dr. Mabel Andrews. Osteopath Dr. Mabel Andrews lived and worked at 1102 Willis Avenue in Perry. Born in 1875, Andrews trained at Still College of Osteopathy, now Des Moines University. In 1923, she brought a lawsuit against the King's Daughters Hospital, claiming that the medical staff prevented her from treating patients the way she saw fit. However, the judge ruled in favor of the hospital board. Andrews continued to practice in Perry and lived to be 91 years old.

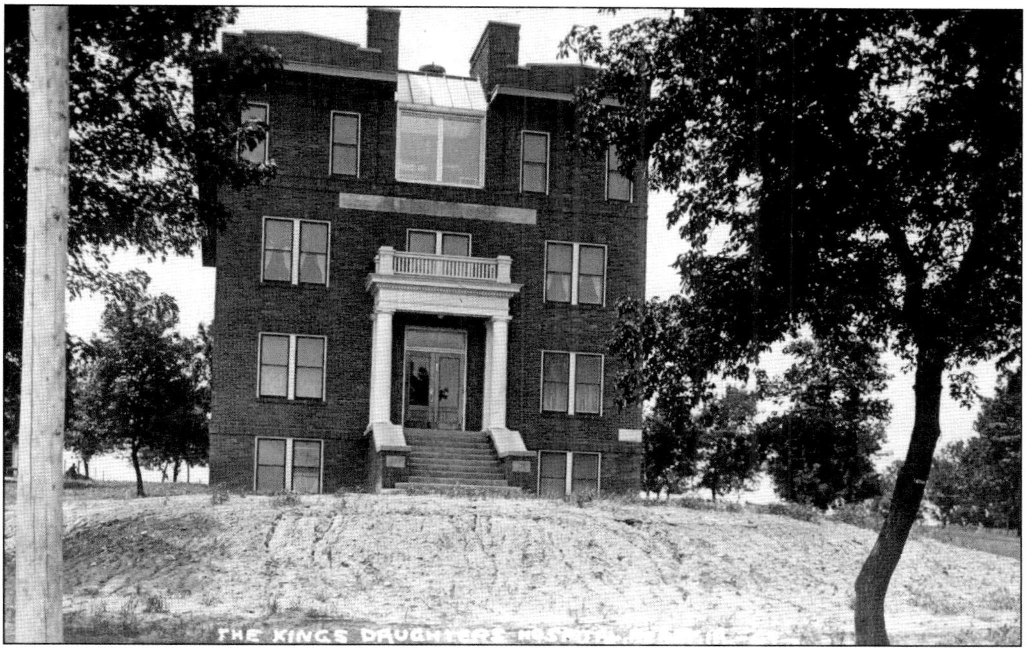

KING'S DAUGHTERS HOSPITAL. Perry's first hospital took its name from the International Order of the King's Daughters, founded in New York City in 1886 by Margaret Bottome, wife of a Methodist minister. Chapters dedicated to this "sisterhood of service" soon spread across the county. The Alpha Circle of the King's Daughters, located in Perry, raised the funds to build the hospital in 1914. The King's Daughters Hospital served the community until the Dallas County Hospital was built in 1956. The building was then sold to the Lutheran Association and became part of a home for the elderly until it was demolished in 1978.

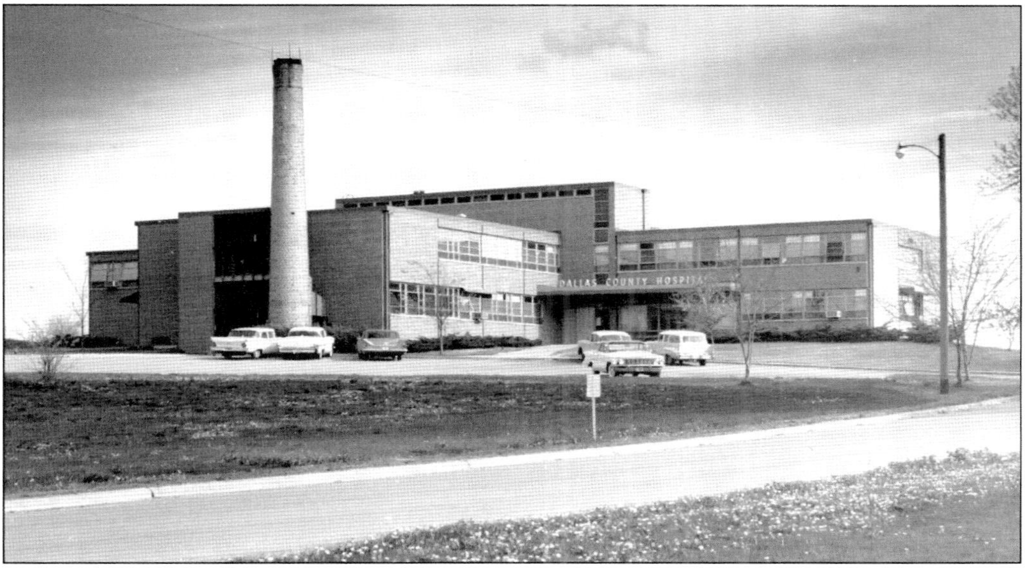

DALLAS COUNTY HOSPITAL. Dallas County Hospital, built to serve Perry after the community outgrew the King's Daughters Hospital, was dedicated in 1956. It continues to operate on the same site.

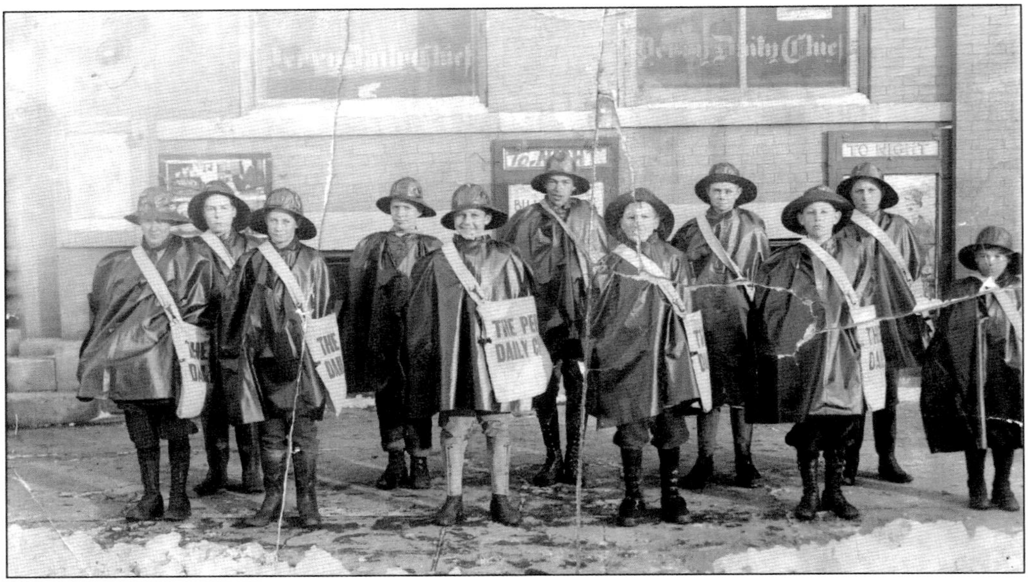

PERRY CHIEF CARRIERS. The first issue of the *Perry Chief* appeared in 1874. Other Perry newspapers included the *Advertiser* and *Reporter*, though neither is still in existence. The *Perry Chief*, now a weekly, was a daily newspaper from 1894 to 1964. *Perry Chief* carriers in 1903 include, from left to right, Ralph Simpson, James Betz, Donald Kerlin, Donald Gardener, Dick Overton, Theo Overton, Elmer Darmer, Alfred Warner, Harry Smith, Hiram White, and Donald White.

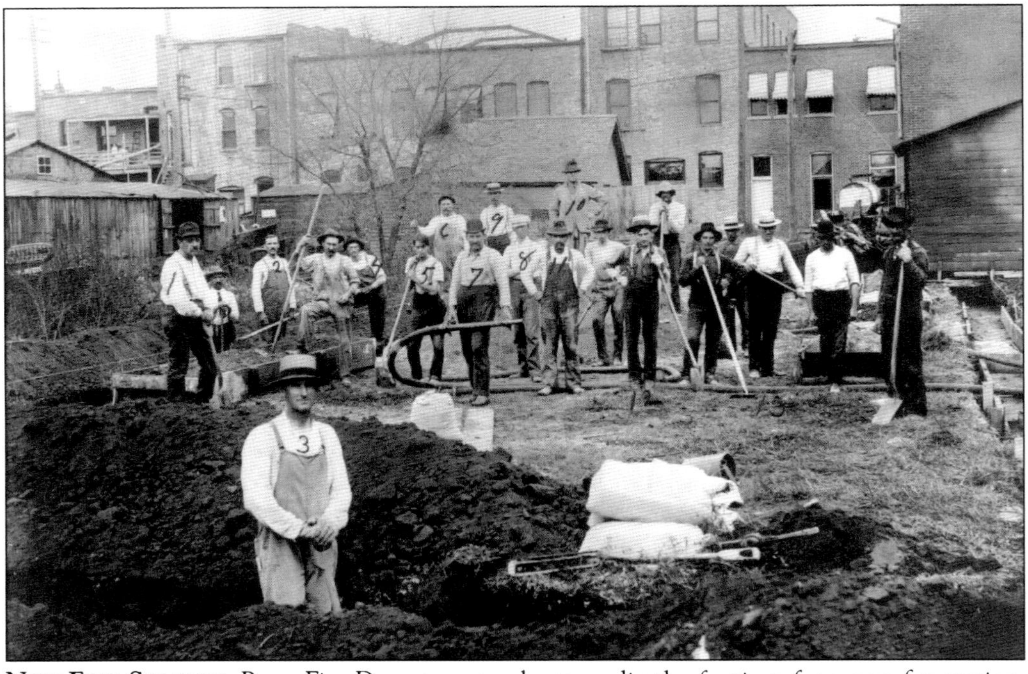

NEW FIRE STATION. Perry Fire Department volunteers dig the footings for a new fire station. Construction began in April of that year. Perry Brick and Tile Works created the bricks for the building.

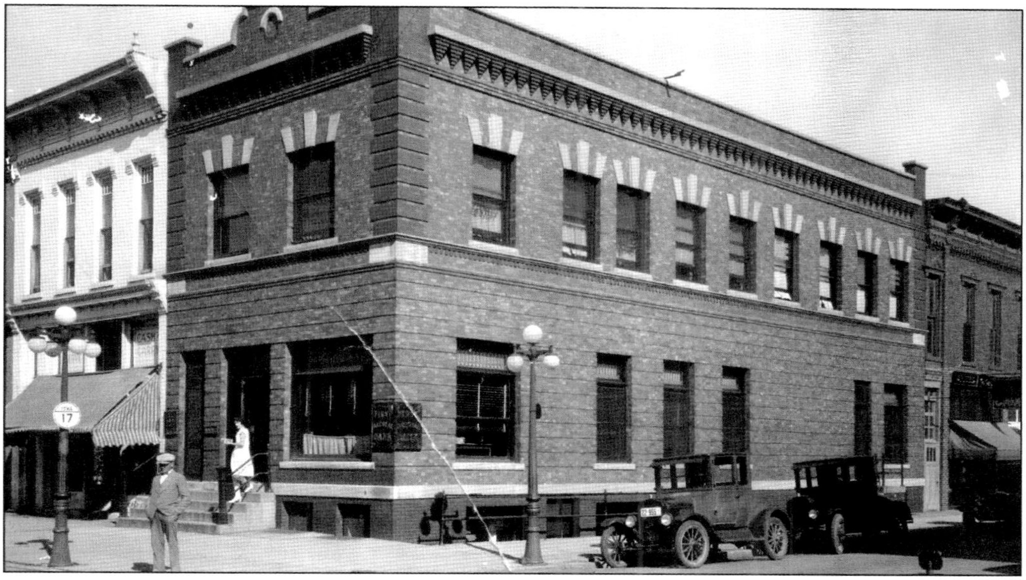

FIRST NATIONAL BANK. First National Bank, which opened in 1883, was located at the corner of Second Street and Willis Avenue. An expansion in 1953 and 1954 took over the two buildings to the west of the corner. In 1961, the bank installed the first drive-up window in Dallas County. At this time, Highway 17 went through Perry on Willis Avenue; a road sign is visible in the photograph. The bank building now houses Town/Craft, a resource center for small towns that is a joint project of Hometown Perry, Iowa, Iowa State University School of Design, and Iowa State Extension.

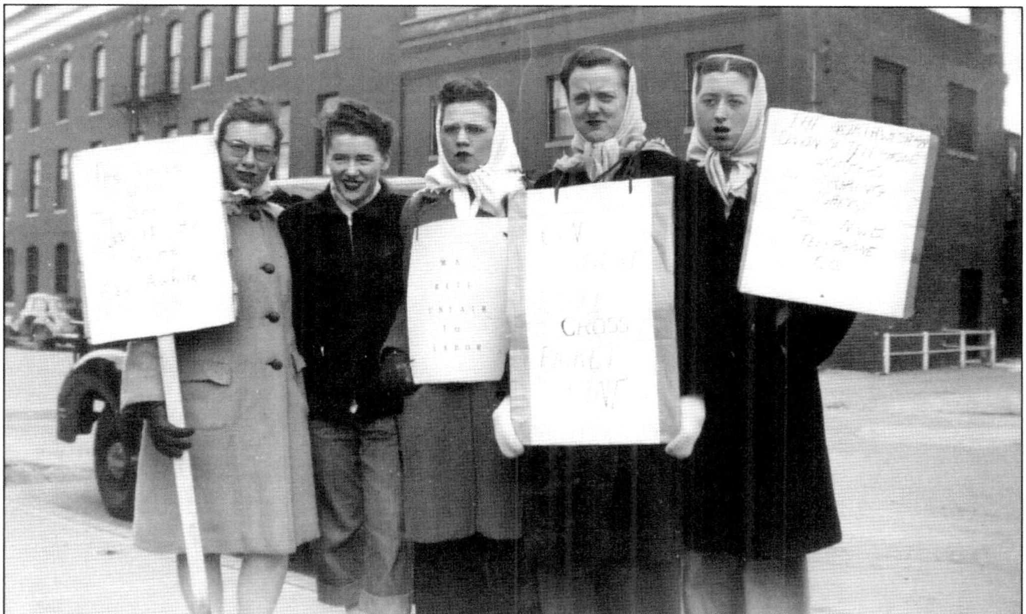

LADIES ON TELEPHONE STRIKE. Employees at Northwestern Bell took part in a nationwide strike from April 7 to May 6, 1947. Pictured here from left to right are Barbara Parket, Ruth Bailey, Nellie Brewer, Ann Rohner, and Phyllis Judd.

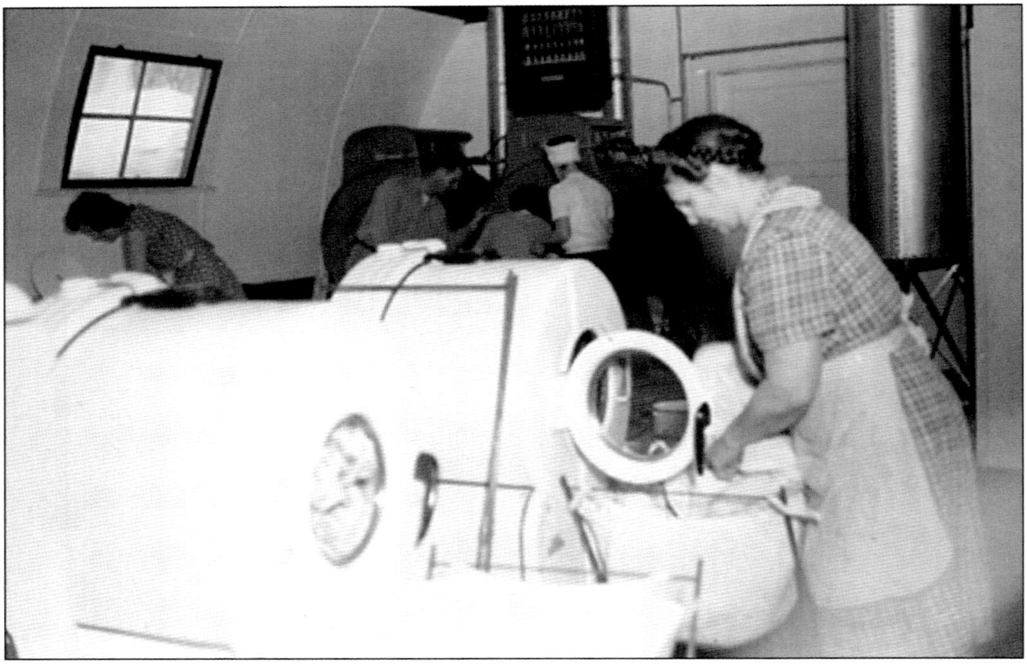

SERV-U LAUNDRY NO. 2. Owner Clyde Latimer, in back beside the dryers, and Bernice Ebert work at the Serv-U Laundry. Clyde and Vina Latimer owned the business, one of the first in Iowa, from 1946 through 1956. It started as a self-serve laundry and then developed into drop-off laundry service. The Latimers sold the business in 1956.

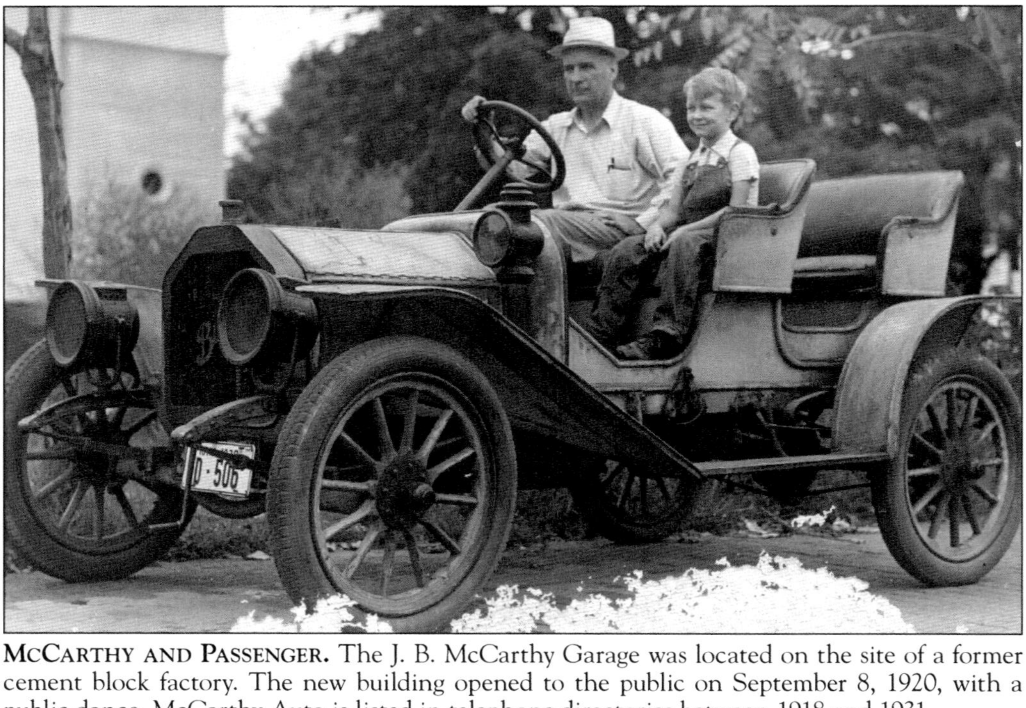

MCCARTHY AND PASSENGER. The J. B. McCarthy Garage was located on the site of a former cement block factory. The new building opened to the public on September 8, 1920, with a public dance. McCarthy Auto is listed in telephone directories between 1918 and 1931.

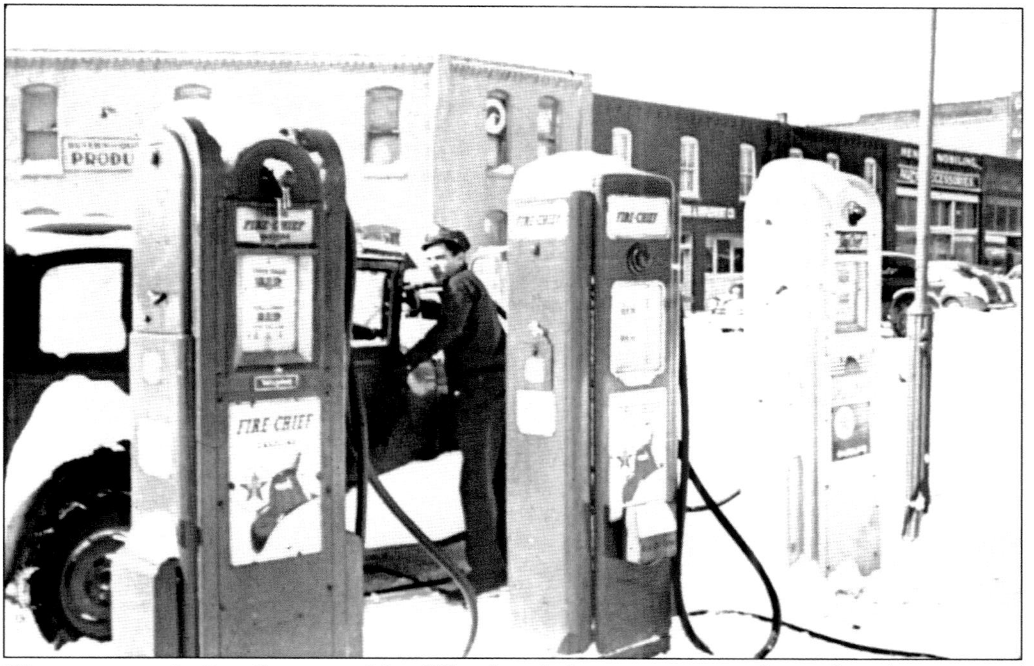

WHEELWRIGHT'S GAS STATION. Max Wheelwright's gas station was located at the corner of Second Street and Otley Avenue. There had previously been other gas stations at this location. Beginning in 1946, the business expanded to become Wheelwright Motors, selling Dodge and Plymouth automobiles.

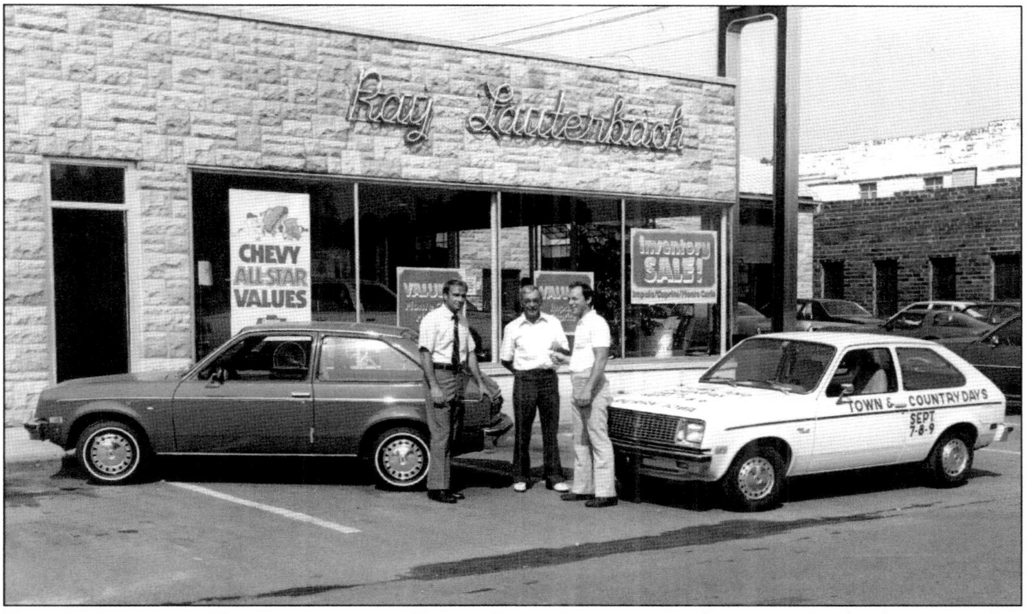

RAY LAUTERBACK CHEVROLET AND BUICK DEALERSHIP. Perry has supported a large number of car dealerships over the years. In July 1949, garage owner Jack Traverse built a new Chevrolet garage at 805 Railroad Street. Traverse and his partner, C. H. Bucher, sold their Chevrolet-Buick dealership to Ray Lauterback of Des Moines in 1954.

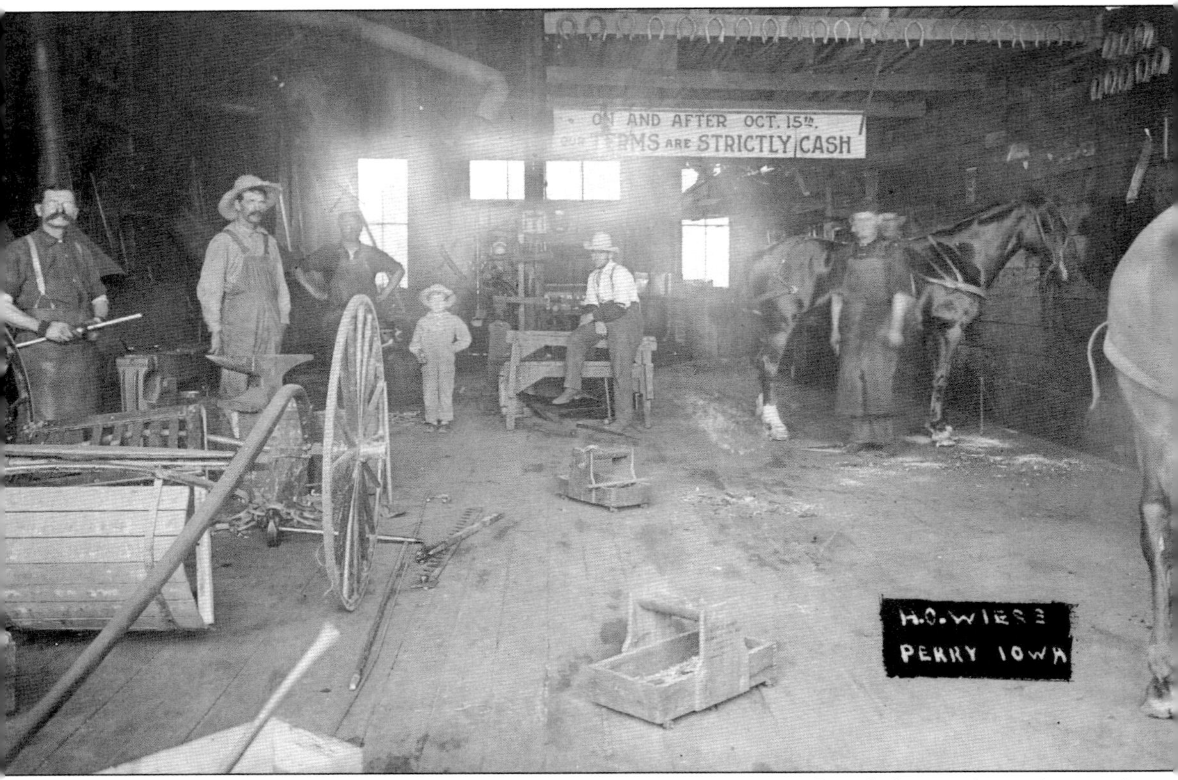

H. O. WIESE BLACKSMITH AND MACHINE SHOP. H. O. Wiese founded a machine shop and welding business in Perry in 1899. In this photograph, the shop's location is believed to be Railroad Street at Otley Avenue. Eventually Wiese branched out into manufacturing plows and launched New Process Plow Welding Company. The business eventually grew into Wiese Industries, still a major employer in Perry today.

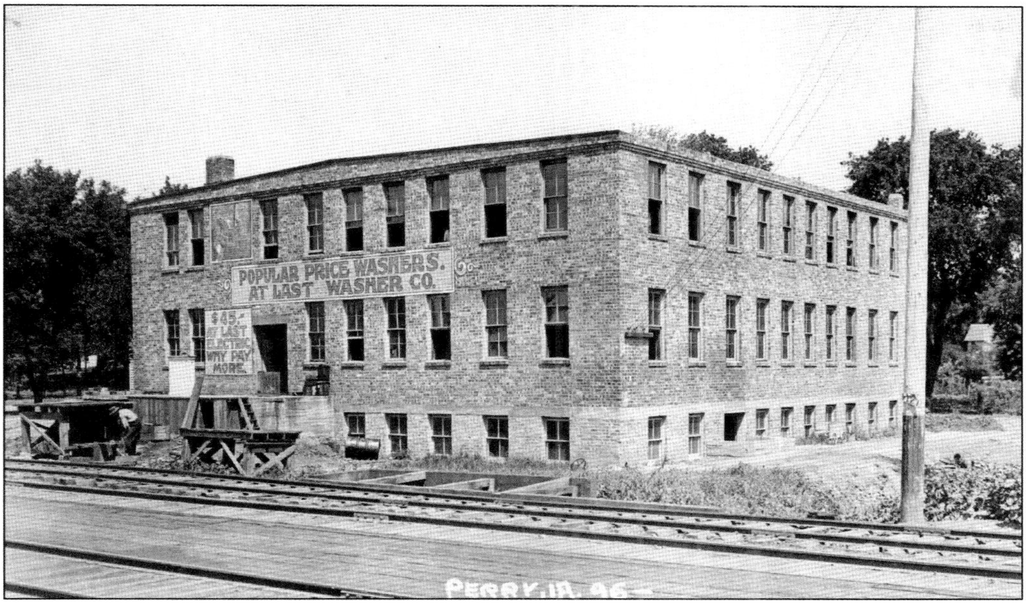

At Last Washing Machine Company. At Last Washing Machine Company was established on West Second Street by A. S. and E. C. Kibby. Located on the previous site of rival Globe Manufacturing, At Last Washing Machine Company operated from 1907 to 1916, manufacturing one of the first electric washers. By 1916, the factory was on the east side of First Avenue just north of the railroad tracks. It lasted until 1929 when A. S. Kibby died.

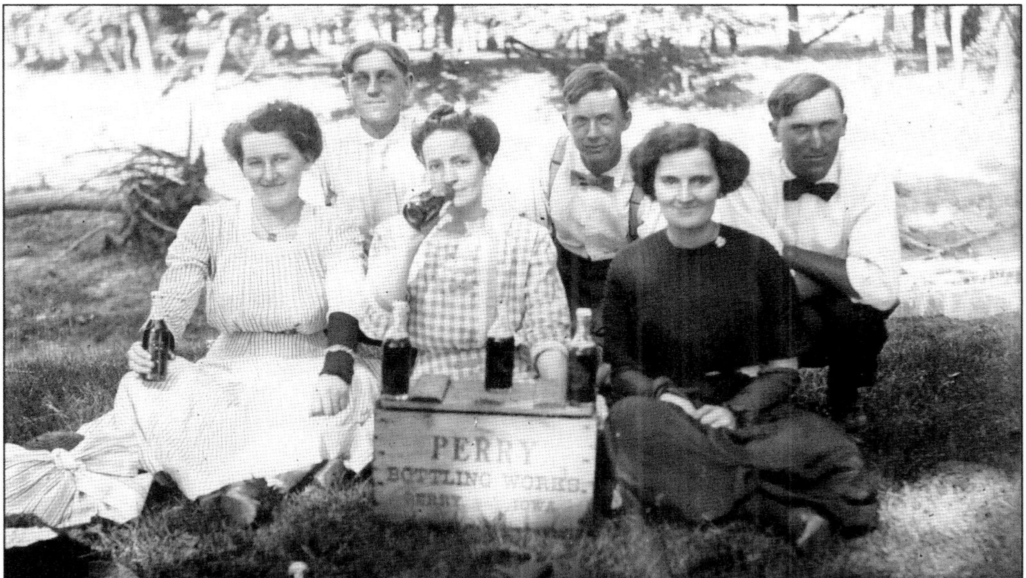

Drinking Soda. The men and women here are drinking soda bottled at Perry Bottling Works. Hub Shively ran the bottling works from the late 1800s until its sale to Frank Jurgens in 1928. First located on the west end of Willis Avenue, the company bottled Perry Cola. In May 1937, it moved to Second Street. The company later became Perry Bottling Company, which produced Nichol Kola, a drink called Little Joe, and Grapette Soda.

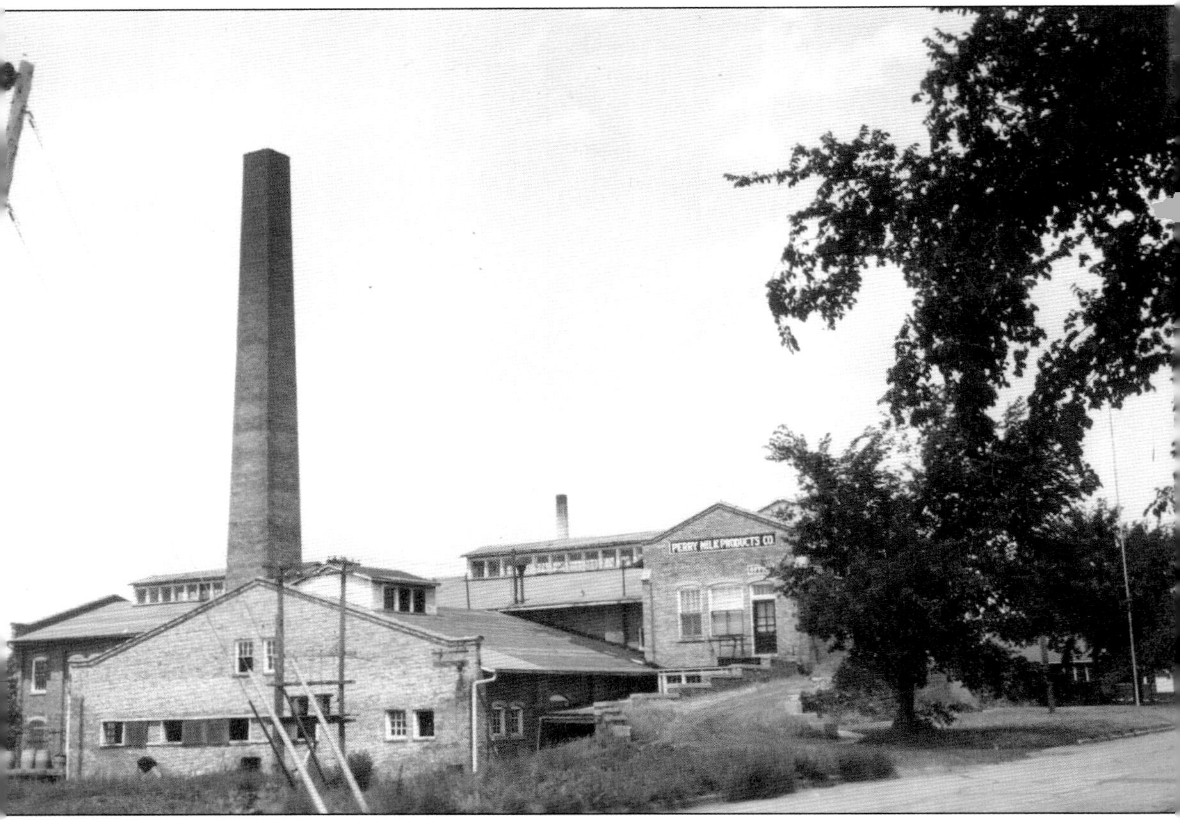

PERRY MILK PRODUCTS. Located at the corner of First Avenue and Estella Street, Van Camp Packing Company opened as a milk-condensing factory in 1908. In 1915, the business was sold and renamed Perry Packing Plant. In August 1922, it became Perry Mik Products and later became a division of Meadow Gold, specializing in ice-cream products. It produced condensed milk, cheese, ice-cream mix, and, later, candy.

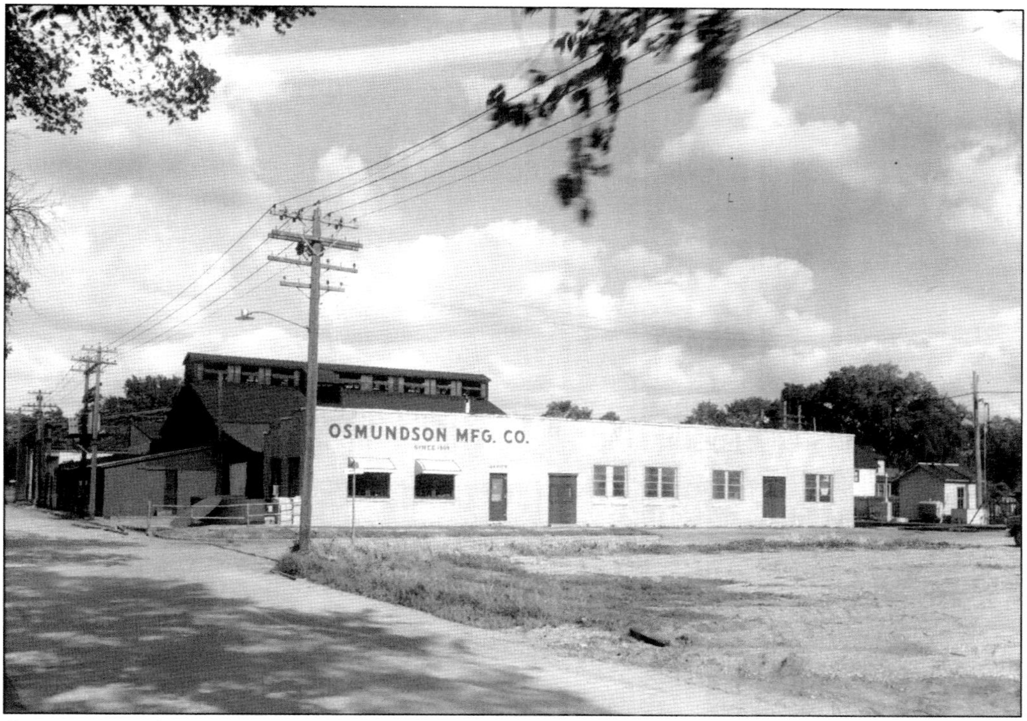

OSMUNDSON MANUFACTURING COMPANY. Henry Osmundson emigrated from Norway and came to Perry in 1905. After he invented a spade for ditching and tilling, in 1906, Osmundson opened a factory east of the Milwaukee Road depot to manufacture the spade. He commuted by train from Slater to Perry daily. His son Howard joined the business in 1911 and became sole owner in January 1917. In 1973, a new plant opened west of Perry. The business is still owned by the same family and employs more than 100 people.

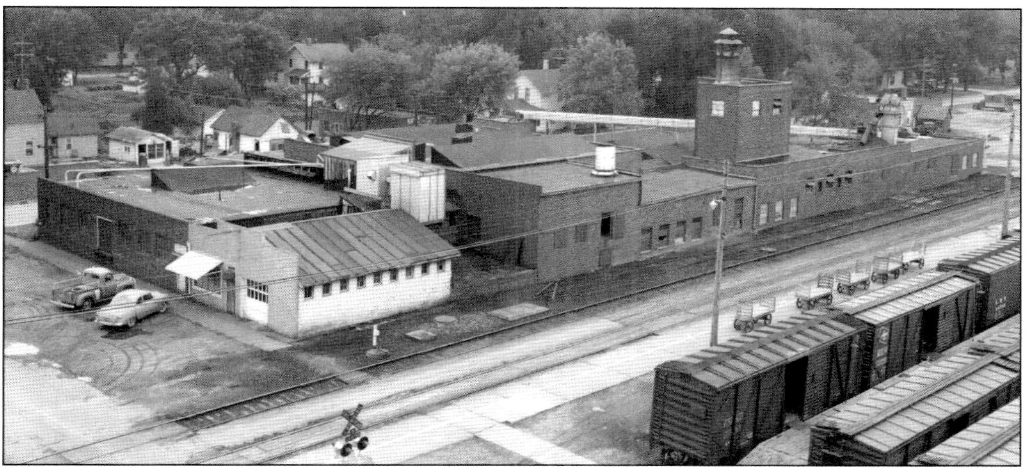

PROGRESSIVE FOUNDRY. Richard Tietjen started Progressive Foundry, then Perry Foundry, in 1919. In October 1920, Tietjen and his sons expanded the plant to employ 40 workers. By 1946, the plant had grown to cover an area equivalent to half of a square block, and it produced gray iron casting for manufacturers throughout the Midwest. In 1981, Mike Hodges and Pete VanKirk bought the business. VanKirk continues to run the foundry.

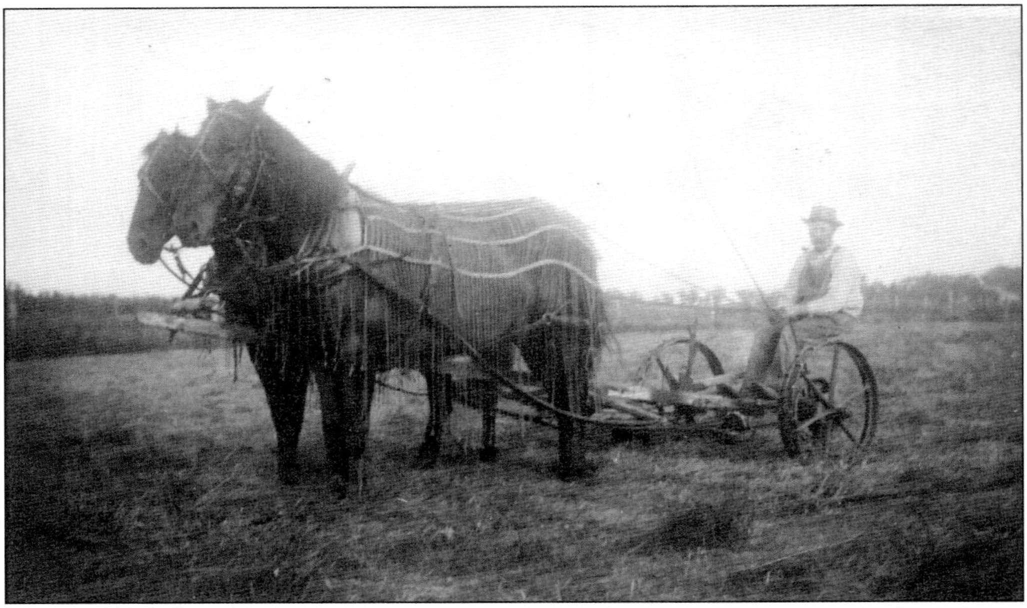

MOWING HAY. Since its beginnings, the area around Perry provided an opportunity for making a living through farming. The history of Perry agriculture highlighted in these pictures exemplifies the larger history of the industry. Here, around 1900, John Elmer Spaudlin mows hay with a horse-drawn mower.

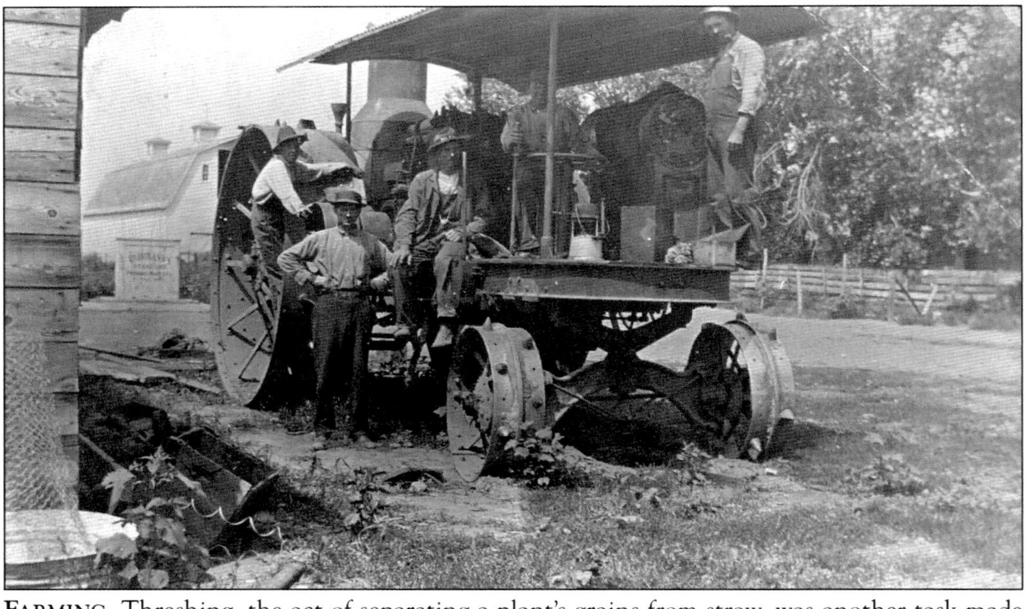

FARMING. Threshing, the act of separating a plant's grains from straw, was another task made easier through mechanization. Here, around 1913, Joe and Fred Conner work with other farmers to accomplish the task. This steam-powered tractor pulled a threshing machine. The family also had a team of horses to help with other tasks.

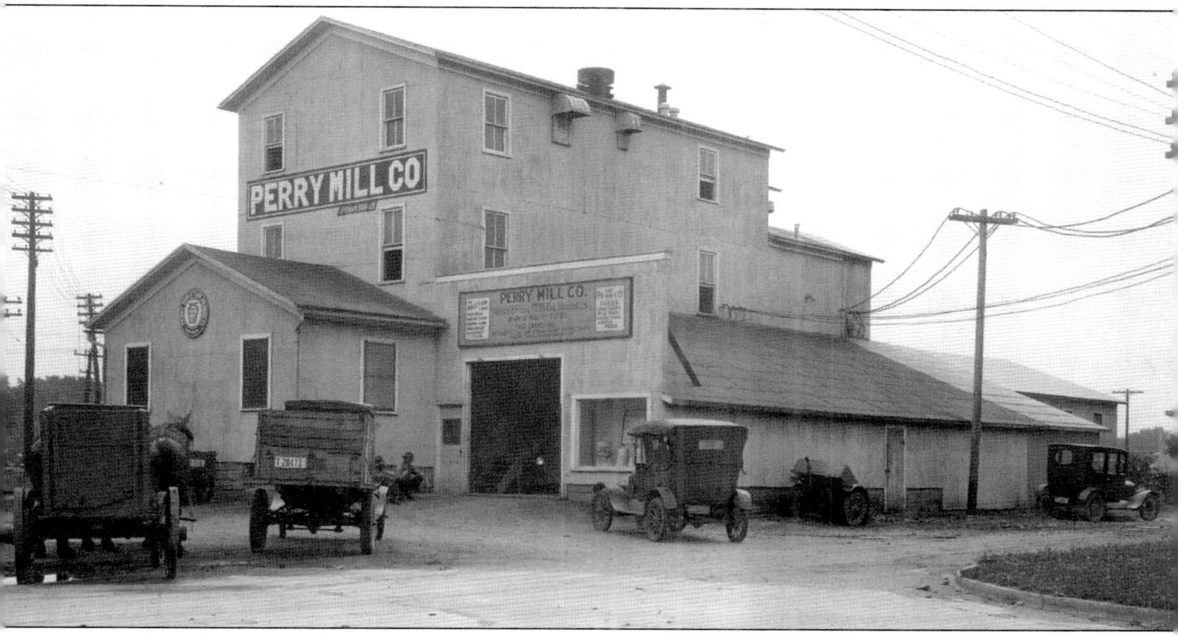

PERRY MILL COMPANY. Enough farming took place in the Perry area that the town could support its own mill. In 1914, J. O. Holdefer built the Perry Mill Company at the corner of First Street and Otley Avenue. He operated the business until 1955 when he sold it to Jack Whiton. Whiton Feeds remains in operation at the same location today.

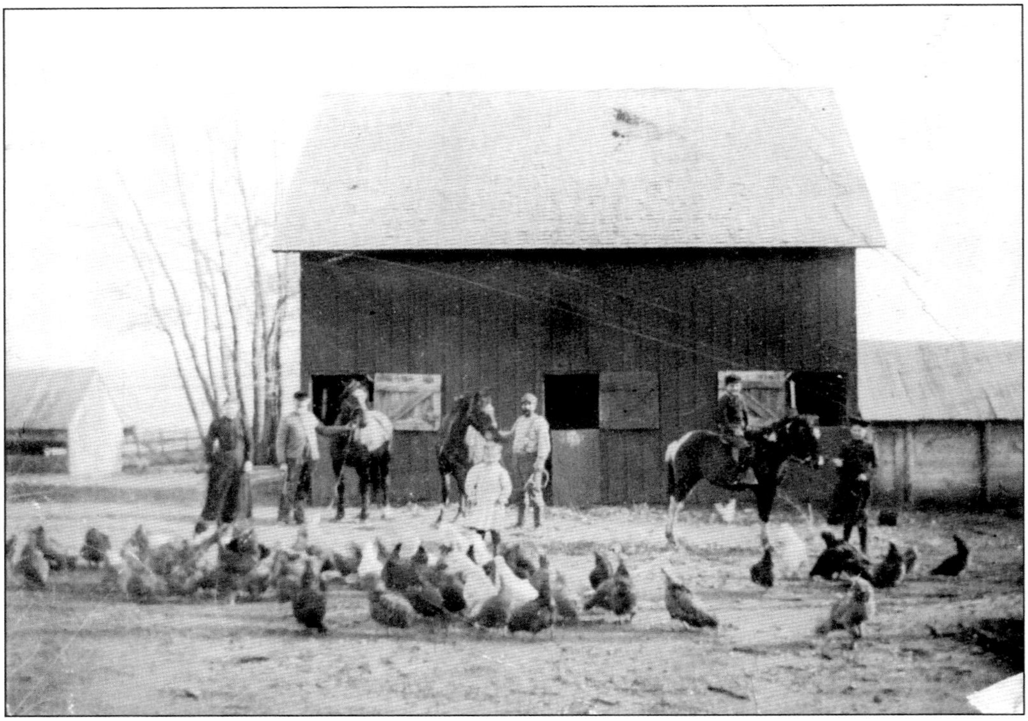

SCHEIB BARN. Although Iowa farmers today primarily grow corn and soybeans, in earlier generations, family farms grew a variety of crops as well as raising animals. Here around 1920, one can see the variety of animals on the Scheib family farm, now a century farm.

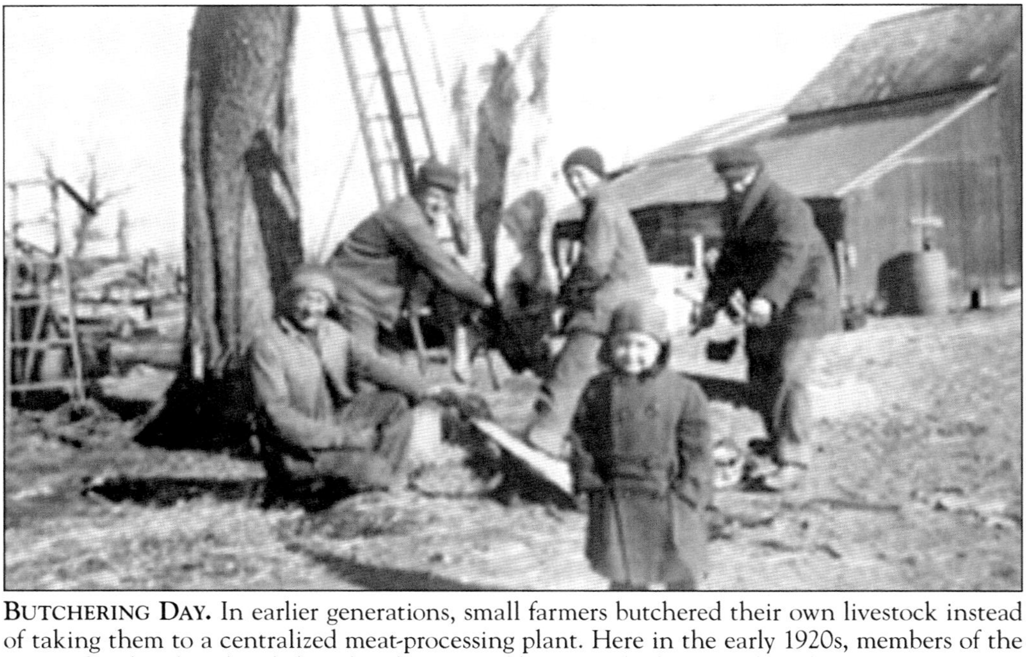

BUTCHERING DAY. In earlier generations, small farmers butchered their own livestock instead of taking them to a centralized meat-processing plant. Here in the early 1920s, members of the Moore family take a break from butchering and hanging the hogs on their farm near Perry.

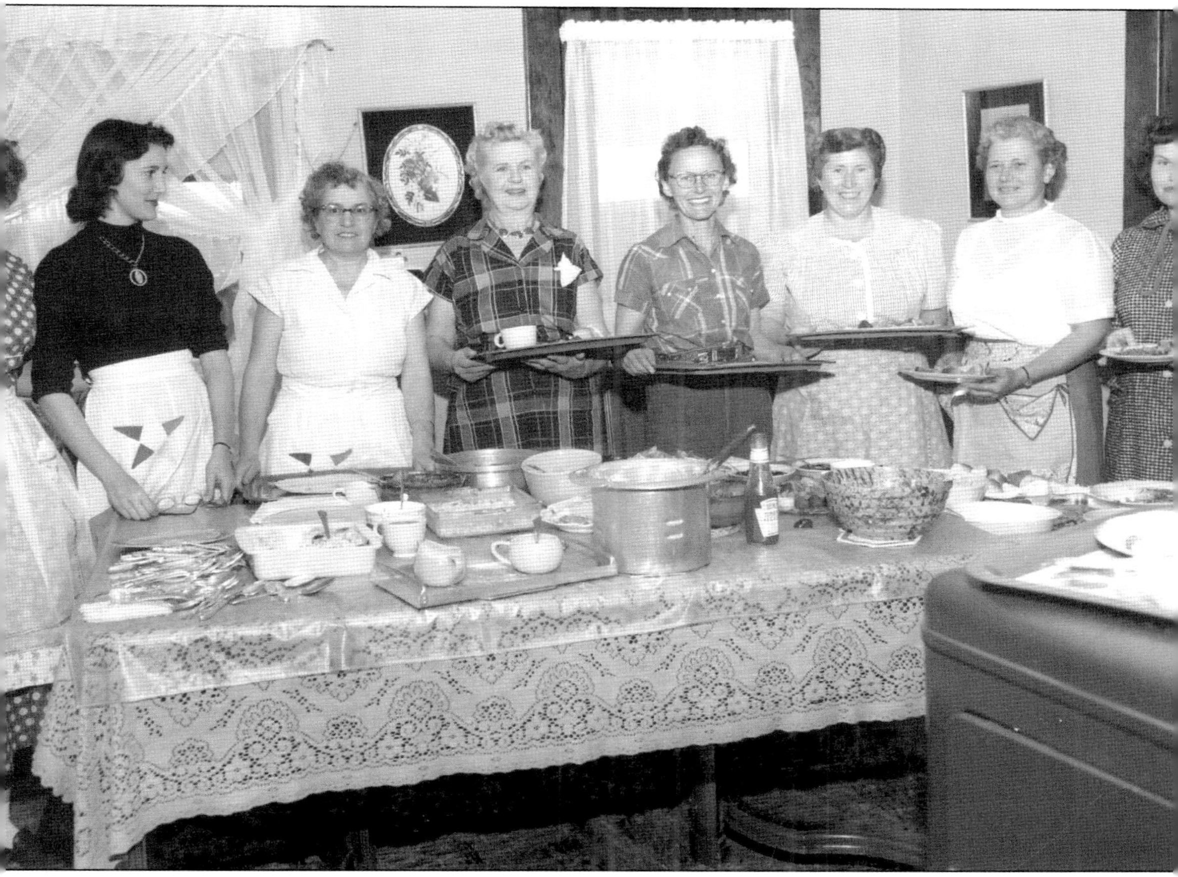

Ladies Serving the Meal. At any event in Perry, food was a highlight. In this picture, typical of the mid-20th century, women are ready to serve. They have prepared a meal for farmers who volunteered to harvest a crop for a neighbor.

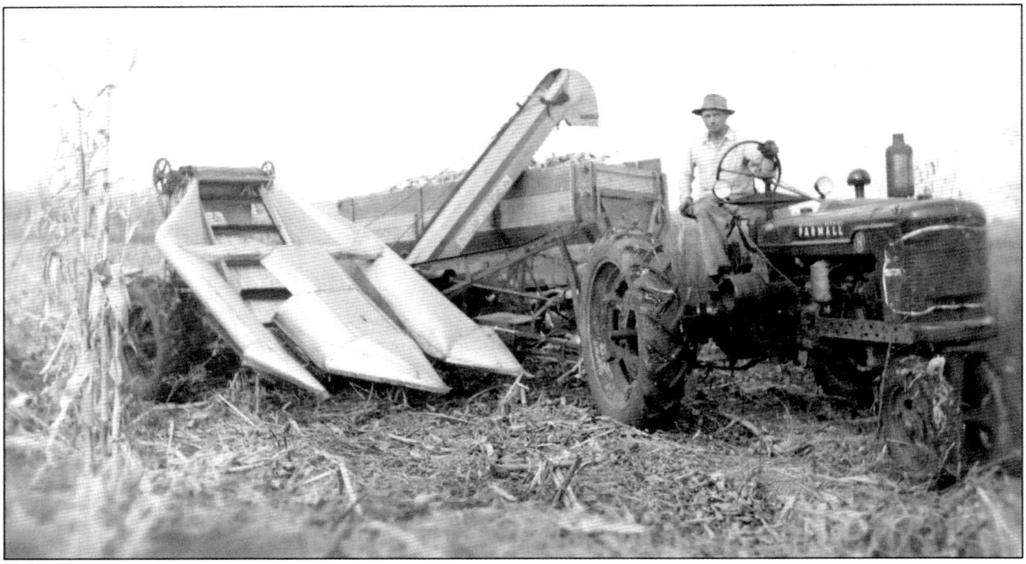

PICKING CORN. By the middle of the 20th century, farm production was more mechanized. Here George Whiton picks corn using a New Idea two-row corn picker.

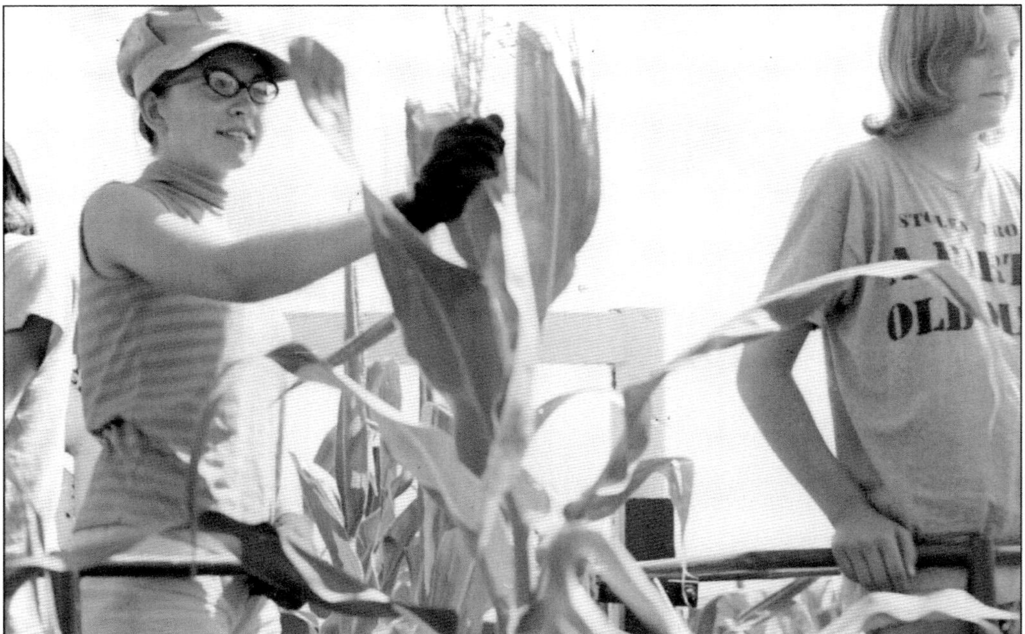

MOEWS DETASSELERS. As it has everywhere else, agribusiness has grown beyond the family farm in Perry. Moews Seed Corn Company, a seed-processing plant at the junction of Highways 169 and 141, opened in June 1966. Each summer, Moews employs many workers for the time-honored tradition of detasseling corn. The process of detasseling, removing a pollen-producing tassel from a corn plant in order to hybridize two varieties, must be done by hand. In Iowa, this is many teenagers' first summer job.

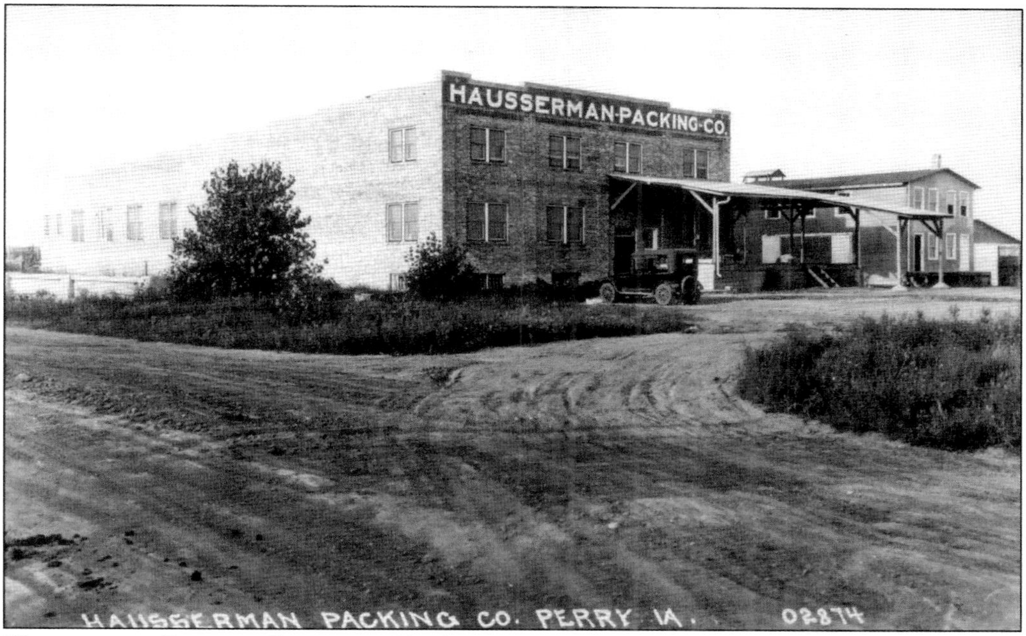

HAUSSERMAN PACKING COMPANY. Charles Hausserman immigrated to the United States at age 19 and moved to Perry from Jefferson in 1894 when he bought a butcher store on the north side of the downtown triangle. He began construction on the Hausserman Packing Company plant in 1919. Completed a year later, it was located on Eighteenth Street north of the Milwaukee Road tracks. Hausserman was killed crossing these tracks in 1921.

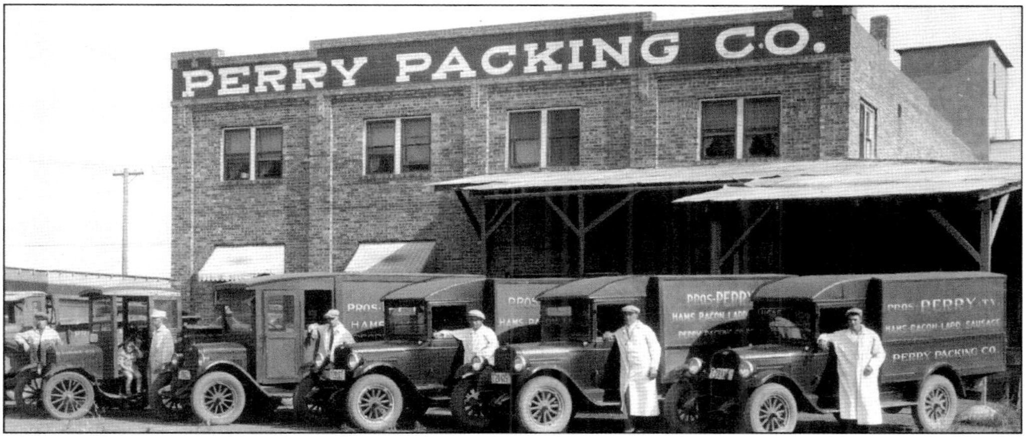

PERRY PACKING COMPANY. In business from 1926 to 1930, Perry Packing Company took the place of the former Hausserman Packing Company on Eighteenth Street. Arnold Brothers took over the plant in 1936, and Swift and Company owned the plant from 1953 to 1956.

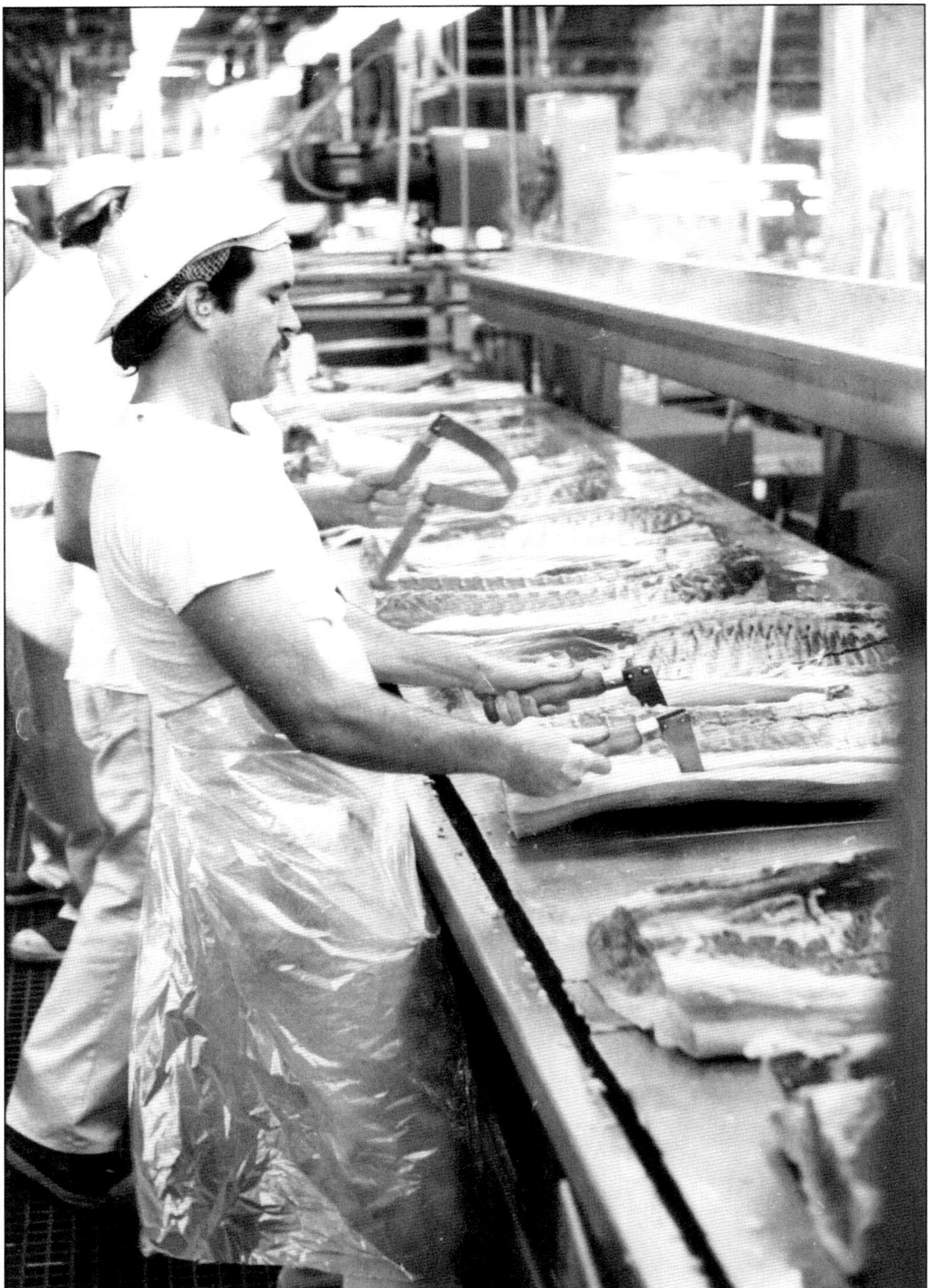

Line Workers at Oscar Mayer. Meatpacking has long been an important industry in and around Perry. The packing plant that had been Hausserman and then Perry Packing became Swift and Company in 1953. In 1962, a new plant was built west of downtown, and Iowa Beef Packers (IBP) of Denison purchased it in 1963. In 1965, IBP sold to Oscar Mayer, which operated the plant until 1988. In 1989, IBP (now Iowa Beef Processors) purchased the plant once more, and in 2000, IBP changed its name to Tyson Fresh Meats. It continues to operate in Perry today.

Three

EDUCATION

Author Lewis Atherton states that, as soon as they could, settlers opened a school. Before the town of Perry was founded, a country school opened in 1867. Over and over, residents of the community mentioned the value of education for themselves and especially for their children. The history of education in small midwestern communities is about local concern and support of schools.

The first schools to open were one-room country schools where grades one through eight were usually taught. Country schools were open near Perry until the middle of the 20th century. Many residents remember walking to the school through the seasons, helping their teachers with the stove, and teaching the younger children. The teachers were often young women who had been to normal school, living in the neighborhood with a family.

As the population of the town increased, schools were built. The schools at first were located so that the town children could walk to school in their neighborhood. Eventually these grade schools were torn down and replaced with a larger elementary school for all the children in the community. The high school, which was originally placed in the middle of the town, moved as well. At present, all the public schools—elementary, junior high, and high school—are located near each other on the east end of Perry.

As the photographs show, the community also supports a parochial school. St. Patrick's Catholic School originally included high school but now provides education through the eighth grade.

At one time, there was a normal college and a business school, chautauqua programs, and other educational venues. As the newest immigrants make their home in Perry, bilingual educational programs have become increasingly important.

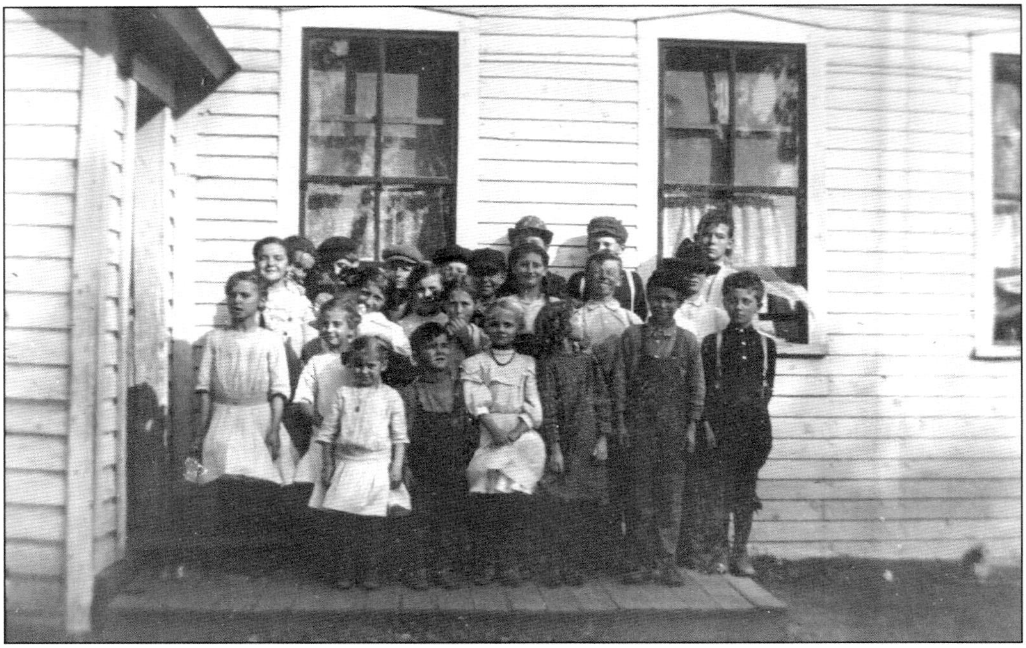

Alton School Students. Alton School, the first in the Perry area, was built near the Perry roundhouse in 1865. The last country school in the area to close, it was in use from 1867 to 1961. When it closed, there were only six students registered for classes, two less than the minimum required. In July 1964, the building was moved to Forest Park Museum in Perry, where it remains as an exhibit.

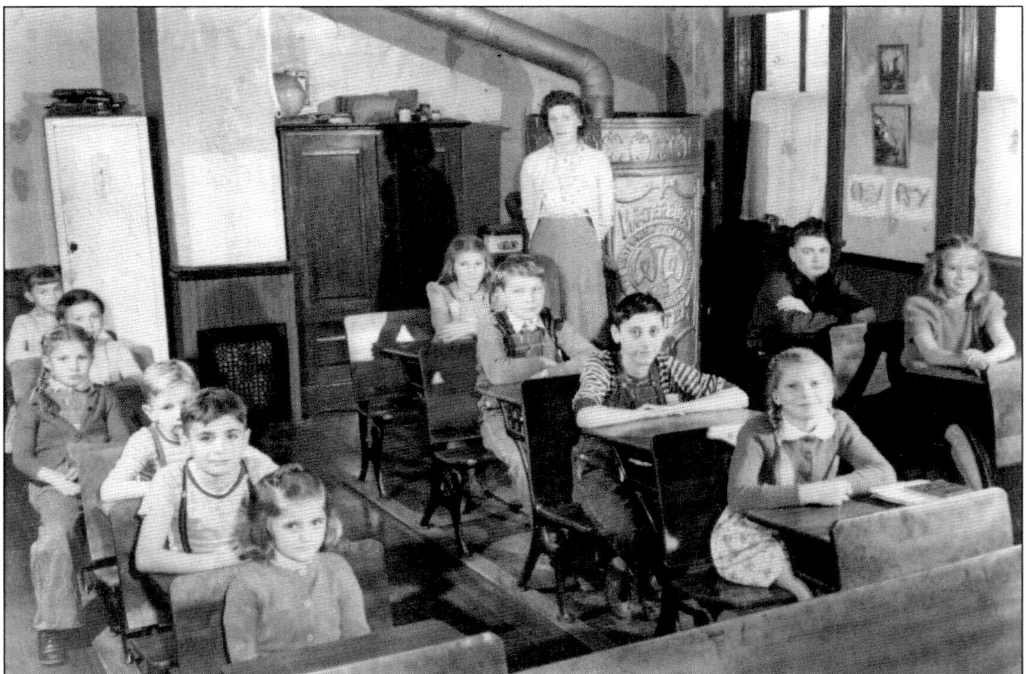

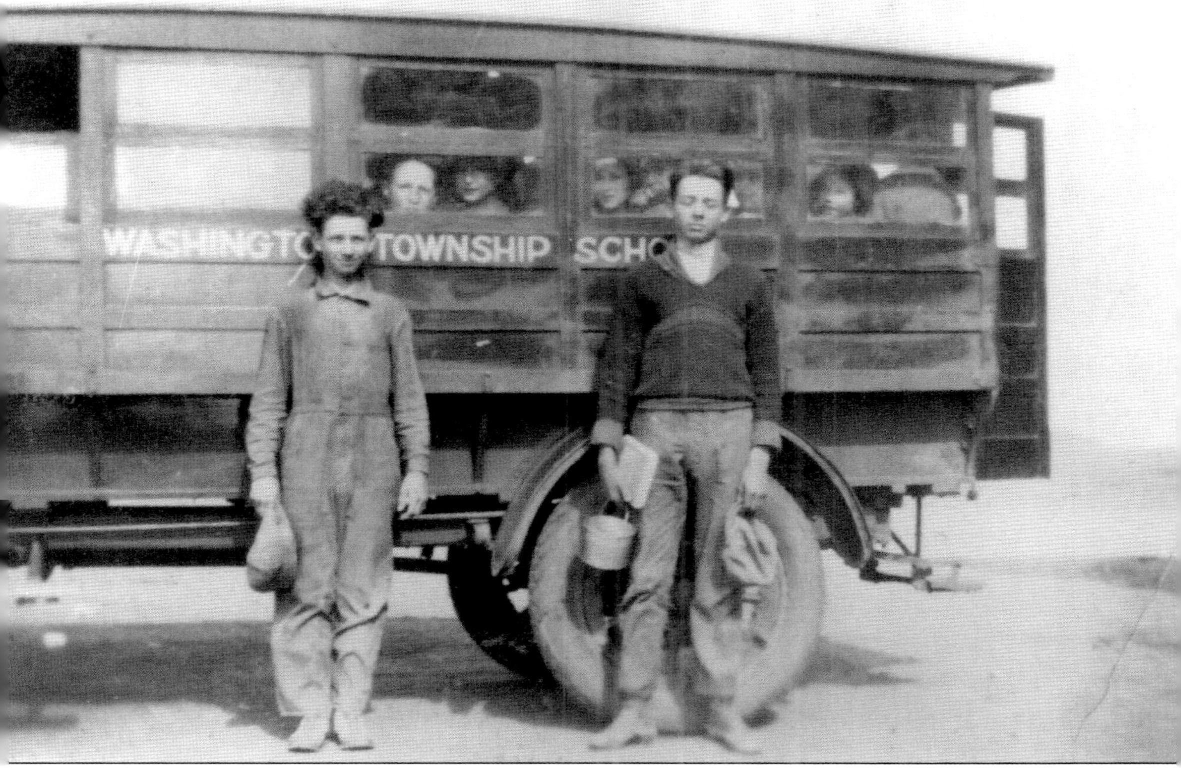

WASHINGTON TOWNSHIP SCHOOL BUS. Washington Township School was unique, a type of consolidated country school. Located about five miles south of Perry, Washington Township voted in 1920 to consolidate the nine independent school districts within it. The first graduating class of three students finished in 1923. The school had all grades and even had basketball teams.

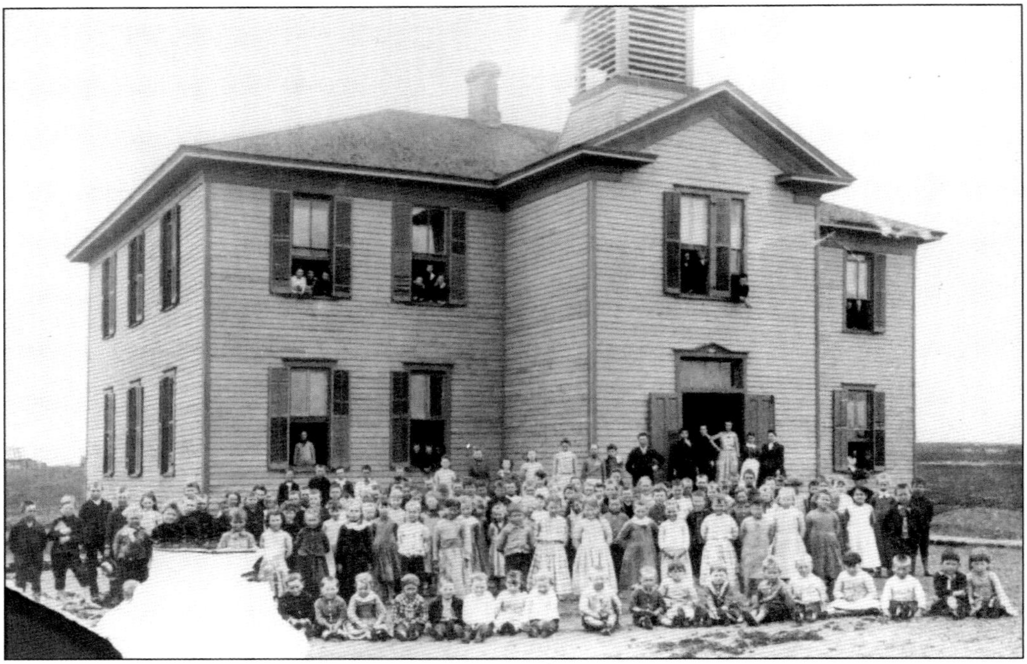

ANGUS SCHOOL. Built in 1882 and 1883 at a cost of $5,000, Angus School served the coal-mining town of Angus, now no longer in existence. Occupying the two-story building was a grade school on the first level and a high school upstairs.

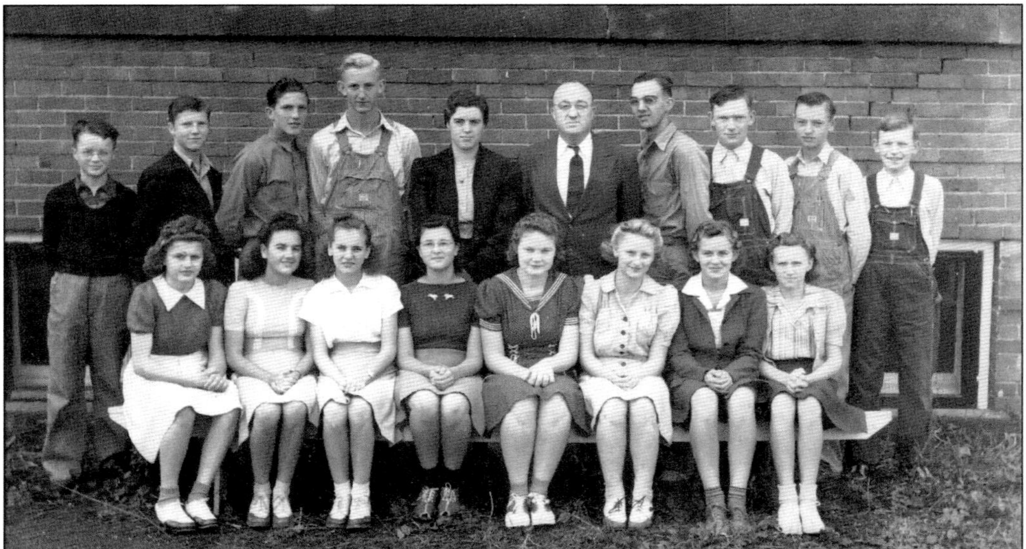

BOUTON SCHOOL STUDENTS. This was the last group of high school students to attend Bouton School in Bouton, a small community five miles east of Perry. The first students in Bouton walked to a country school east of town, but when Bouton's population increased to 100, in 1910, the Bouton Independent School District formed and built a school. Although the school initially served all grades, by 1942, the school only had one graduating senior, so the high school ceased while the lower eight grades continued. The building was demolished in 1968.

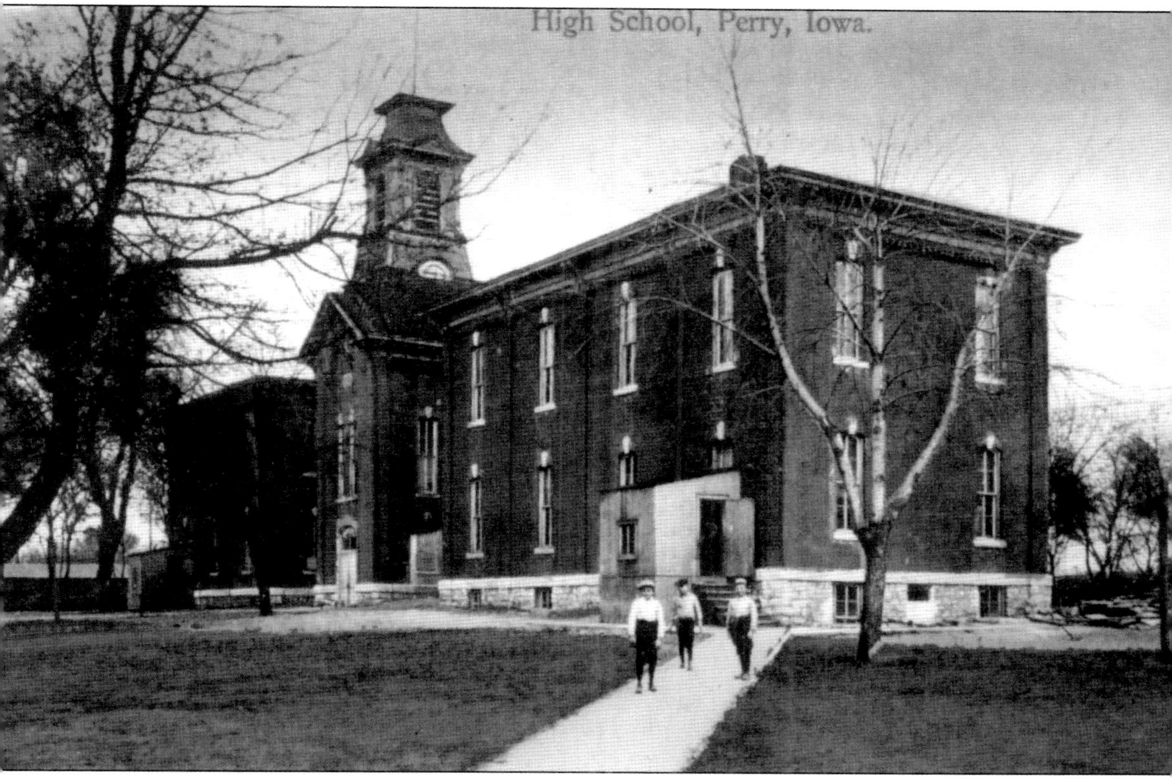

WASHINGTON SCHOOL. Washington School, also called Second Ward School, opened on December 6, 1876, in the 1400 block of Second Street on the site of the present Perry Post Office. The cost of the site was $1,000. In its second year, the teaching staff consisted of four teachers. It was the first high school in Perry, but it also housed elementary classes. Although the school's last high school class left in 1910, it was used as an elementary school until 1914, after which it was briefly occupied by Globe Manufacturing. After being damaged by fire in 1916, it was demolished in 1917. In 1921, the land was turned into a park.

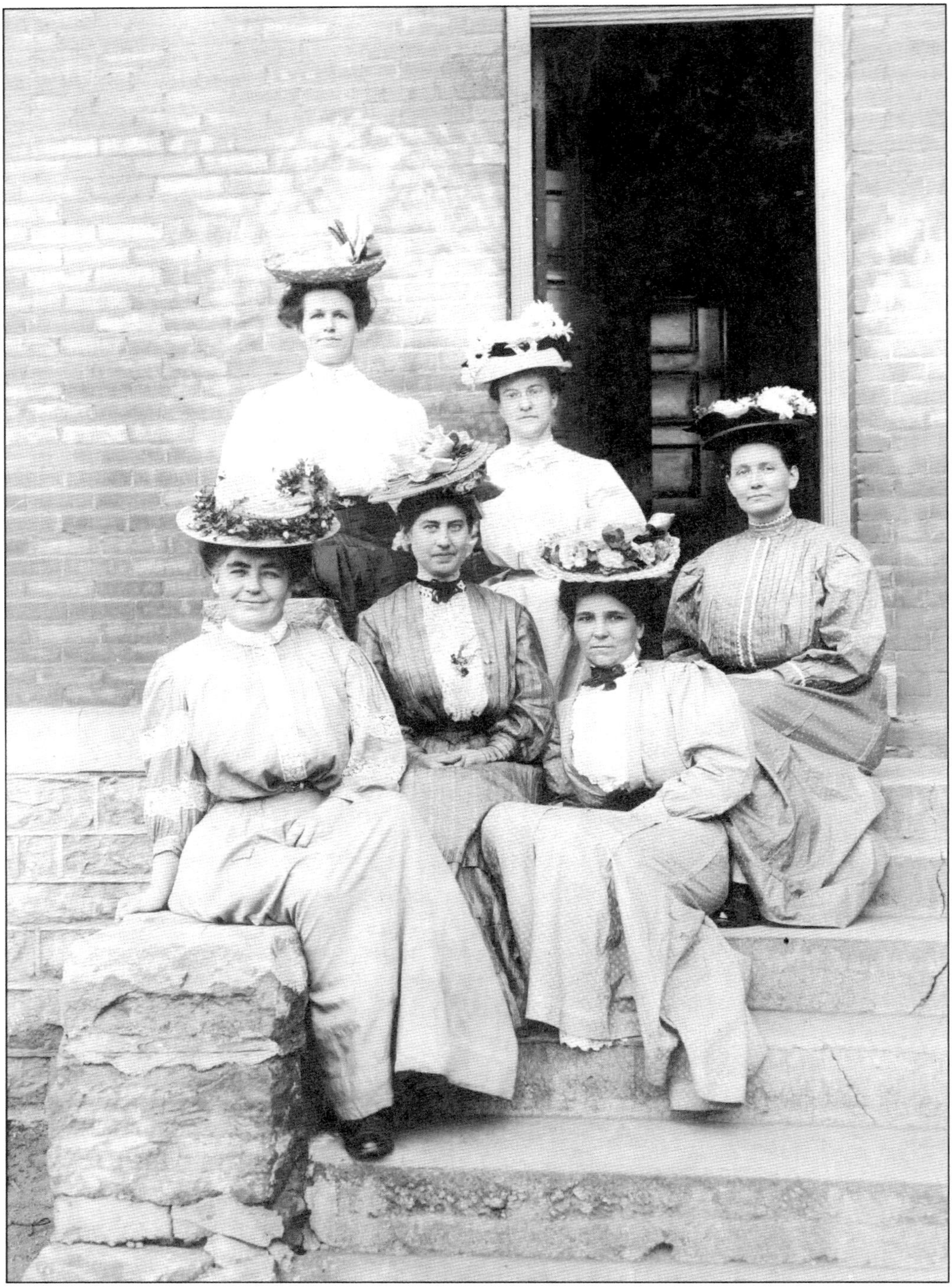

Early Teachers on School Steps. These are likely teachers at the Washington School, located at Second and Pattee Streets in Perry, around 1900. From left to right are (first row) Julia Grady, Ethel Kent, and Edith Piatt; (second row) Kate Dana, Lillian Parmenter, and Emma Huffman.

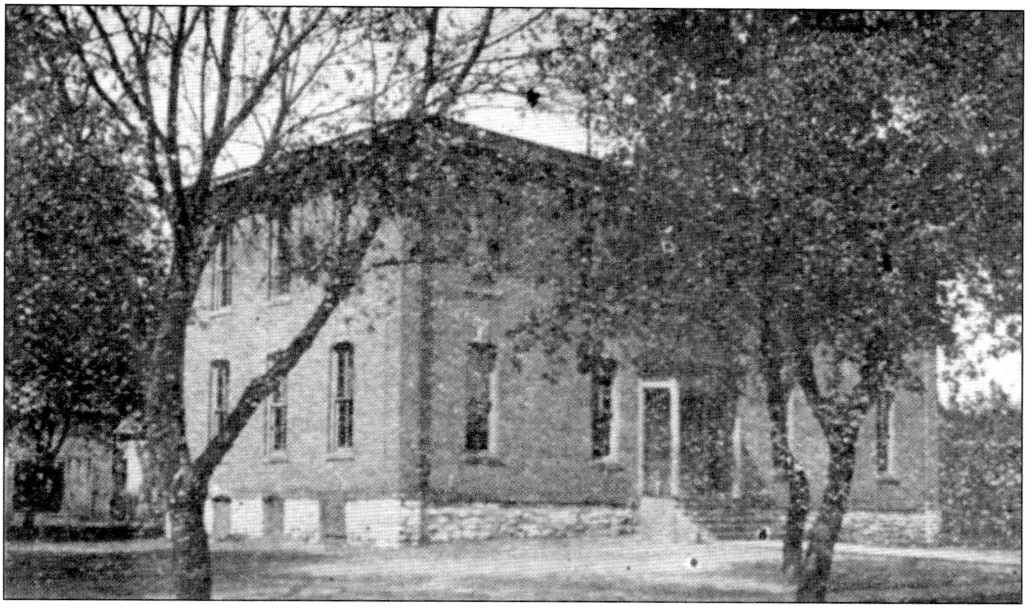

OTLEY SCHOOL. Otley School, also called the First or South Ward School, was built in 1890 between Fifth and Sixth Streets on Otley Avenue in Perry. Later Lincoln Elementary School was built to the east on the same block. Originally built with two rooms, the school saw the addition of two more in 1893. The building ceased to be used as a school by 1914 and was later demolished.

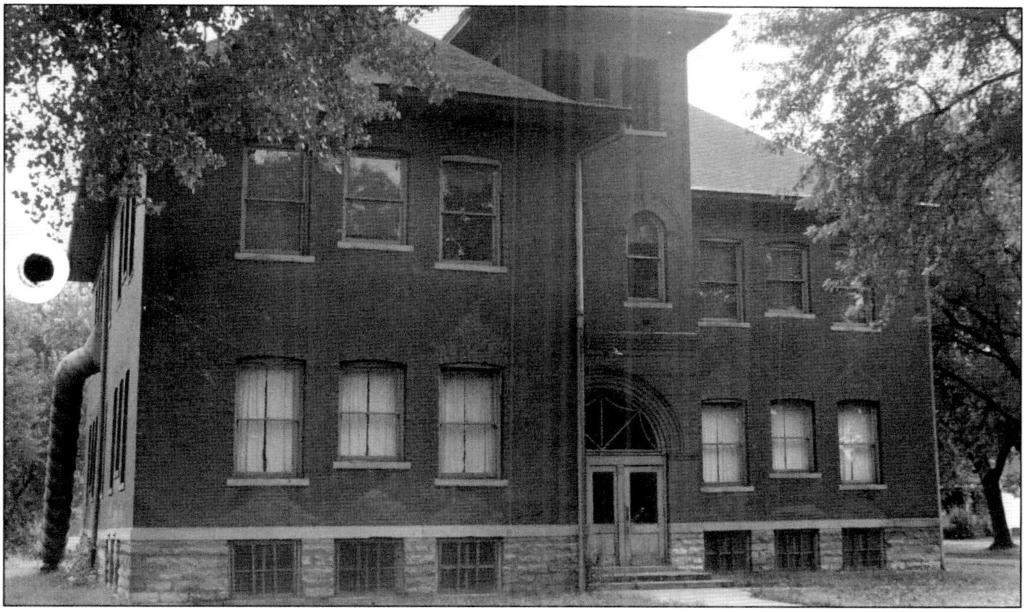

WILLARD SCHOOL. Built in 1900 at the northeast corner of Seventh and Lucinda Streets, Willard School served students up to sixth grade. It had three rooms on each floor and was the first in Perry to be named for something other than the ward it was in. In 1940, it ceased being used as a school and was converted to a youth recreation center for a time before its demolition in February 1967.

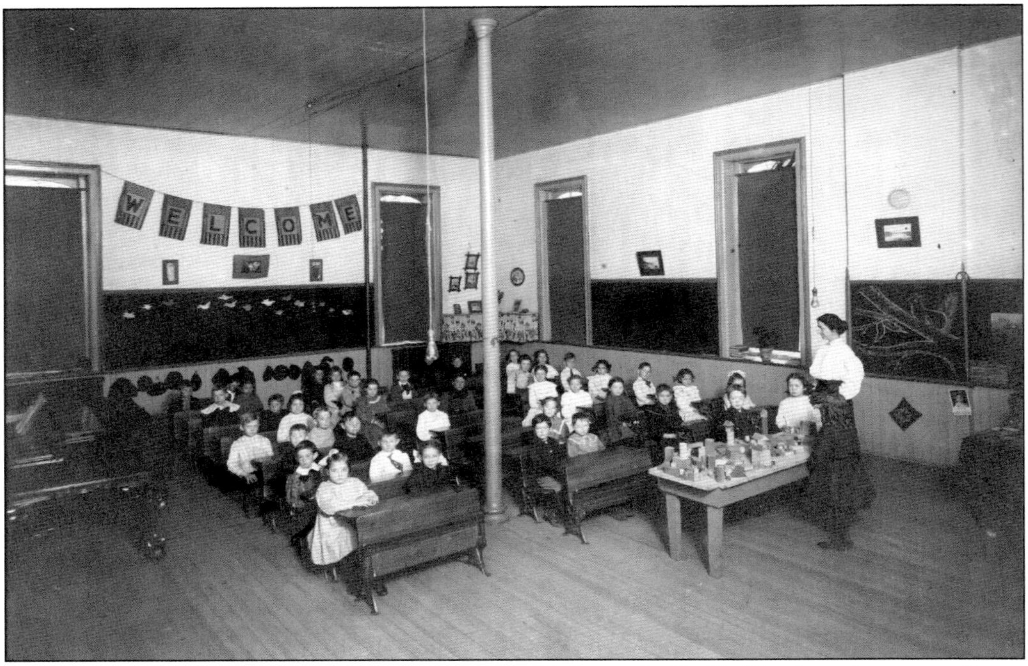

CLASSROOM INTERIOR. This schoolroom is most likely in the Diddy Block in downtown Perry. It was used as an overflow classroom for elementary students that normally were housed in the Washington School around 1910.

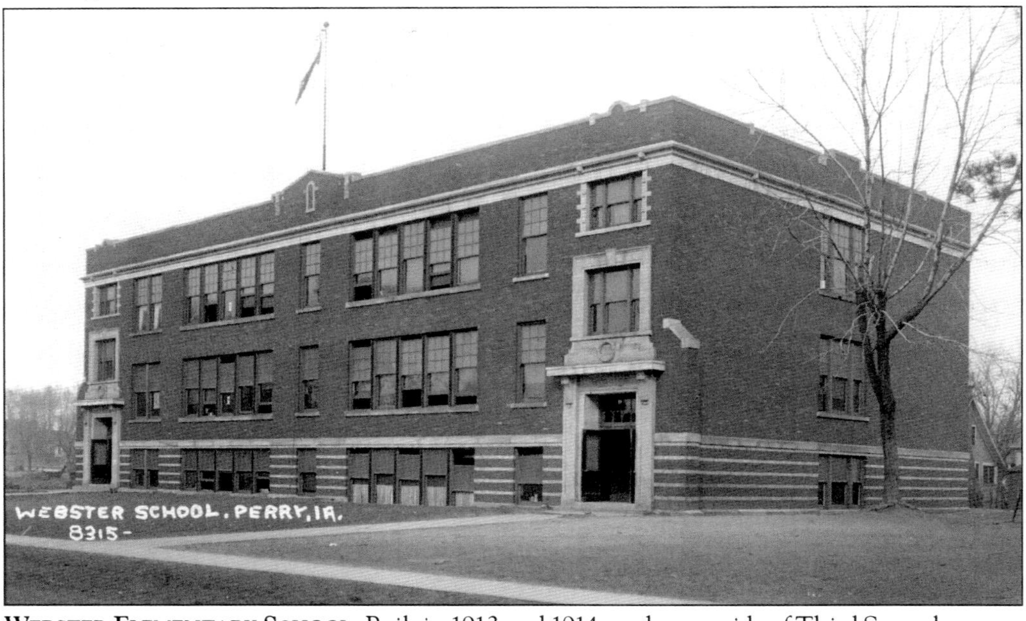

WEBSTER ELEMENTARY SCHOOL. Built in 1913 and 1914 on the east side of Third Street between North and Paul Streets, Webster Elementary School opened on March 9, 1914. Originally named the Third or North Ward School, its new name was chosen in hopes that "children would be as bright as Noah or Daniel Webster." It closed when the new Perry Elementary School opened in the fall of 1992 and has since been demolished.

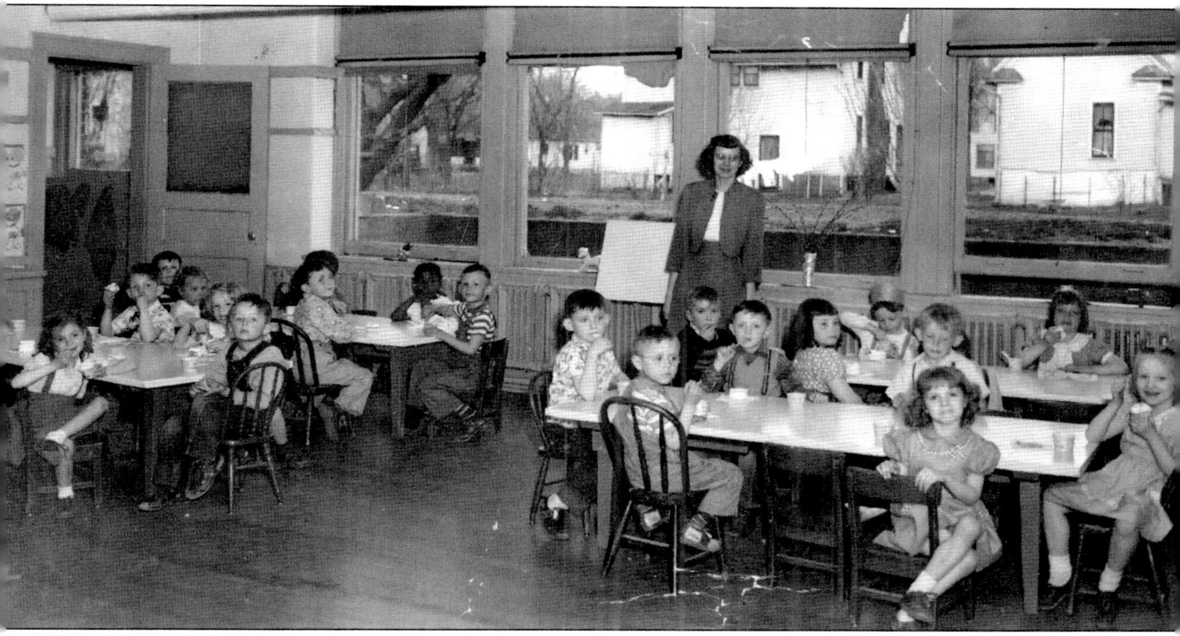

CLASSROOM AT WEBSTER ELEMENTARY SCHOOL. In the mid-1950s, when the population of Perry was about 7,000, Webster Elementary School had nearly 300 students and 13 teachers. All told, the three elementary schools (Webster, Lincoln, and Roosevelt) enrolled about 800 students. In 1956, to relieve overcrowding in the school, a section of the first grade began meeting at the Christian Science church at Fifth Street and Otley Avenue.

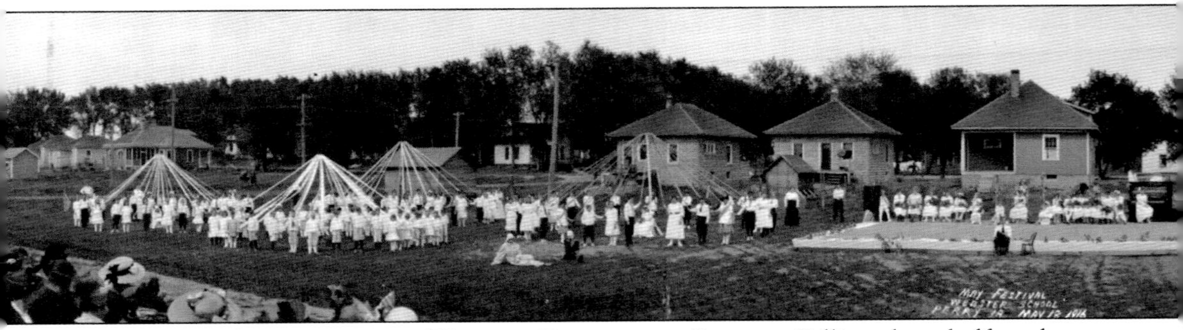

MAY DAY CELEBRATION AT WEBSTER ELEMENTARY SCHOOL. Falling about halfway between the spring equinox and summer solstice, May Day (May 1) is a holiday dating back to ancient Rome. In the early 1900s, May Day was celebrated in the schools. At least through the 1930s,

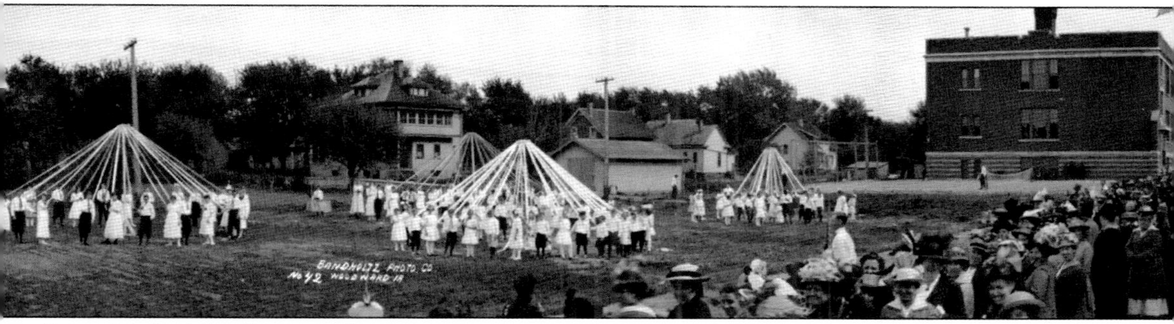

Perry High School crowned a May queen in connection with the celebration. Here Webster Elementary School students celebrate the holiday.

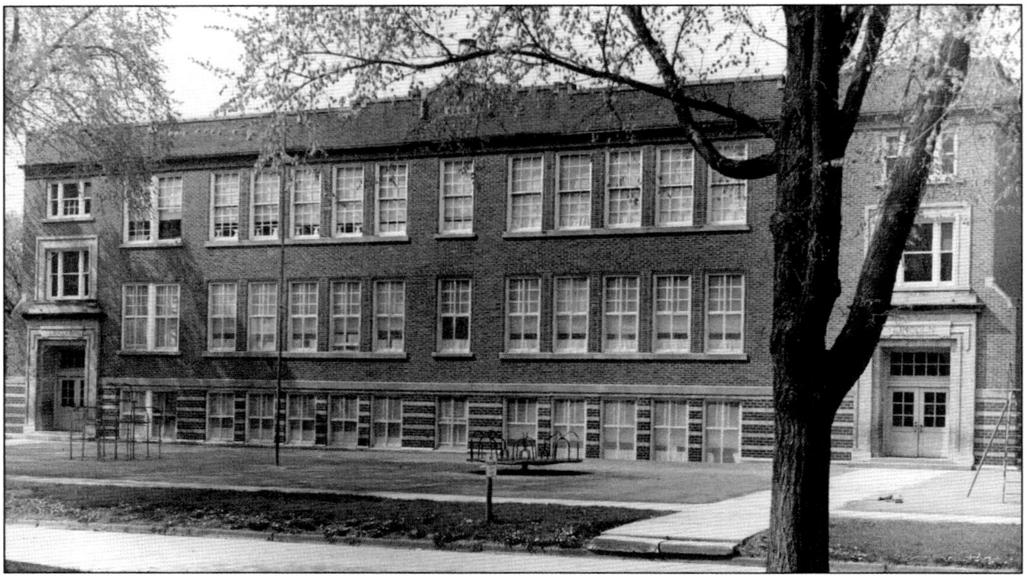

LINCOLN ELEMENTARY SCHOOL. Lincoln Elementary School was built in 1914 on the 500 block of Otley Avenue to replace the old Otley School. It closed when the new Perry Elementary School opened in the fall of 1992 and has since been demolished. Florence Skinner's class at Lincoln (around 1954) is pictured below.

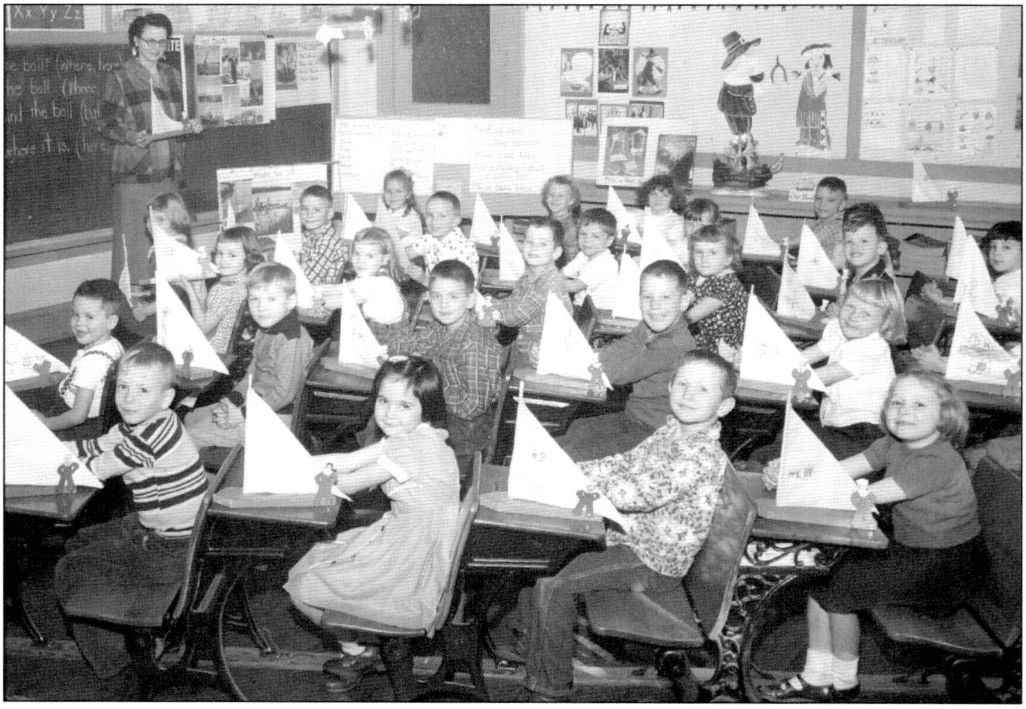

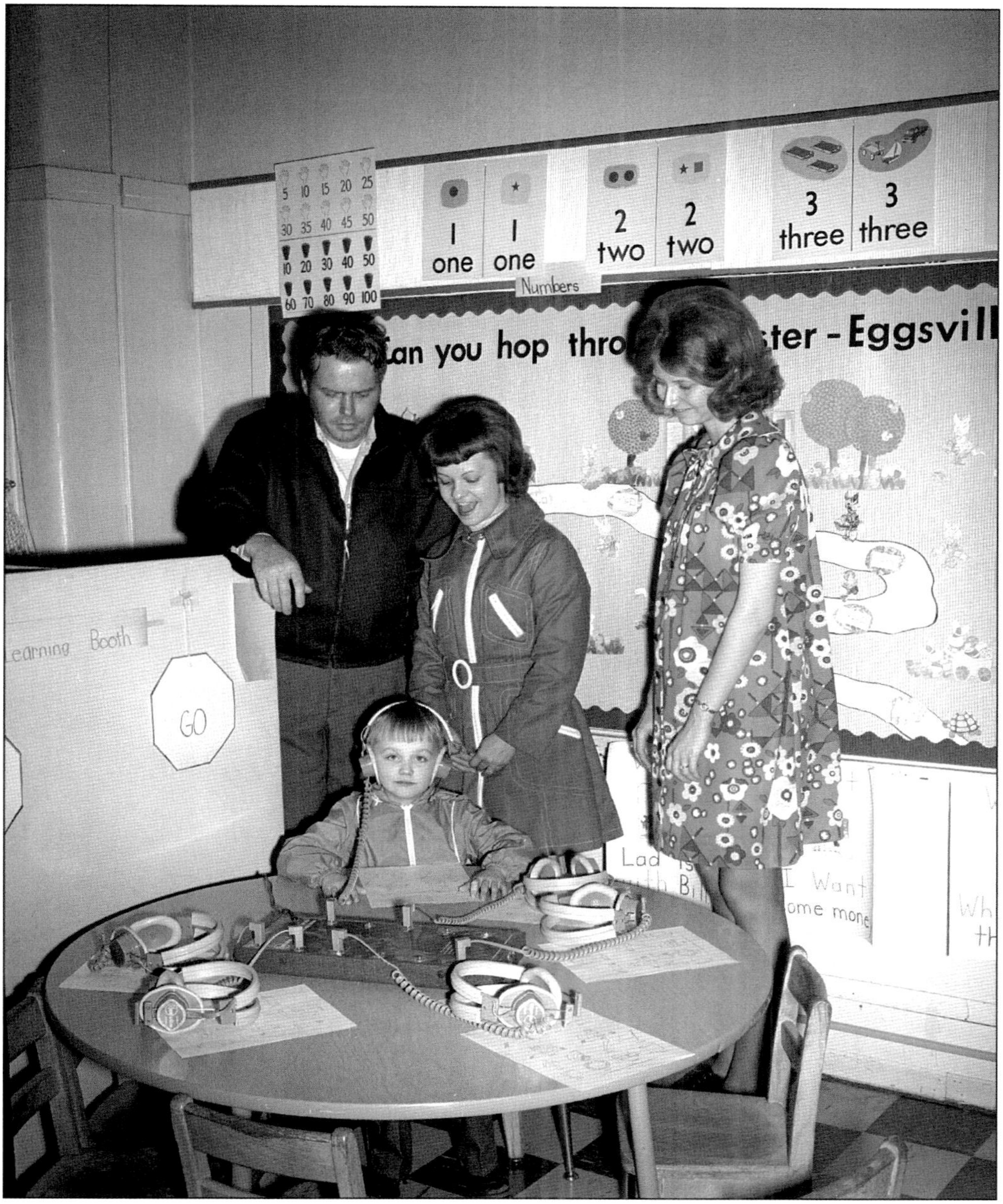

FIRST-GRADE DISPLAY NIGHT AT LINCOLN ELEMENTARY SCHOOL, 1973. Standing from left to right are Curt VanDorn, Mrs. VanDorn, and teacher Diane Jones. Seated is Jimmy VanDorn, a first grader at Lincoln Elementary School.

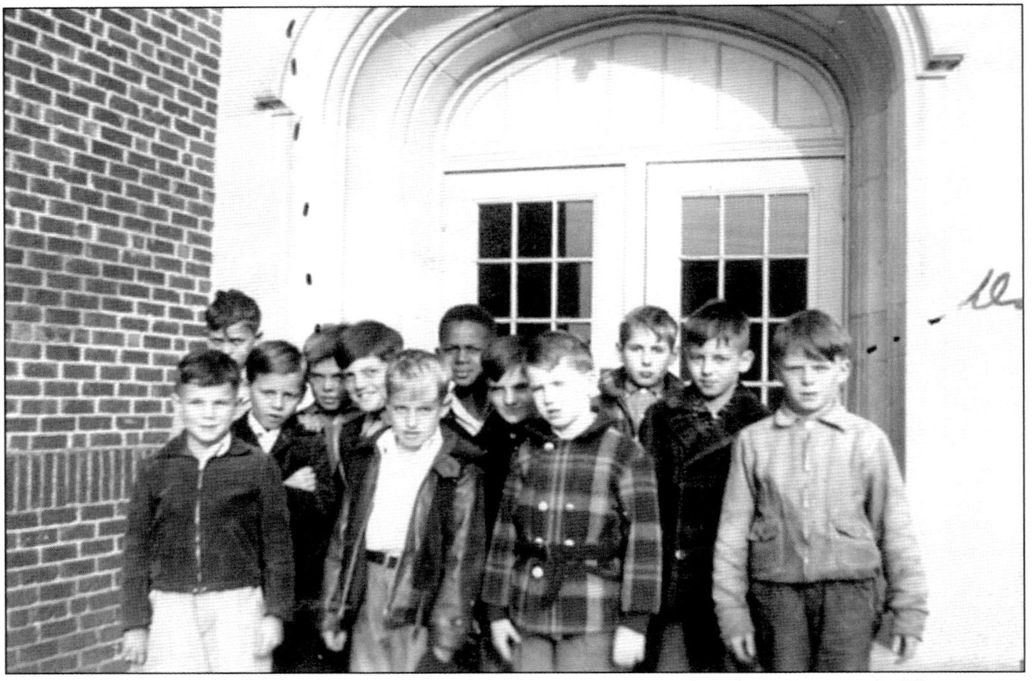

Theodore Roosevelt Elementary School Students. Theodore Roosevelt Elementary School, located between Willis Avenue and Warford Street and West Eighth and Ninth Streets, opened in the fall of 1922. During its first year, only four rooms were occupied, but it grew quickly. It closed in 1992 when the new Perry Elementary School opened and has since been demolished.

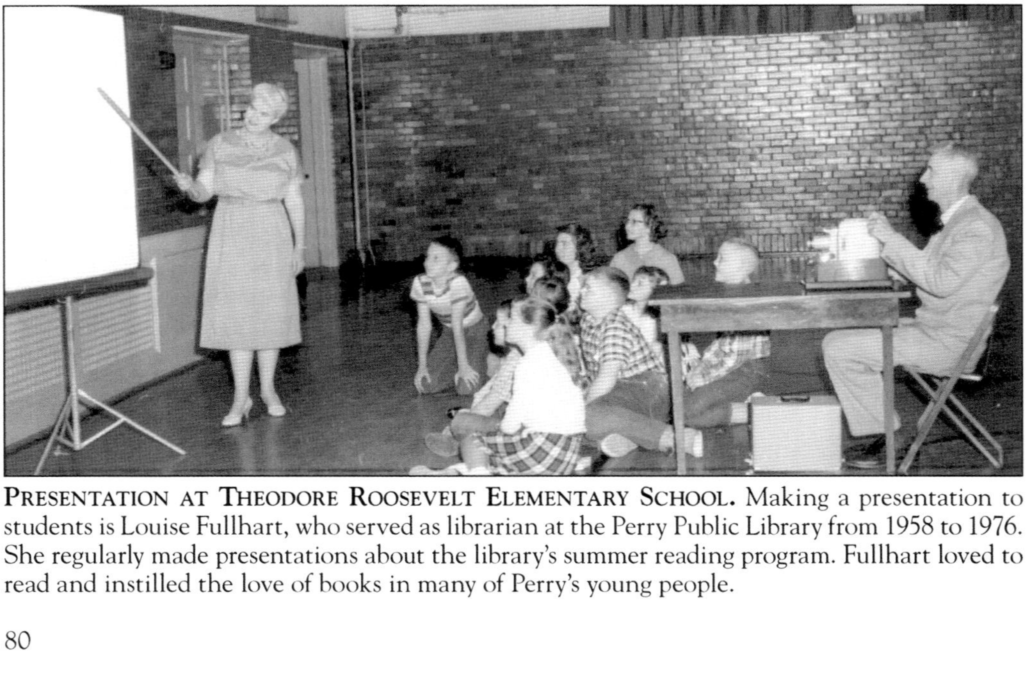

Presentation at Theodore Roosevelt Elementary School. Making a presentation to students is Louise Fullhart, who served as librarian at the Perry Public Library from 1958 to 1976. She regularly made presentations about the library's summer reading program. Fullhart loved to read and instilled the love of books in many of Perry's young people.

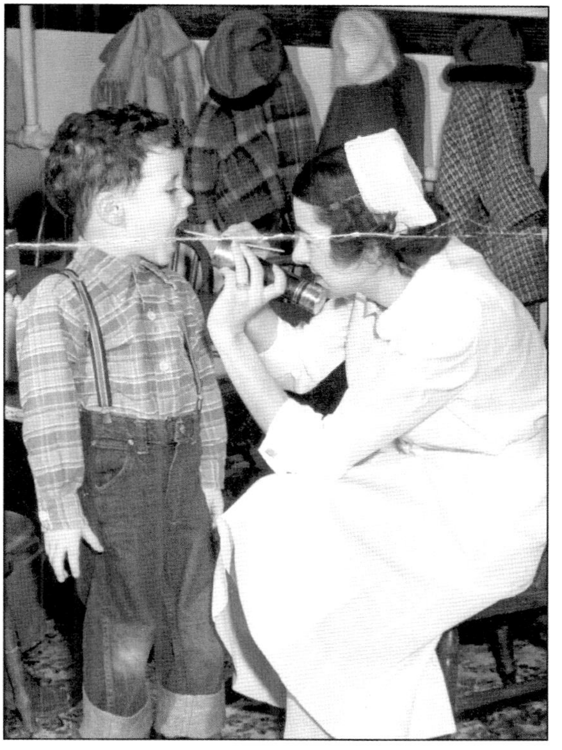

School Nurse. Nell Flockhart, the school nurse, checks Marty Haas in 1954. School nursing has been a public health specialty since 1902. Nurses care for students who become ill during the school day and promote preventative measures. Flockhart also worked for Dr. R. F. Deranleau in Perry.

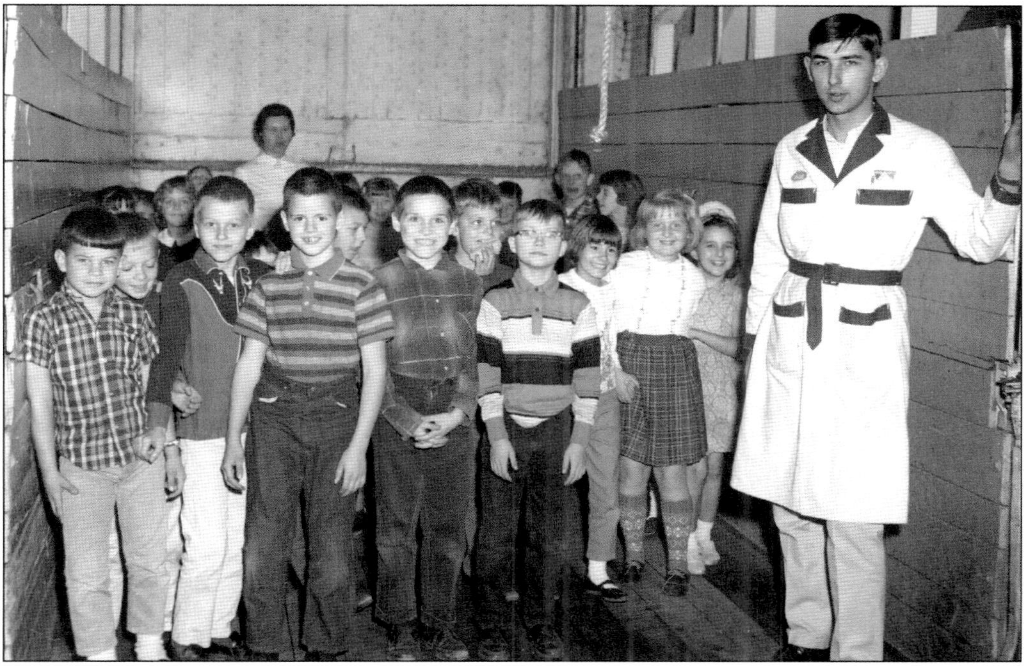

Field Trip to Ford Garage. By 1965, field trips became a part of the schools' curricula. Here students visit Burk Ford, which sold and serviced cars. It was one of many such service stations in Perry.

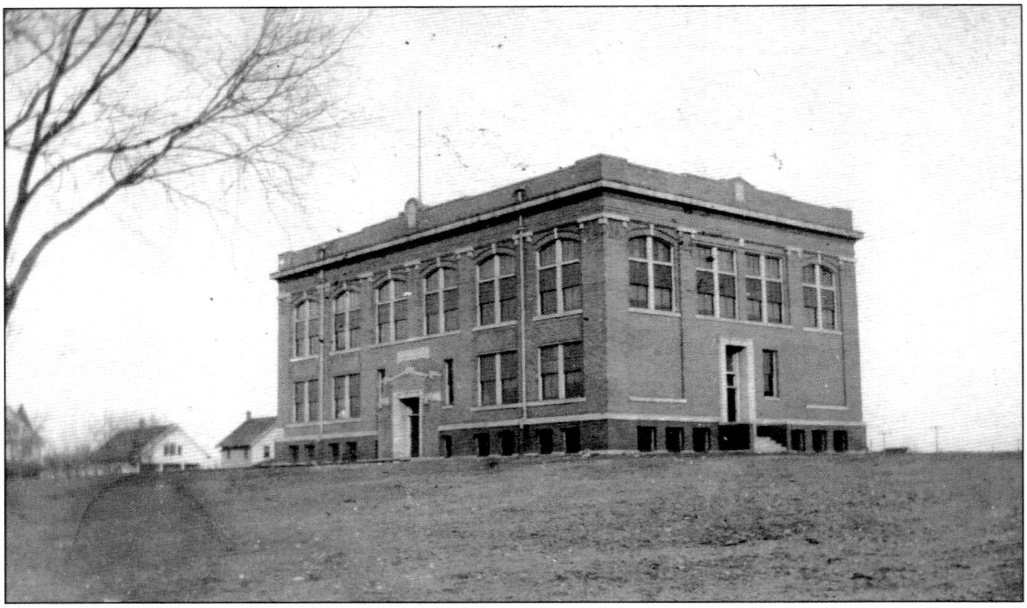

PERRY HIGH SCHOOL. Perry High School opened in February 1911 between Tenth and Twelfth Streets on Willis Avenue on a site formerly occupied by George Heaton's house and barn. One addition was added in 1936 and another in 1946. In the fall of 1960, high school students moved to a new building, and this school became a junior high for sixth through eighth grades. The school closed in 2002.

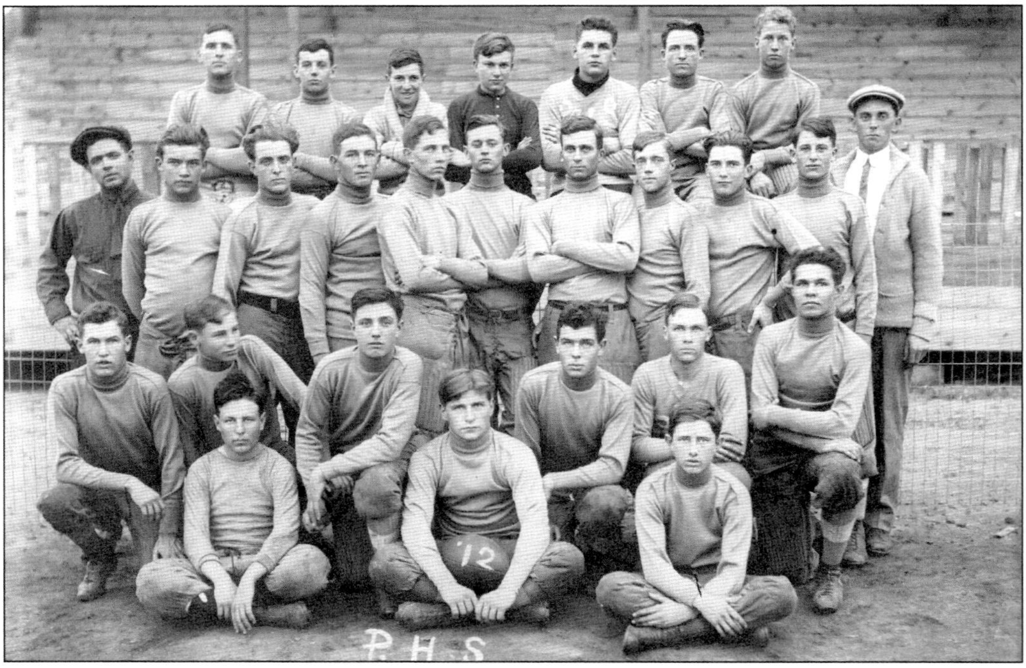

PERRY HIGH SCHOOL FOOTBALL TEAM. In the early days of Perry High School football, games took place at the Tri-County Fairgrounds. The first game played at the high school took place in October 1931 in which Perry defeated Roosevelt High School from Des Moines 6-0.

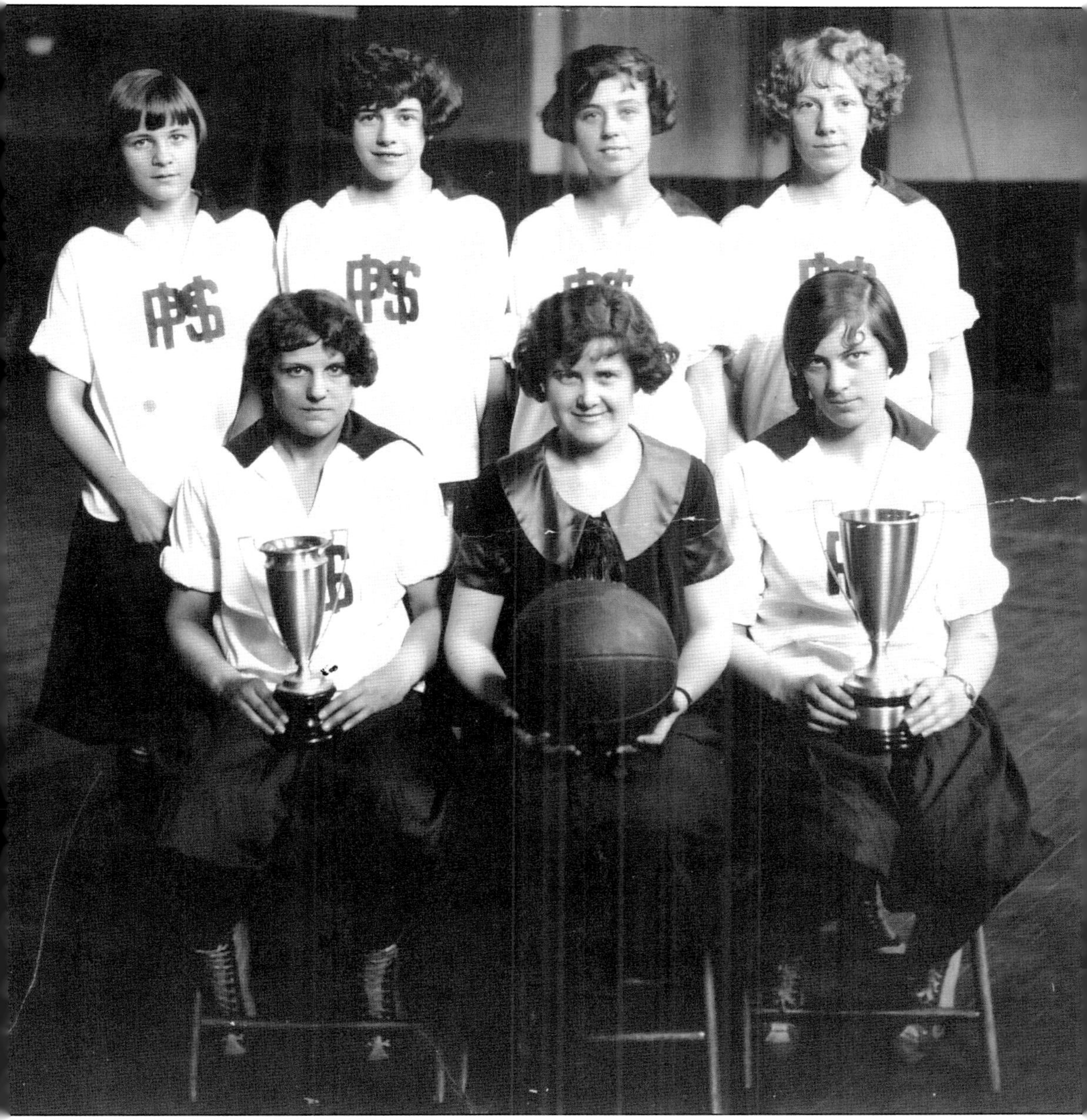

GIRLS' BASKETBALL, 1925. From the beginning, Perry High School offered not only classes but also a variety of extracurricular activities for students, including sports, music, and journalism. The first girls' basketball team formed in Perry in 1910.

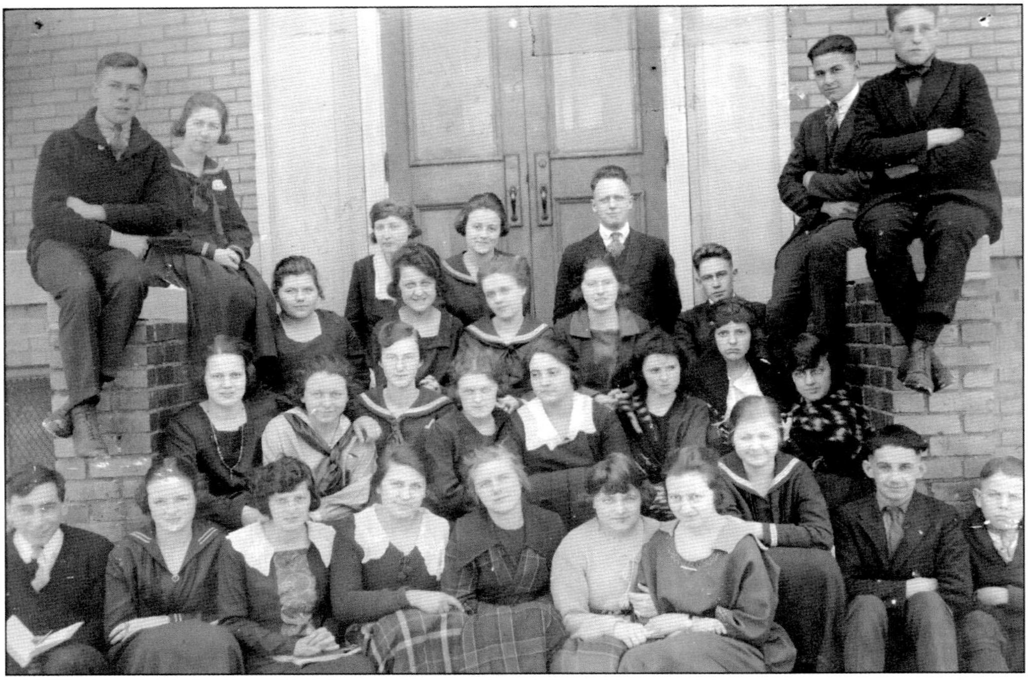

Perry High School Editorial Staff. Through the high school's history, the editorial staff has produced a yearbook, *The Eclipse*, and a newspaper, the *Telital*. The *Telital* was first published in November 1926. The journalism honor society Quill and Scroll started in 1932 when 17 students were inducted.

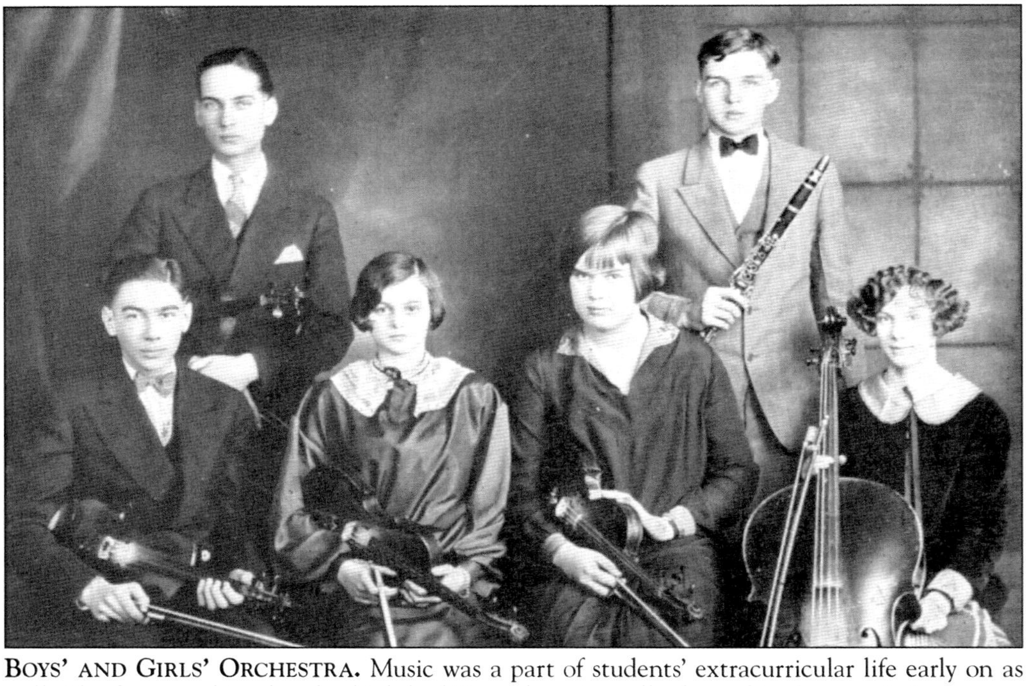

Boys' and Girls' Orchestra. Music was a part of students' extracurricular life early on as well. The first marching band, which had 38 students initially, formed in August 1933.

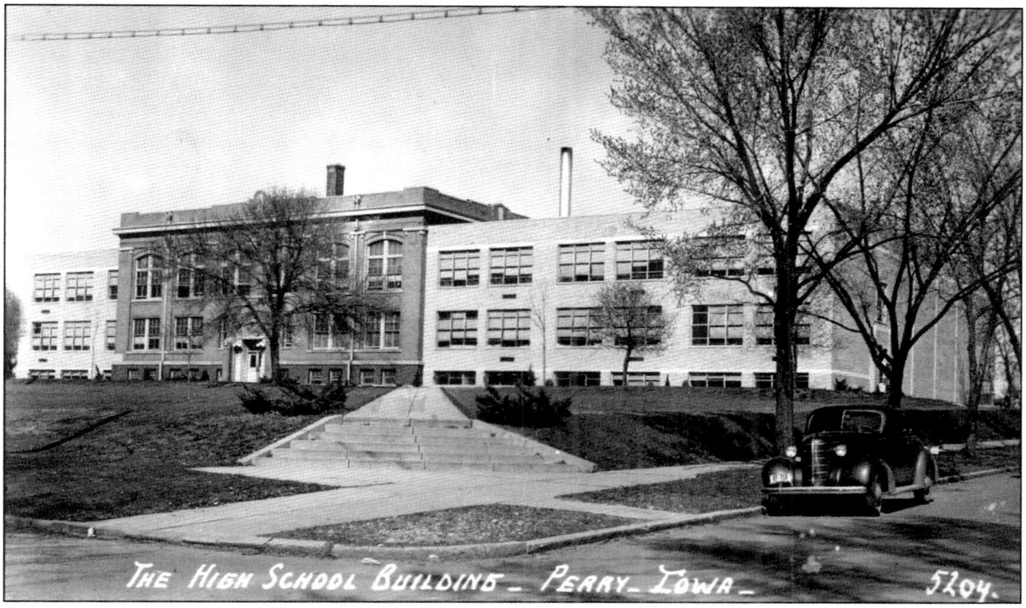

PERRY HIGH SCHOOL BUILDING. New additions to the high school building, constructed in 1936, are visible here. After this building ceased to be used as a school in 2002, it housed other nonprofits and services such as Head Start and a church congregation.

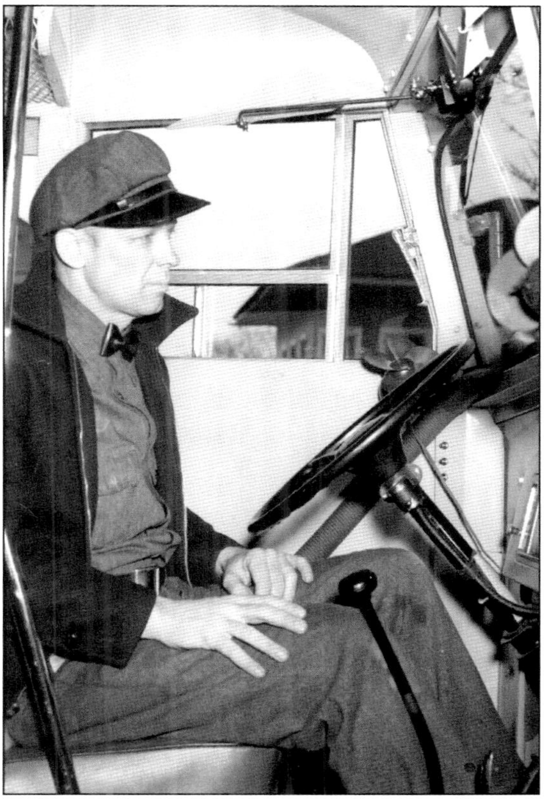

BARNEY JOHNSON. Barney Johnson drove the first school bus in Perry in the late 1930s. The bus took sports teams to compete in events in other towns and was also used to pick up commodities for the school from a central office in Adel, the county seat.

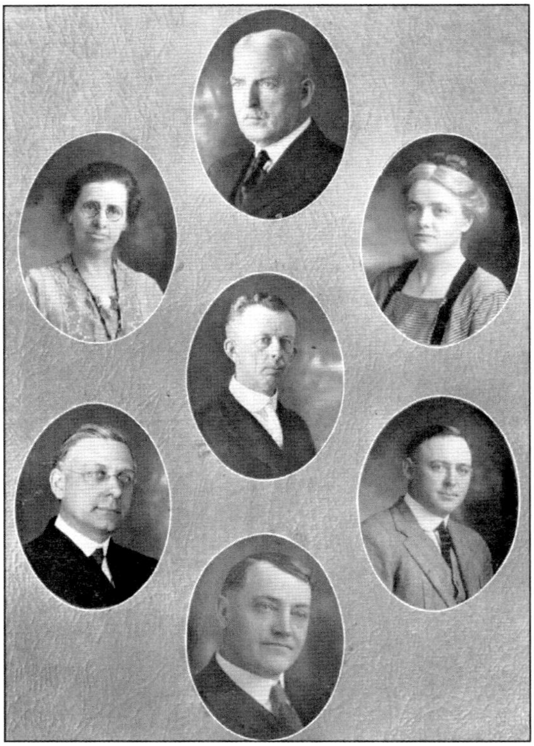

Board of Education. Members of the 1922 board of education were H. L. Thomas, president; W. H. Winegar, secretary; W. H. Pattee, treasurer; W. B. Robinson; Mrs. C. D. Jones; Mrs. R. D. Echlin; and A. J. Krohnke.

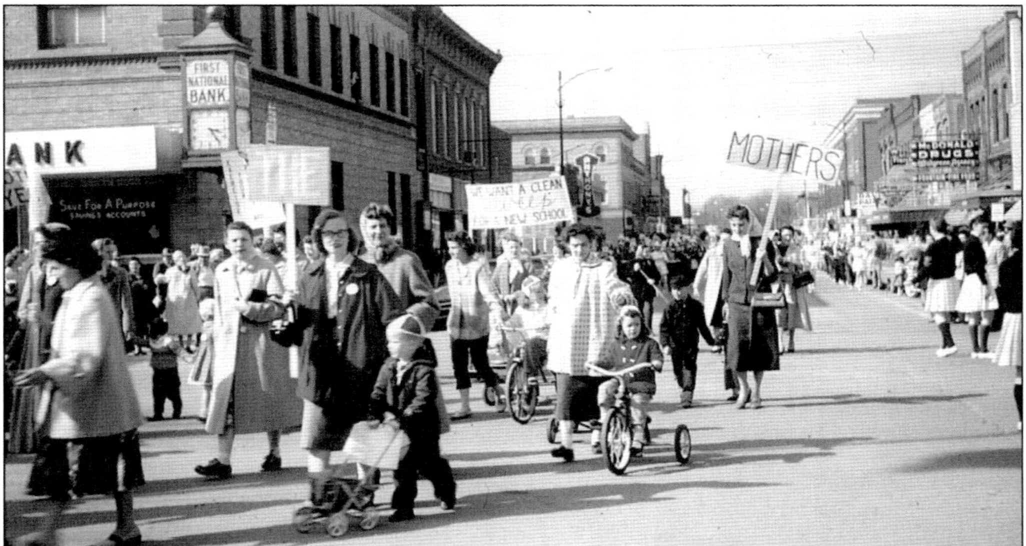

Mothers March for Better Schools. A bond issue for a new high school was proposed as early as March 1956. Voters were asked to authorize $627,000 to purchase a site on the east side of Perry and build a new building. That year, the bond was defeated by a margin of 95 votes. Another vote in May 1956 did not succeed either. When the issue came before the voters again in April 1958, a parade of more than 2,000 Perry school students and their mothers demonstrated in support of it, and the bond passed.

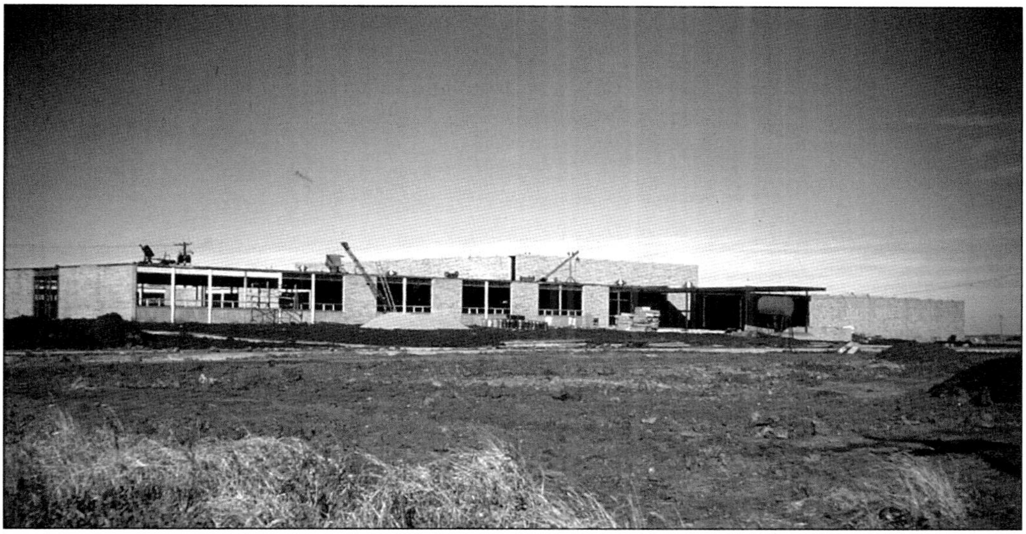

New High School under Construction. Ground was broken for the new school on Eighteenth Street in December 1958. Construction began in March 1959, and the building was dedicated in September 1960. Not long after, the building expanded again with more classrooms and vocational rooms built in 1966. Once the building was completed, the former high school building was used as a middle school for grades six to eight.

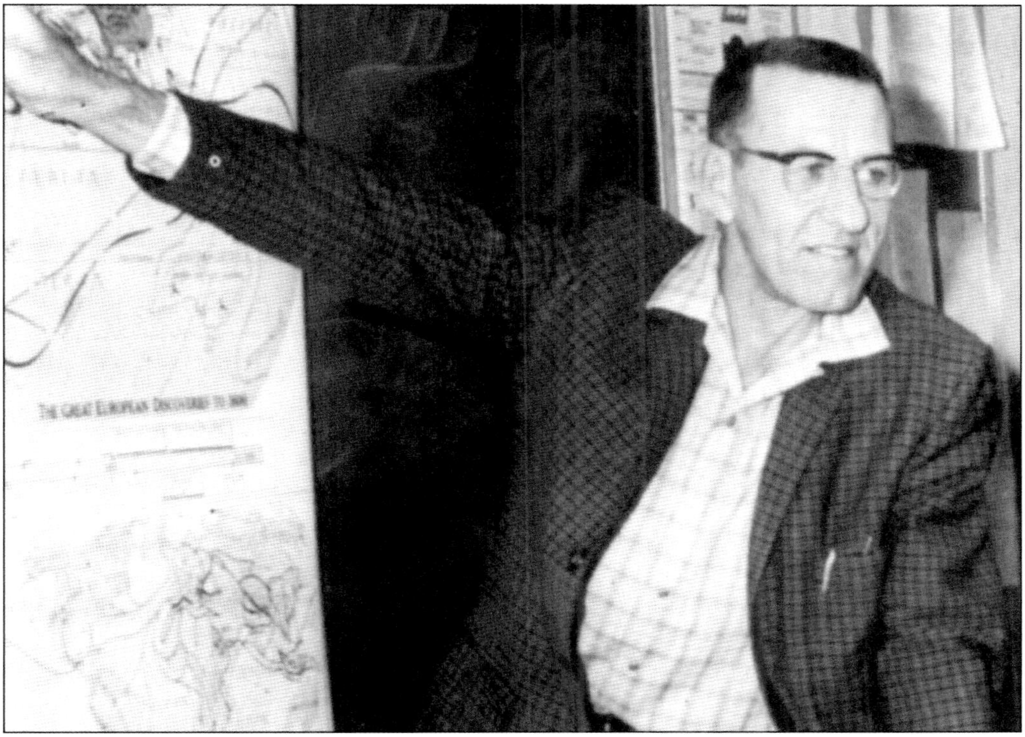

Judson Reimer. Judson Reimer taught economics and government at Perry High School for more than 20 years. A former football player at Central College in Pella, Reimer also held the position of football coach at the high school.

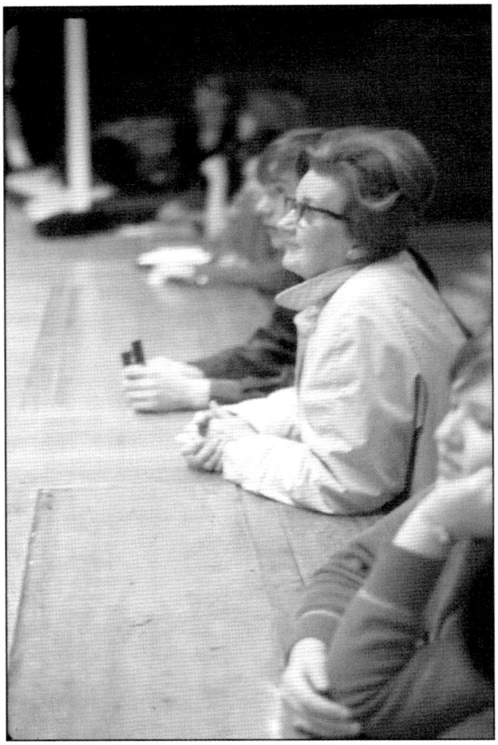

MARGARET CROUCH. Margaret Crouch (left) taught literature and led the drama department at Perry High School for many years during the 1960s and 1970s. During her tenure, the program became known for elaborate and professional productions of both plays and musicals, including *The Mikado* (below), *Gypsy*, *Peter Pan*, and *Twelfth Night*.

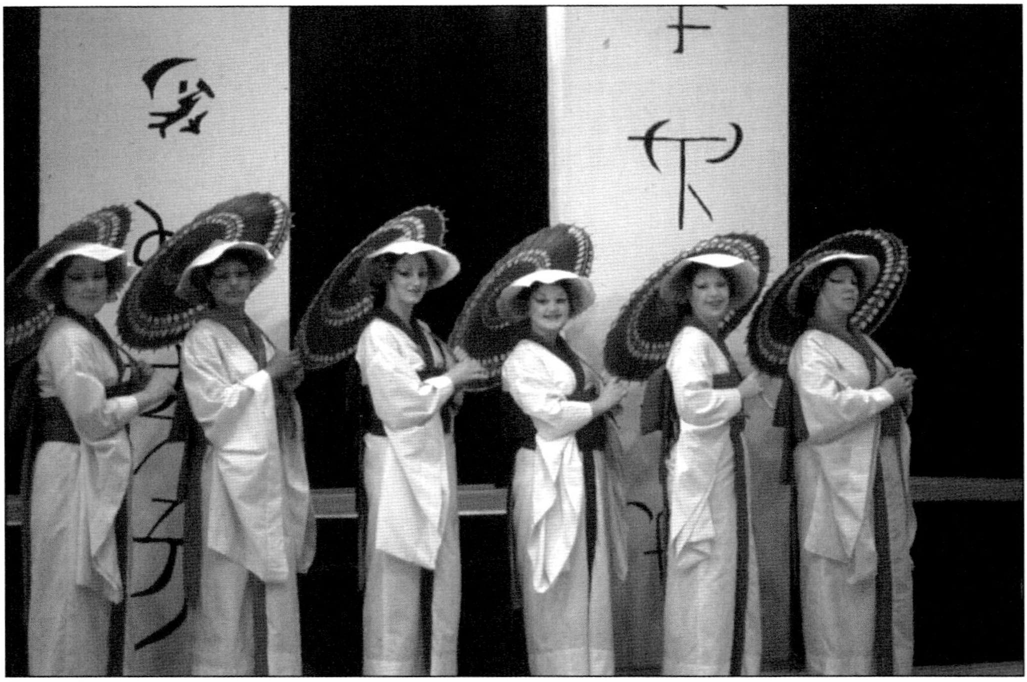

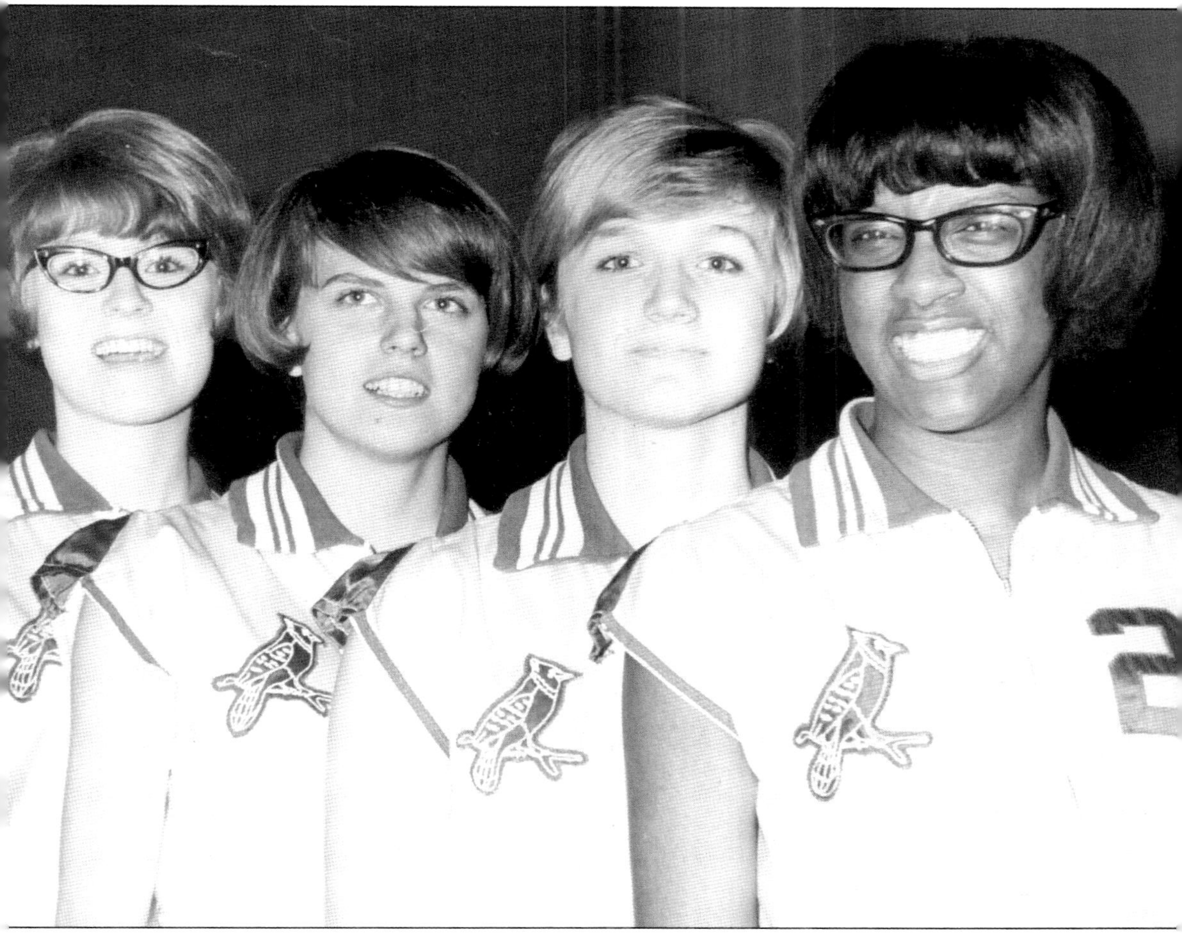

GIRLS' BASKETBALL GUARDS. Perry High School's girls' basketball team went to the state tournament five times in a row in the mid-1960s. Players included, from left to right, Deb Bell, Deb Gilbertson, Cheryl Roush, and Jan Davis.

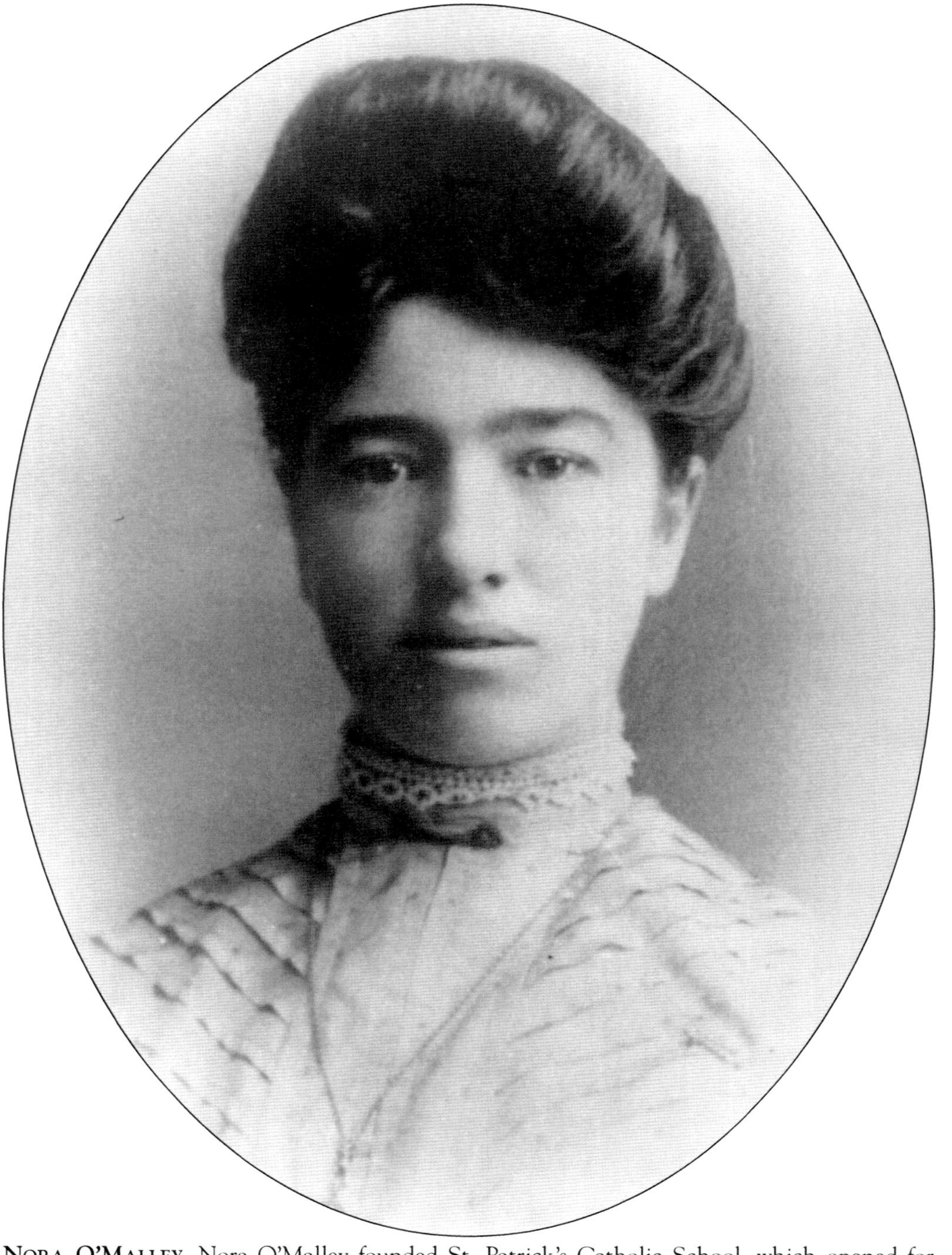

Nora O'Malley. Nora O'Malley founded St. Patrick's Catholic School, which opened for classes in 1920. Interest in a parochial school was evident as early as 1916, when Rev. James Cleary started a fund to raise money for a school. A committee purchased the site on Fifth Avenue for around $10,000 in April of that year. O'Malley, one of its biggest proponents, died just two days before the school's dedication in 1921.

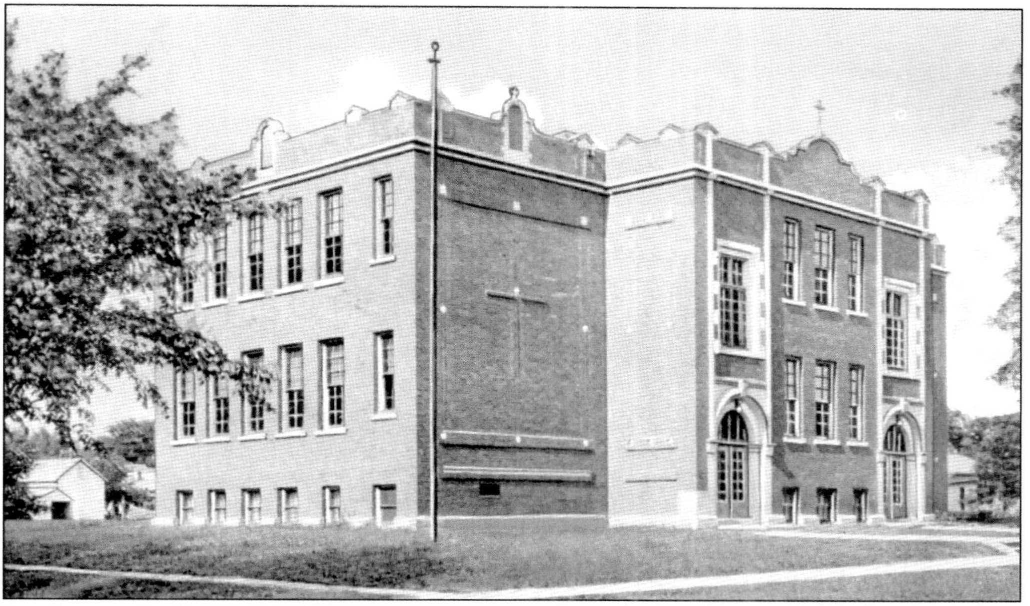

ST. PATRICK'S CATHOLIC SCHOOL. Five nuns served as teachers at St. Patrick's. Initially the school's curriculum included a two-year high school course; its first high school graduation came in May 1924. A gymnasium and two-story classroom building were added in 1957. The high school was discontinued in 1966, but other grades remain today.

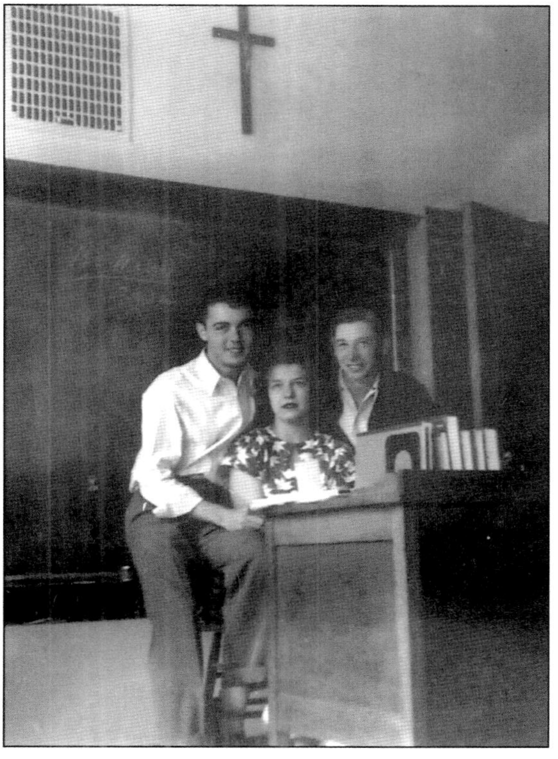

STUDENTS AT ST. PATRICK'S CATHOLIC SCHOOL. Students pose with their teacher in a classroom at St. Patrick's in 1947.

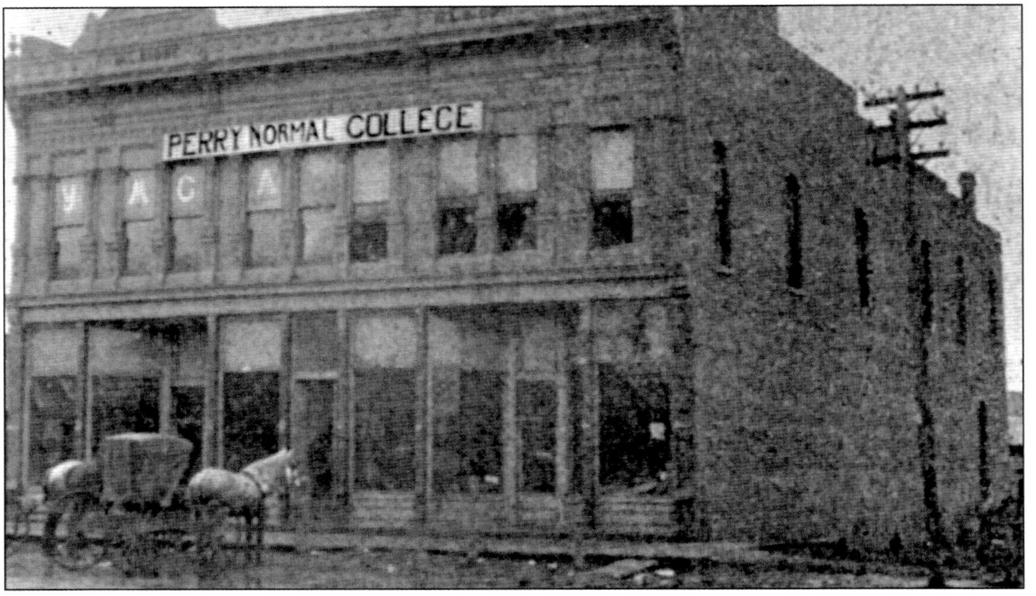

Perry Normal College. Beginning in the fall of 1892, Perry Business College offered classes in downtown Perry. It had as many as 250 students in attendance at one time, and many country schoolteachers received their training there. Early classes were organized by H. C. Wahl, who was later joined by Ed Hulley and then William M. Tarr. The school's name changed to Perry Normal College in 1898. By 1900, it was incorporated and owned by 31 local residents. In 1909, C. Durant Jones assumed ownership of the college, and in 1912, he moved it to a new building at 1305 Otley Avenue. It dissolved sometime after 1921.

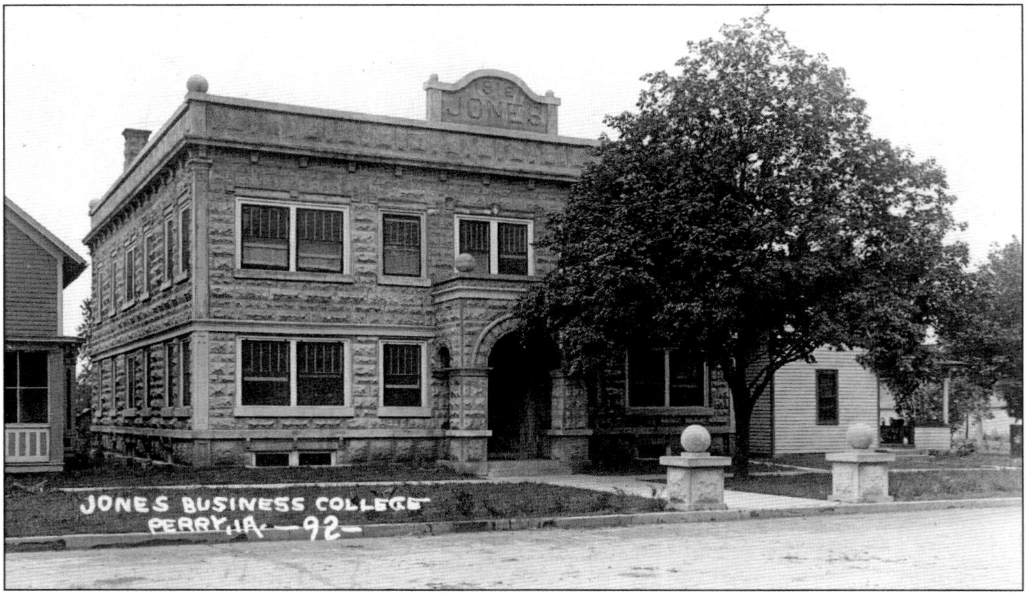

Jones Business College. Formerly the Perry Normal College, the Jones Business College, located at 1305 Otley Avenue, was built by prominent Perry businessman C. Durant Jones in 1912. Jones and his family lived in a house directly to the west. Blocks used to construct the building were manufactured in Jones's concrete factory located nearby.

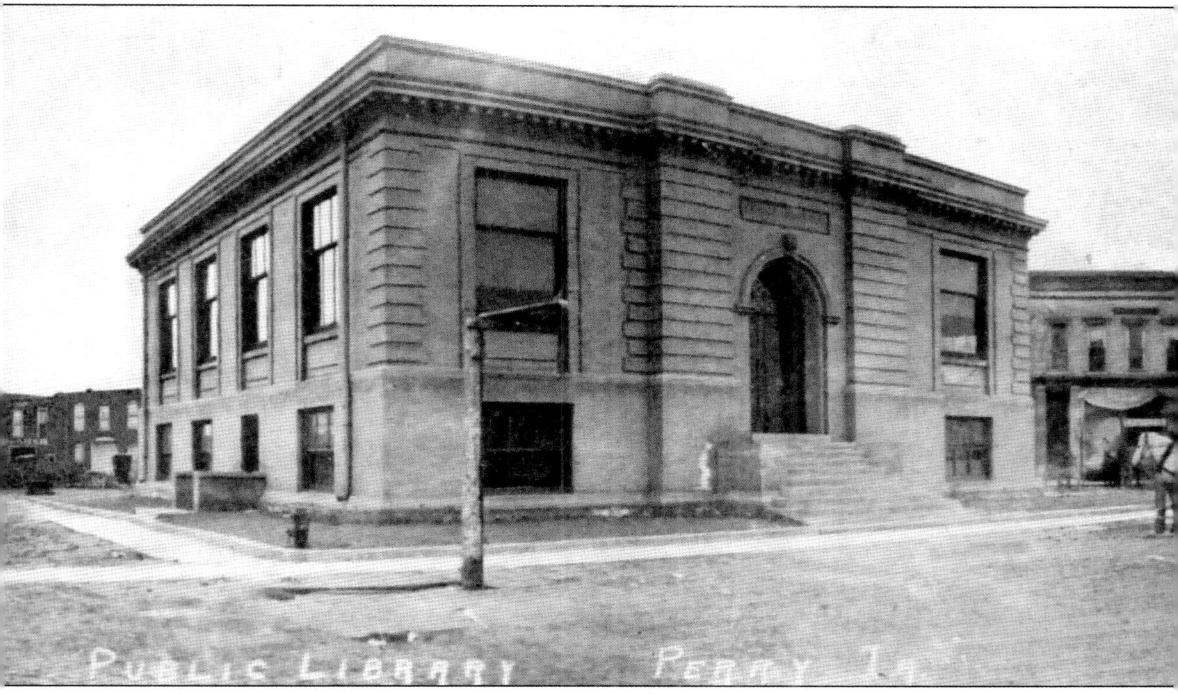

CARNEGIE LIBRARY. The town's library, built with a $10,000 grant from Andrew Carnegie, opened in 1904 with 1,000 titles donated by the Perry community. Its first librarian was Flora Bailey, who served in the position until 1945. The Perry Public Library had its home in the building until 1994, when it moved to a new building across the street. In 2004, the building had a grand reopening as the Carnegie Library Museum, part of Hometown Perry, Iowa.

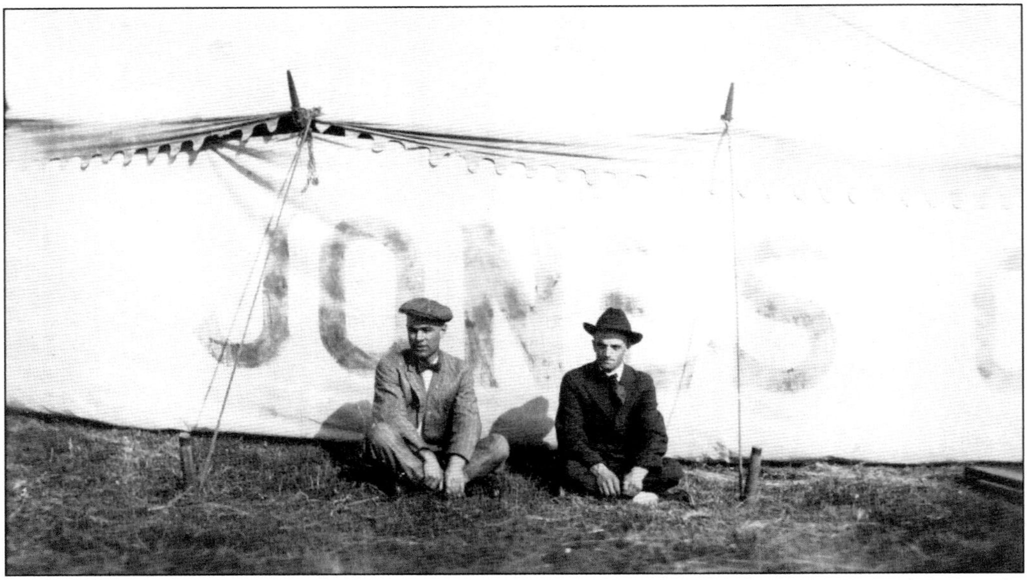

CHAUTAUQUA TENT AND MEN. Beginning in 1878, the Chautauqua Literary and Scientific Circle (CLSC), a correspondence course, formed to offer adults educational opportunities outside the college classroom setting. Another stated goal of the CLSC was to give people an alternative to other leisure-time activities such as drinking and dancing. Out of this movement emerged the circuit chautauqua traveling tent shows that offered lectures and other entertainment. C. Durant Jones of Perry organized one such chautauqua. In 1912, it traveled to more than 130 towns in Iowa. In a bulletin, Jones wrote, "A Chautauqua means recreation of the very best kind for many whose opportunities in this direction are limited. It presents to its patrons a degree of culture which is not easily attainable elsewhere. It creates a community spirit more easily and with less expense than can be attained by any other method."

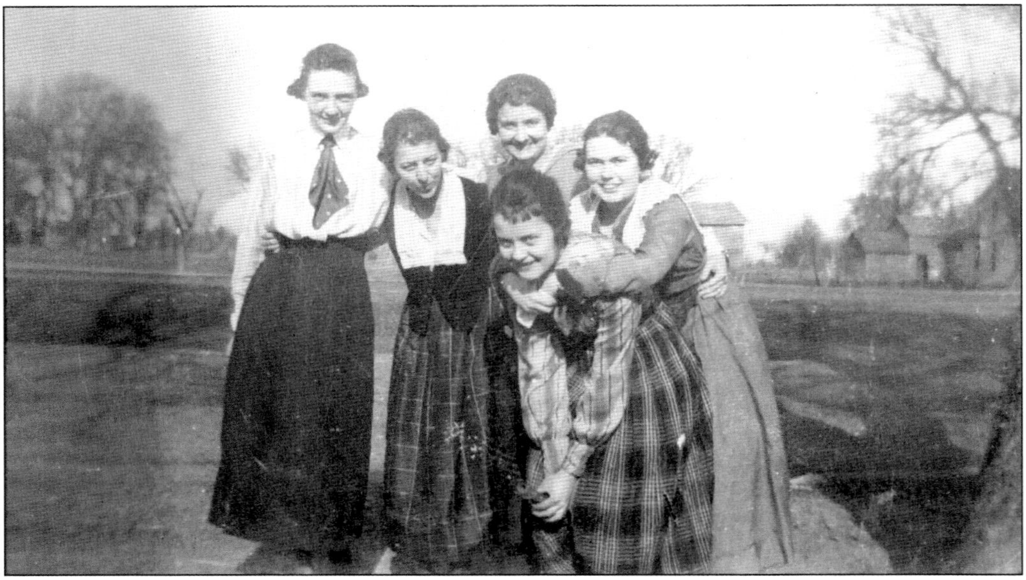

LOUISE DIDDY AND CHAUTAUQUA FRIENDS. Louise Diddy graduated from Perry High School in 1914 and then traveled with the Jones Chautauqua.

Four

FAITH

As well as shopping at a general store and going to school, early settlers to Perry built and attended churches. Even before Perry was officially incorporated, congregations were meeting both in and outside Perry. These photographs show what is evident in describing this community—the diversity of lived experience. At one time, there were more than 16 congregations in this small community with a population that varied between 5,000 and 7,000 people.

In many of Hometown Perry, Iowa's interviews with residents, faith is as an important aspect of their lives. People speak about how their congregation responded when a family member was sick or had passed away. More than that, many spoke about how their faith had gotten them through the hard times of their lives.

As with many early congregations, the pastors were circuit riders, moving from one congregation to another. Yet congregations continued to thrive throughout the history of Perry. Congregations including Methodist, Baptist, Lutheran, Roman Catholic, Christian, Assembly of God, Christian Science, Presbyterian, Episcopalian, and Unitarian flourished. Also at one time, there were three African American congregations. The very small congregations came and sometimes left. Revivals were also part of the history of this community. They were often organized by several congregations and resulted in new members for congregations.

As the photographs show, the congregations were involved in many aspects of community life. Weddings, baptisms, vacation Bible school, and funerals were the traditional events of all the congregations. Also, the congregations were gathering spots for community suppers and musical events.

In present-day Perry, the landscape of faith is altered yet again. With the newest influx of immigrants, there are new congregations. Moreover, the established congregations added additional services for these residents.

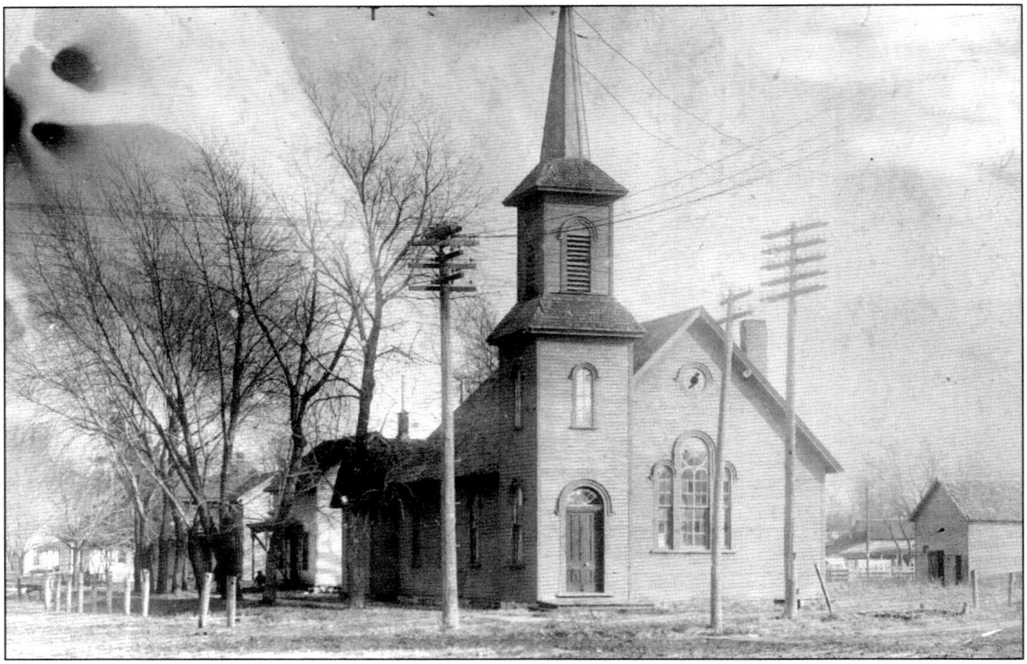

FIRST BAPTIST CHURCH. This church, one of the first in the Perry area, started outside town in 1869 as the Spring Valley Baptist Church. The congregation's first services took place in a schoolhouse. The building pictured here, built between 1870 and 1873, was located on a small triangle between Otley Avenue, Railroad Street, and Second Street. After the congregation built a new church at Fourth and Lucinda Streets, this building was demolished.

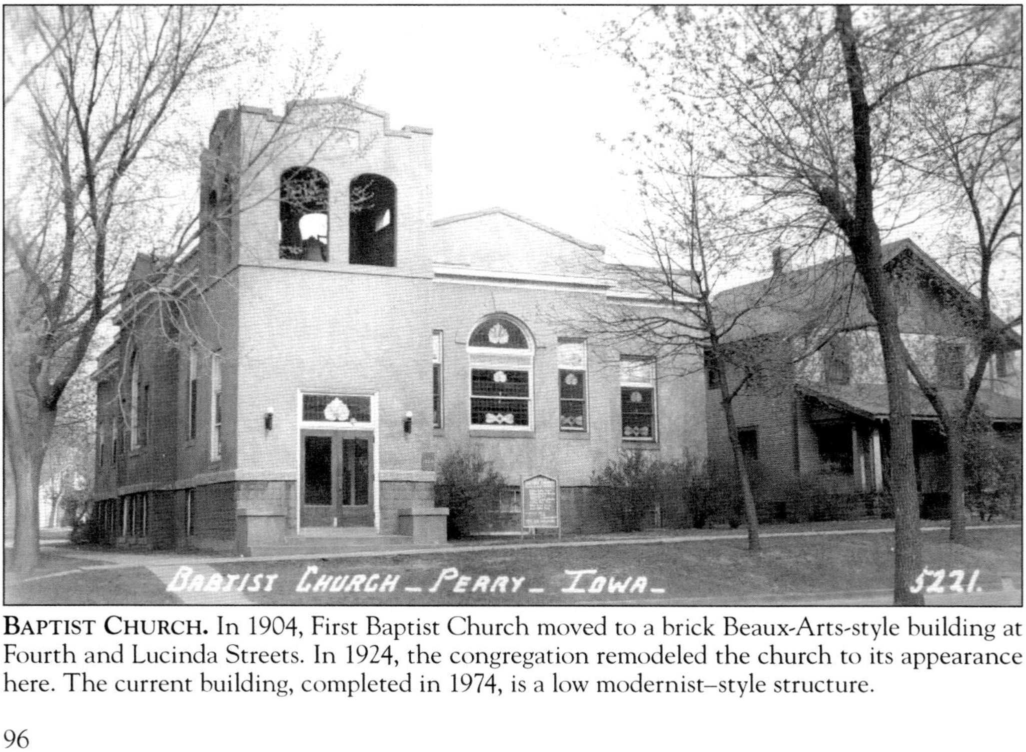

BAPTIST CHURCH. In 1904, First Baptist Church moved to a brick Beaux-Arts-style building at Fourth and Lucinda Streets. In 1924, the congregation remodeled the church to its appearance here. The current building, completed in 1974, is a low modernist–style structure.

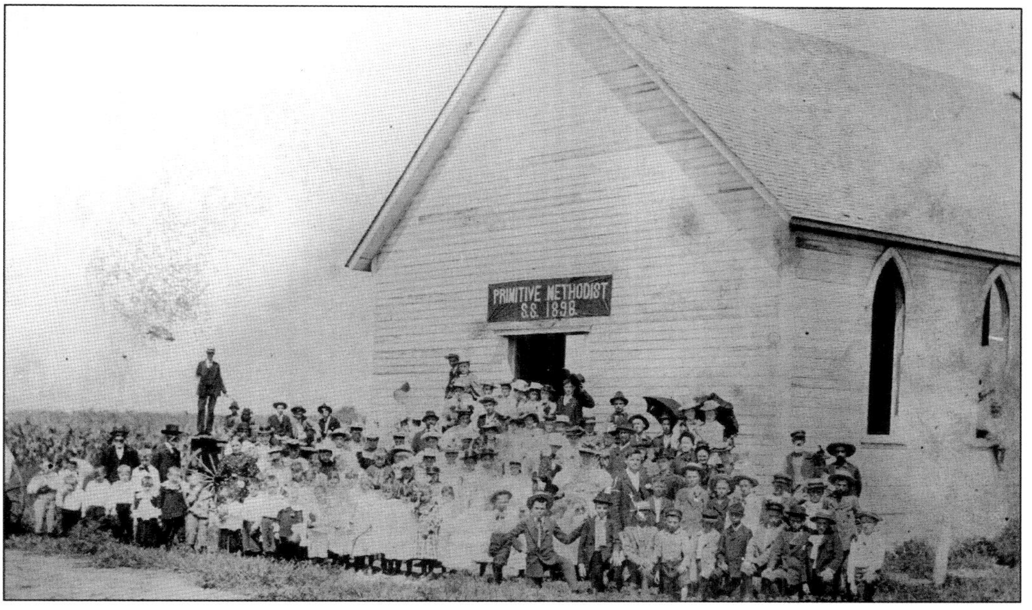

PRIMITIVE METHODIST CHURCH. Located in Angus about five miles from Perry, this was an early congregation led by Rev. William Morris, who also served a congregation in Fraser. Morris and his wife married in England and then immigrated to Rock Island, Illinois. When they arrived in Angus, then a town of 7,000, it had 14 saloons but no churches. Morris was still leading services in Angus 55 years after its founding.

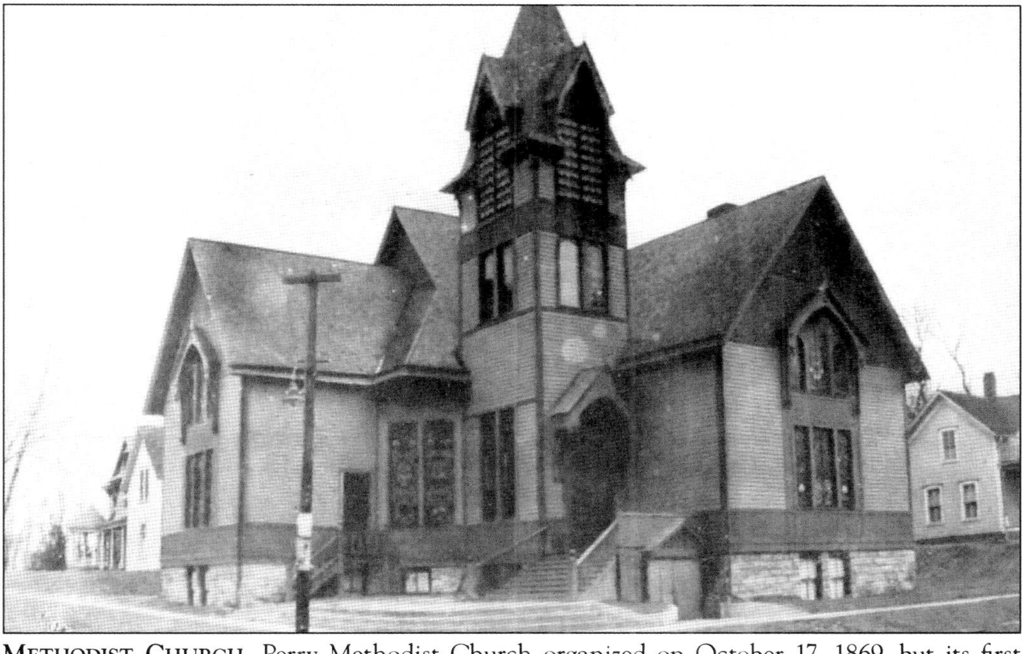

METHODIST CHURCH. Perry Methodist Church organized on October 17, 1869, but its first building, located at Third and Warford Streets, was not built until 1874. This photograph shows the second building. Built in 1891, the church burned in May 1908 after it was struck by lightning. William Jennings Bryan and Carrie Nation both spoke at this church.

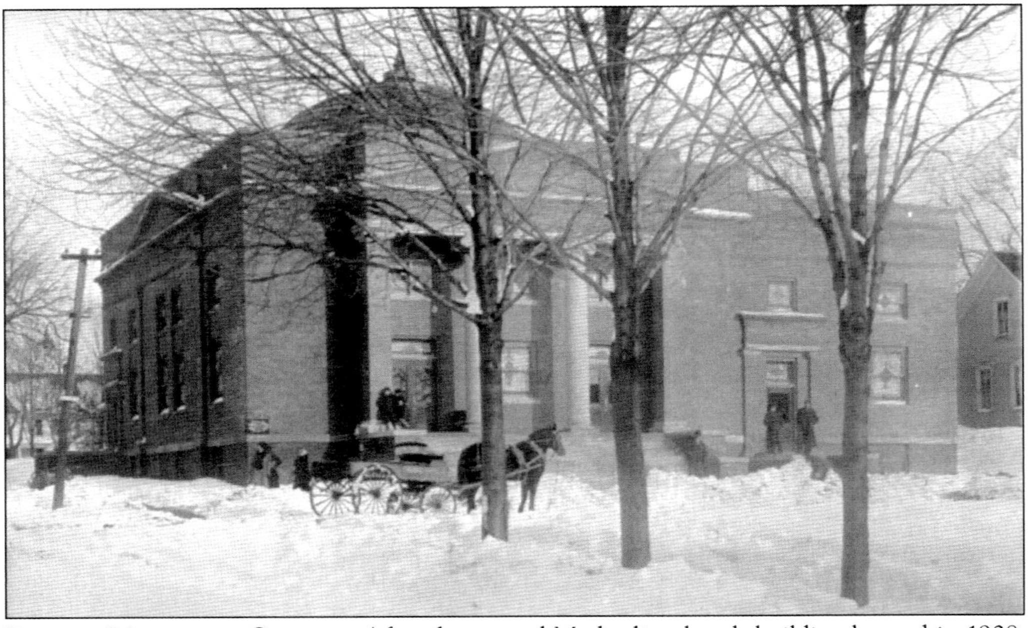

REBUILT METHODIST CHURCH. After the second Methodist church building burned in 1908, this new building was dedicated in March 1909. The new church featured stone pillars and a green tile dome. Sometime prior to 1962, the dome was determined to be structurally unsound and removed. In October 1924, an annex was added on the south side.

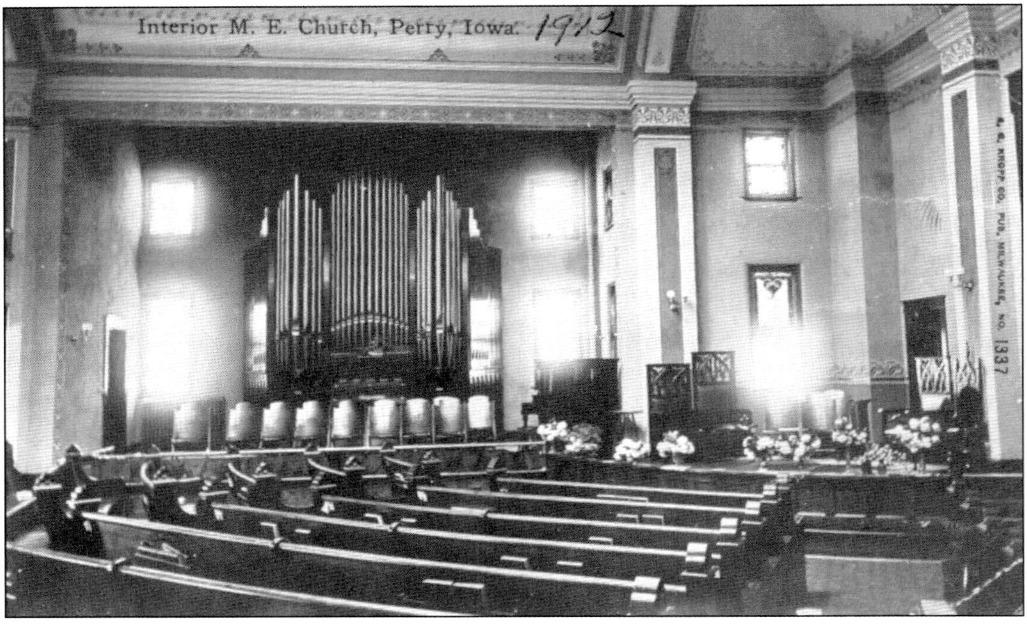

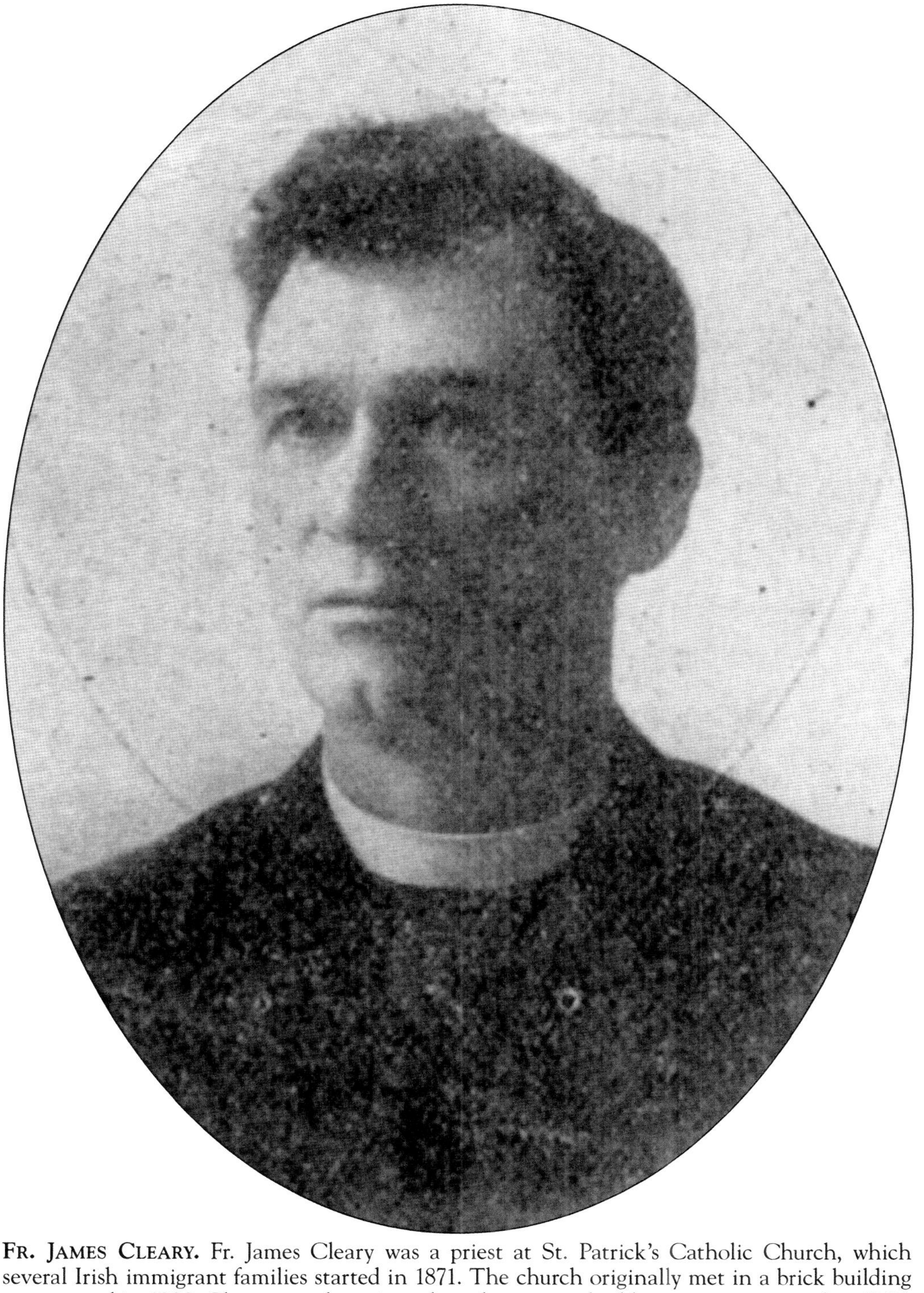

FR. JAMES CLEARY. Fr. James Cleary was a priest at St. Patrick's Catholic Church, which several Irish immigrant families started in 1871. The church originally met in a brick building constructed in 1880. Cleary was the priest when the current building was constructed in 1905. The fourth priest to serve at St. Patrick's, Cleary resigned in 1935.

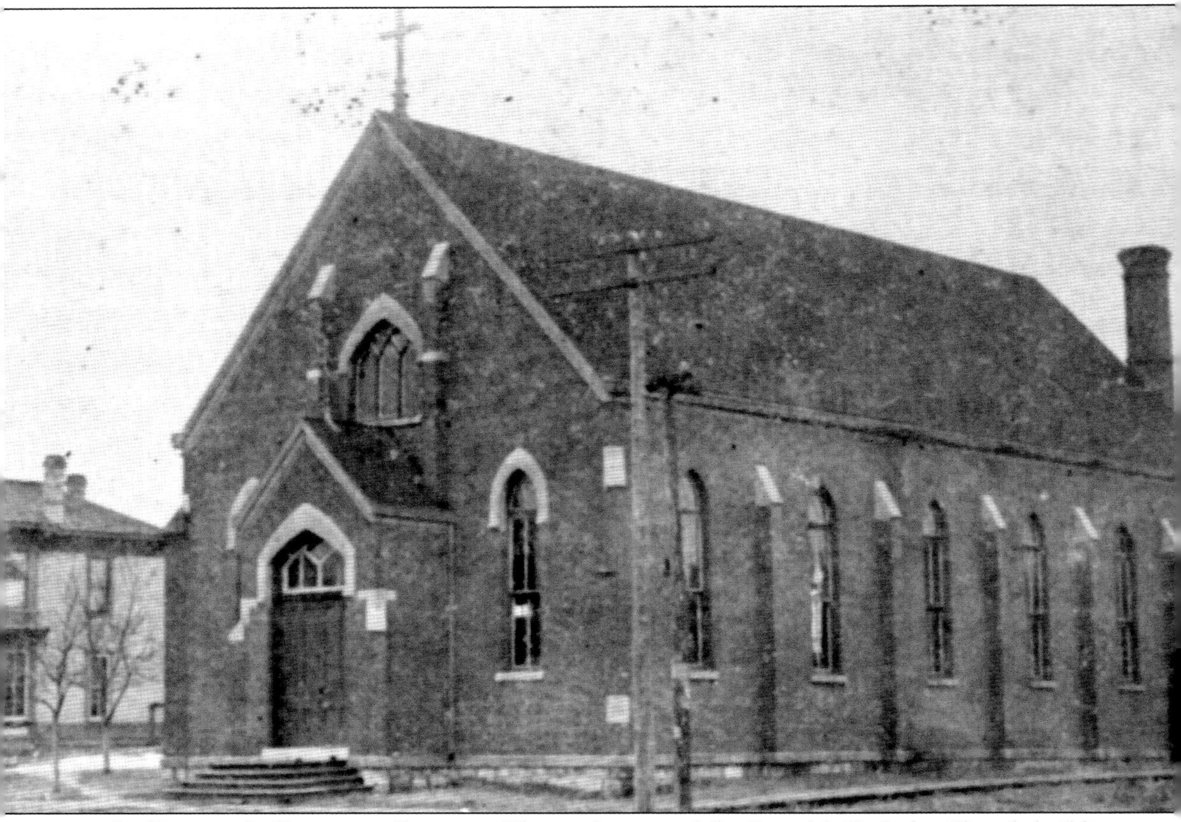

St. Patrick's Catholic Church. This is the second St. Patrick's Catholic Church building, built in 1883 at Third and Lucinda Streets. In order to save money on the construction, parishioners made and fired their own bricks, using clay found southeast of Perry. The building replaced an old wooden church that was moved to the corner of West Eighth and Lucinda Streets and remodeled into apartments in 1914.

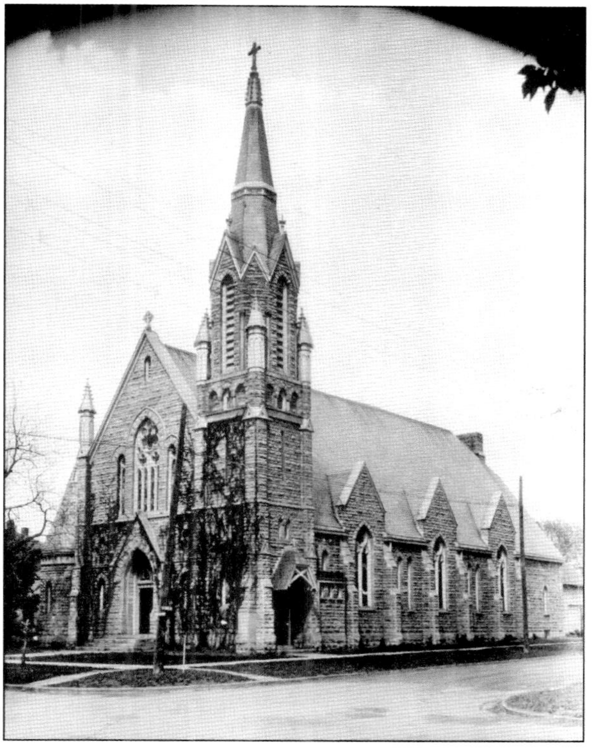

THIRD ST. PATRICK'S CATHOLIC CHURCH. This building (right), still in use as St. Patrick's Catholic Church, was the congregation's third location. Although remodeled, the church still looks much the same today.

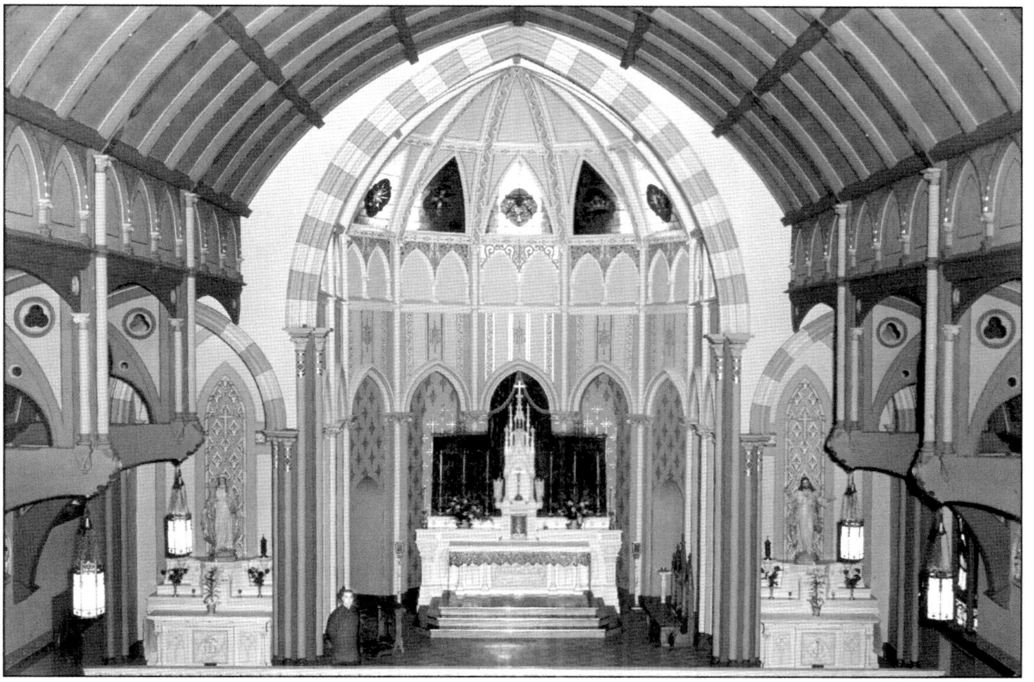

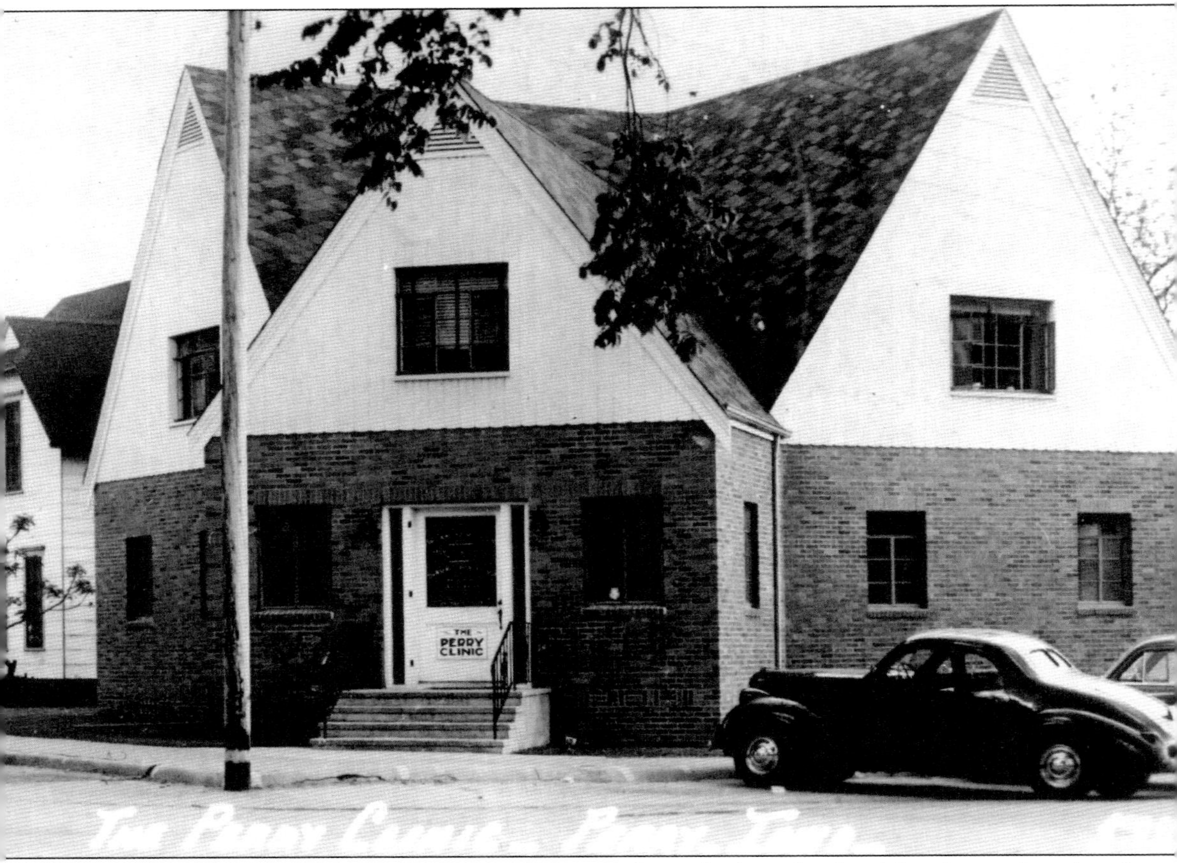

UNITARIAN CHURCH. In 1890, a small group of people from five local families gathered and formed a Unitarian society. In 1894, they built a church located on the southwest corner of Third and Lucinda Streets. The congregation disbanded in 1913, and the building was later purchased by the Assembly of God church. The building also served as the Perry Clinic for some time (as pictured here) but was eventually torn down.

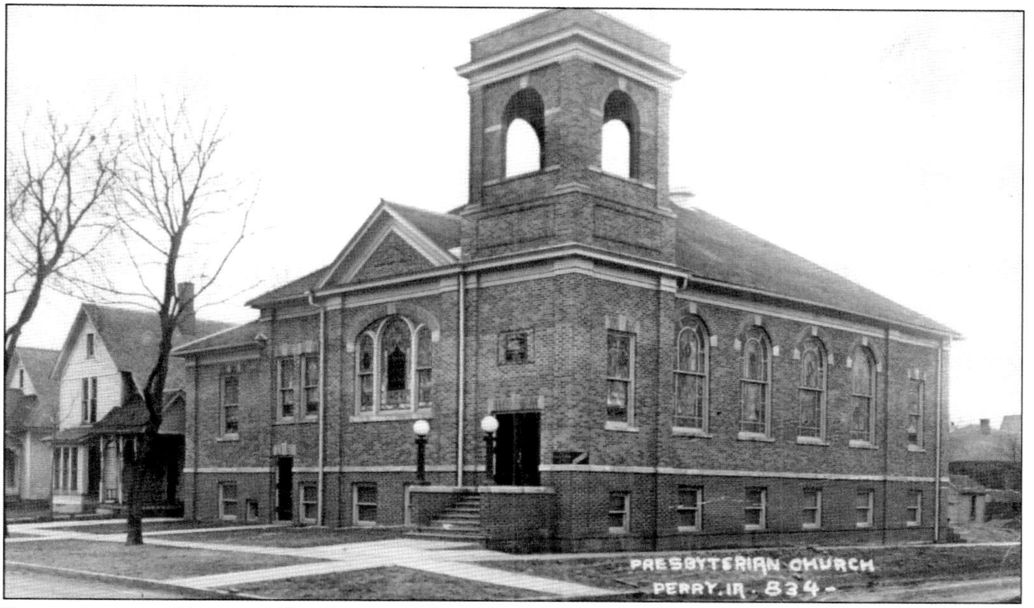

PRESBYTERIAN CHURCH. Presbyterians began meeting in Perry in 1869 as a small home mission headed by Rev. H. H. Kellogg. In August 1880, they formally organized and held their first services at the Des Moines and Fort Dodge Railroad depot. Later they built their first church at Fourth and Pattee Streets and dedicated it on February 1, 1891. In May 1917, the congregation laid the cornerstone for a new church on the same site.

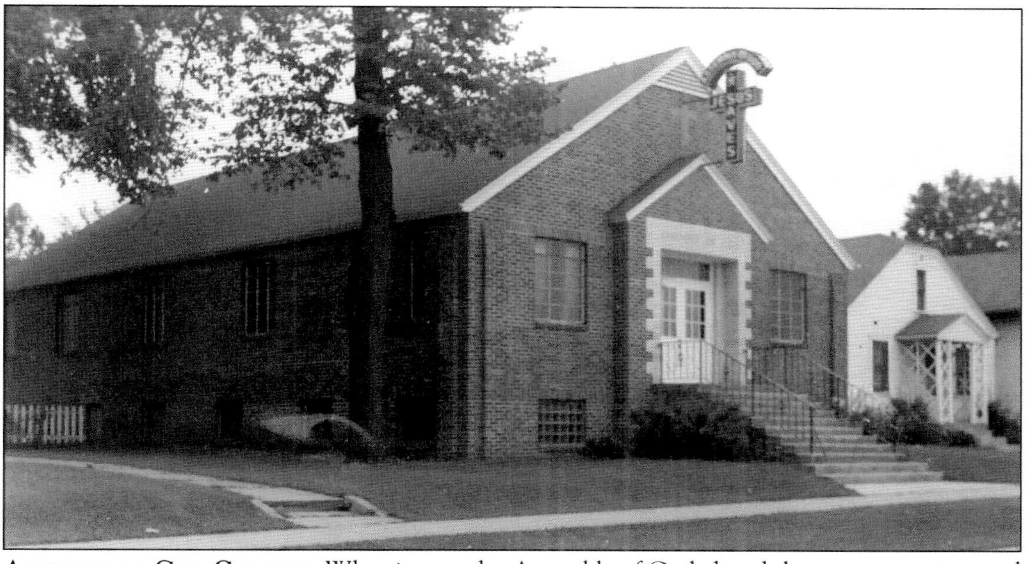

ASSEMBLY OF GOD CHURCH. What is now the Assembly of God church began at a tent revival in 1906. About a dozen Perry residents converted to holiness teaching and opened a mission on Willis Avenue. The congregation switched to Pentecostal teaching in 1910. When the Assemblies of God were formed in 1914, the Perry congregation became affiliated with this denomination. The congregation began renting the former Unitarian church in 1916, and it purchased and remodeled the building in 1929. In 1946, it purchased a lot on Third Street between Lucinda and Warford Streets and constructed the present church, pictured here.

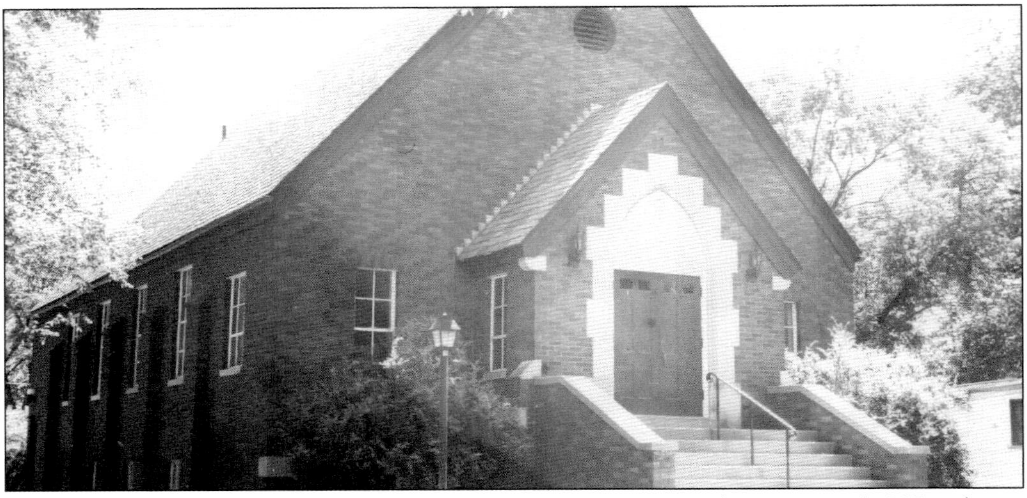

CHRISTIAN SCIENCE CHURCH. Christian Science services in Perry began around 1907 and were most often held in private homes. In 1913, the church formally organized, and services were held in the former Unitarian church and the Jones Business College building. This property on the southwest corner of Fifth Street and Otley Avenue was built in early 1928. Before this date, the congregation held services in Fraternity Hall in Perry. Although the first services were held on January 19, 1933, the church's dedication was delayed until August 5, 1934, due to Christian Science practice that all churches must be debt free. It is not known when the Christian Science congregation in Perry disbanded, but sometime after, the building was used by a Seventh-Day Adventist congregation.

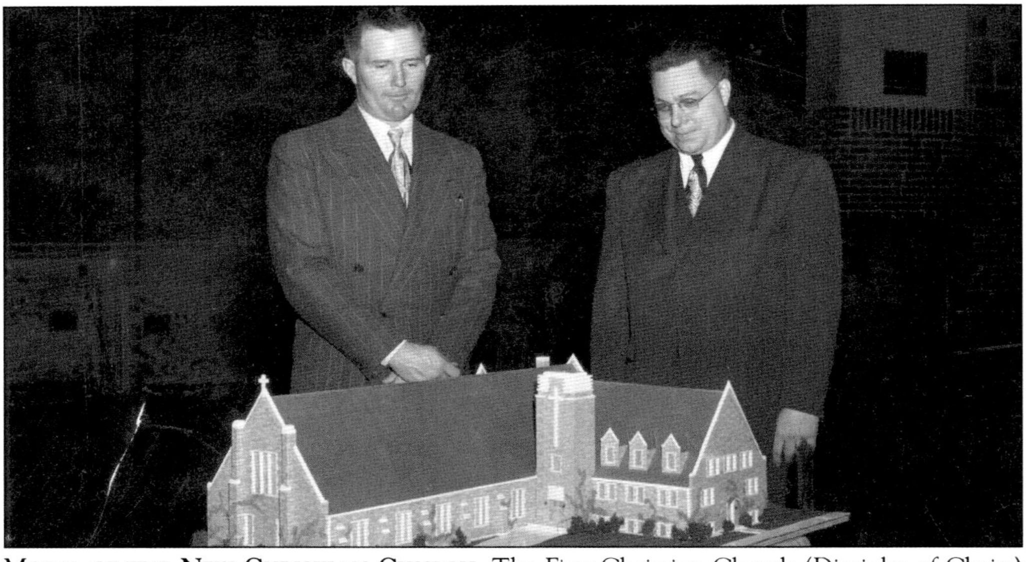

MODEL OF THE NEW CHRISTIAN CHURCH. The First Christian Church (Disciples of Christ) began as early as 1871, meeting in members' homes or in schoolhouses. Its first building was constructed in 1881. In the late 1890s, two tent revivals in Perry contributed so many members to the church that a new building, ultimately located at the corner of Third and Lucinda Streets, became a necessity. In September 1947, the congregation of the Christian church in Perry voted to construct a new building. Groundbreaking took place on April 9, 1950, and the cornerstone was laid on April 22, 1951.

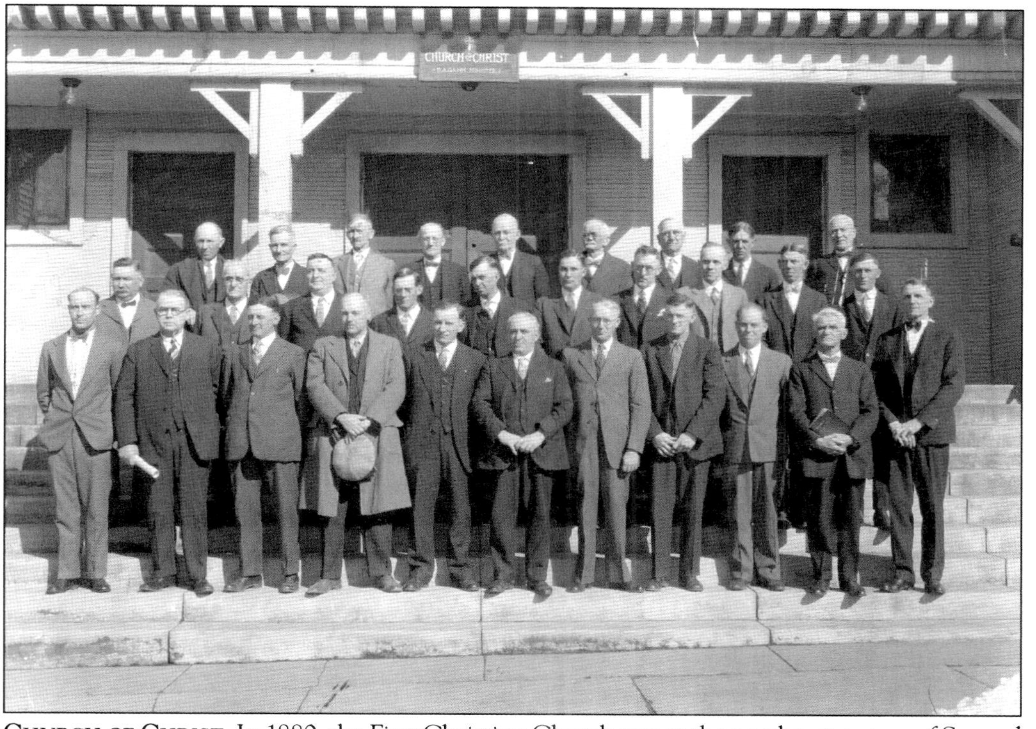

CHURCH OF CHRIST. In 1880, the First Christian Church was at the northeast corner of Second and Lucinda Streets. The congregation built a new church at Third and Lucinda Streets and dedicated it on December 25, 1898. William Jennings Bryan spoke at the church in June 1902, and in April 1906, it housed refugees from the San Francisco earthquake. Although extensively renovated in 1924, the building was damaged by a windstorm in 1949 and declared unsafe. A new church built on the site was dedicated on December 9, 1951.

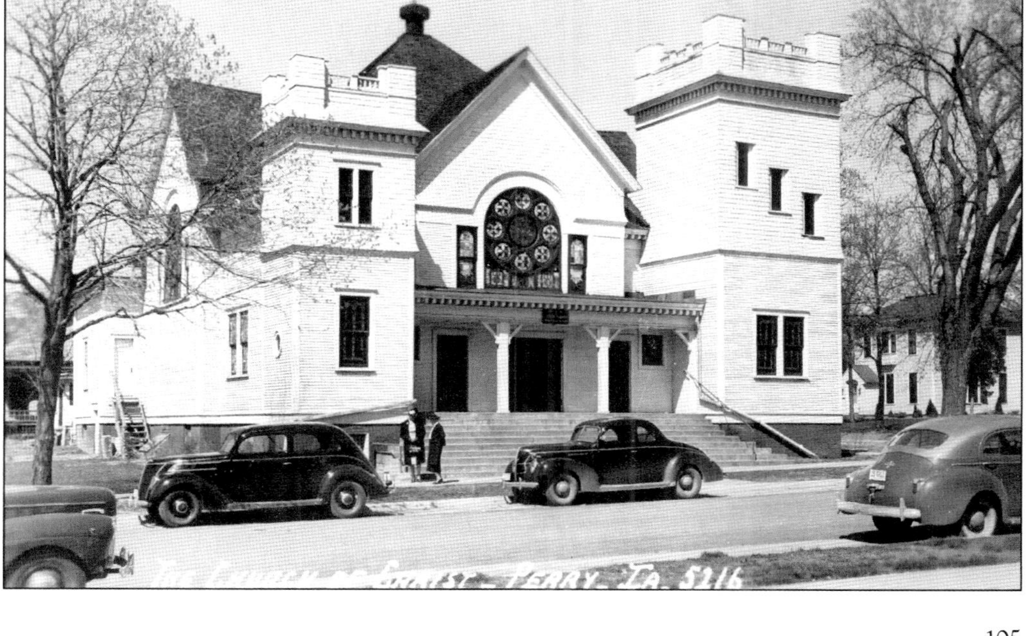

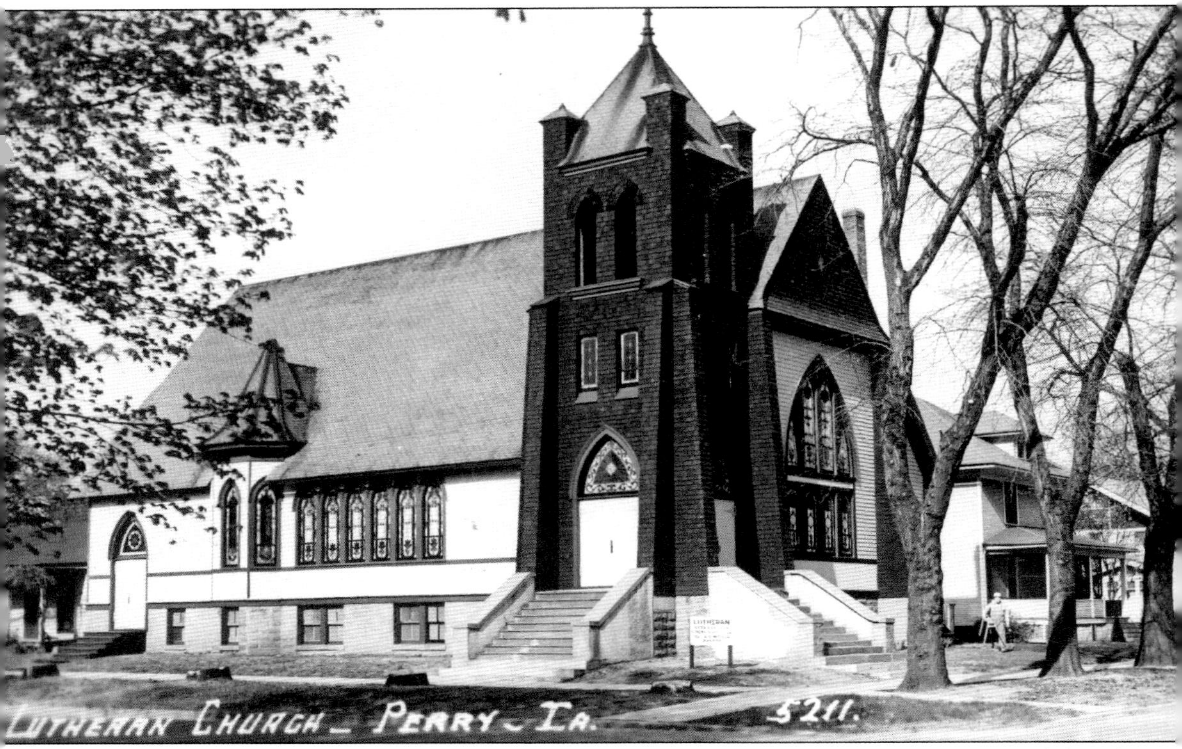

CONGREGATIONAL CHURCH. In December 1883, 18 people met to form a Congregational church in Perry. In 1888, the congregation built its first church on the northeast corner of Third Street and Otley Avenue. A second church was built in 1905 on the corner of Fourth and Warford Streets. It disbanded in September 1940 when no minister could be found to fill a vacancy, and the building was sold in 1941 to Trinity Lutheran Church, originally a mission branch of Bouton Lutheran Church. When Trinity moved to a new building in 1970, the next tenant was Oscar Mayer, which purchased the structure for an activity hall. It is presently Heartland Church of Christ.

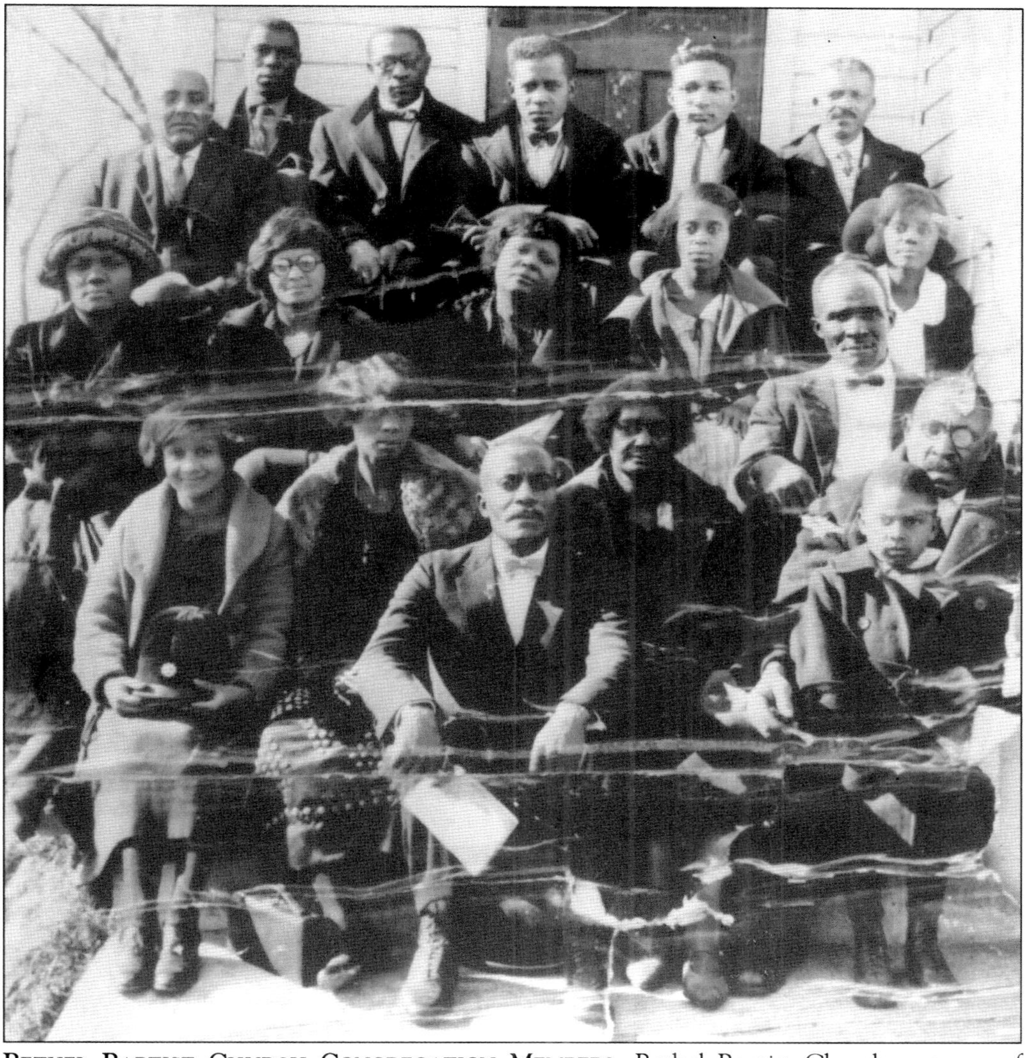

BETHEL BAPTIST CHURCH CONGREGATION MEMBERS. Bethel Baptist Church was one of three African American churches in Perry in the 20th century. Originally part of Zion African Methodist Episcopal Church, Bethel Baptist formed in the fall of 1914. The congregation moved into a building at Seventh and Rawson Streets in 1920 and remained there until its last service in 1999. After being restored, the New Bethel Baptist Church reopened as part of the Hometown Perry, Iowa museum campus in February 2005.

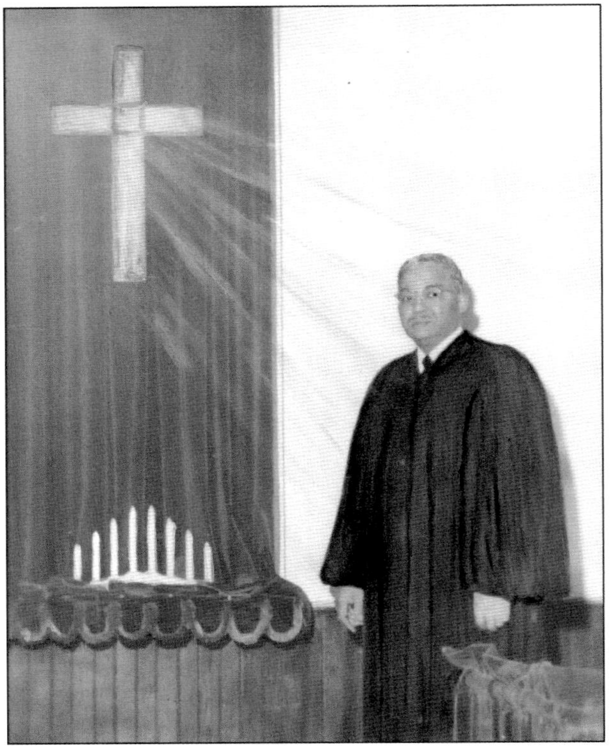

Rev. Horace Lewis. Rev. Horace Lewis served as longtime pastor of Bethel Baptist Church at Seventh and Rawson Streets in Perry. Lewis was ordained a minister in 1947 and died in 1984. Throughout his life in Perry, he was a popular speaker and community leader who promoted racial understanding.

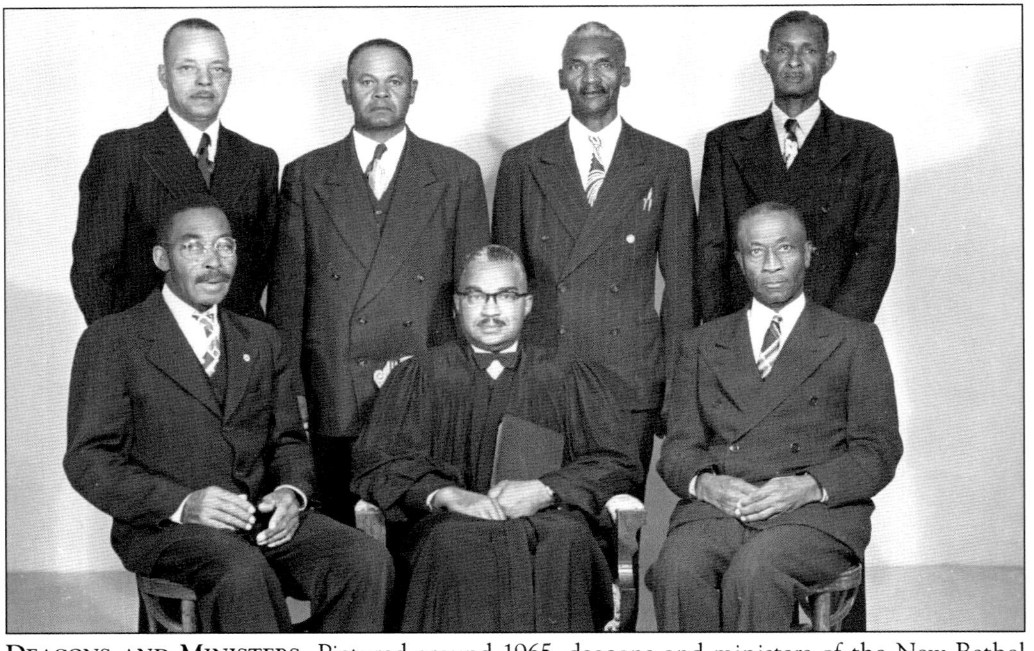

Deacons and Ministers. Pictured around 1965, deacons and ministers of the New Bethel Baptist Church in Perry are (first row) Reverend Ross, Rev. Horace Lewis, and Rev. Arthur Griffith; (second row) Deacon Arthur Johnson, Deacon Dave Maupins, Deacon Allen, and Deacon Dell Woods.

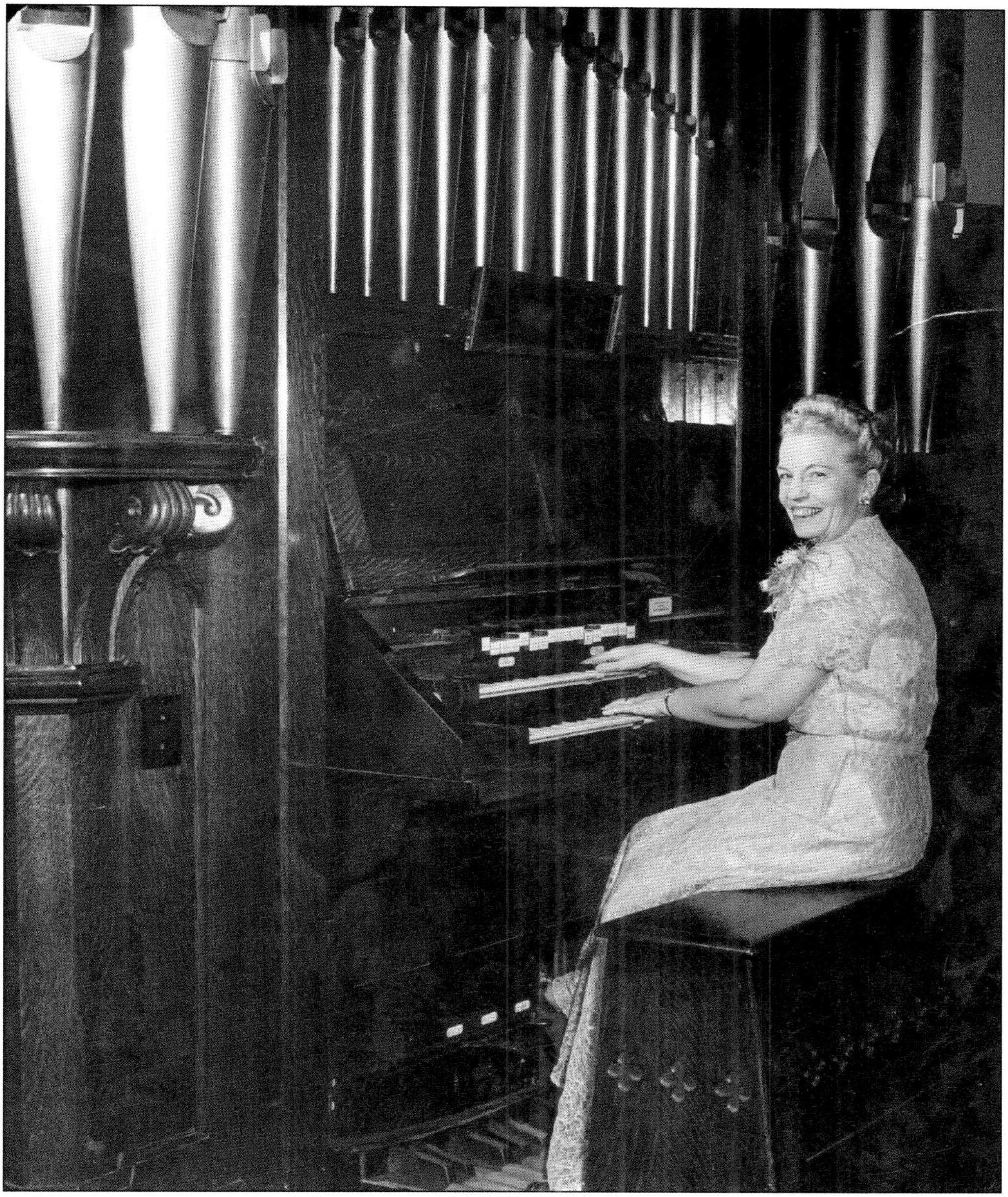

ADA WORTH CHAPMAN. Ada Worth Chapman, wife of Frank Chapman, was the longtime organist at Perry's First Methodist Church. Her parents, George and Viola Worth, ran a music store in Perry for many years. In 1972, Fred Melick, a longtime member of First Methodist, passed away and left a considerable sum of money to pay for a new organ if a new church was built. The congregation built a new sanctuary at the corner of Willis Avenue and Third Street.

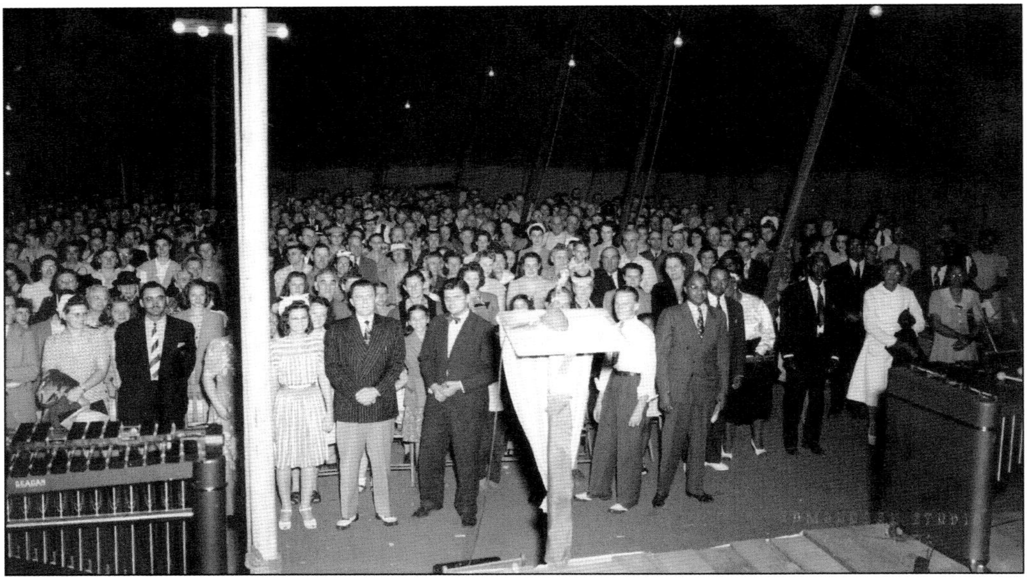

CHURCH REVIVAL MEETING. From the collection of Dora Lewis, wife of New Bethel Baptist Church pastor Horace Lewis, this image depicts a church revival held in a tent in Perry in the 1940s. Tent services were popular in Perry from the late 19th century into the 20th century. It was often a time for many congregations to work together as they worshipped.

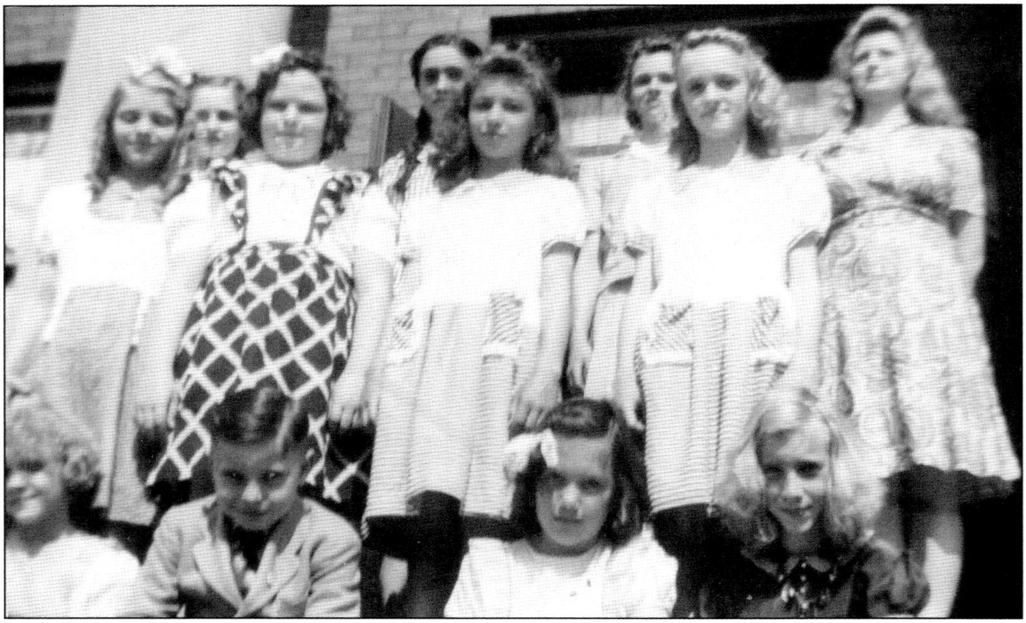

METHODIST CHURCH SUNDAY SCHOOL CLASS. One of the many activities offered by Perry churches of various denominations is Sunday school instruction for all ages. This picture, taken around 1944, comes from Delores Holcomb, who met her husband, Don, through Sunday school when they were children.

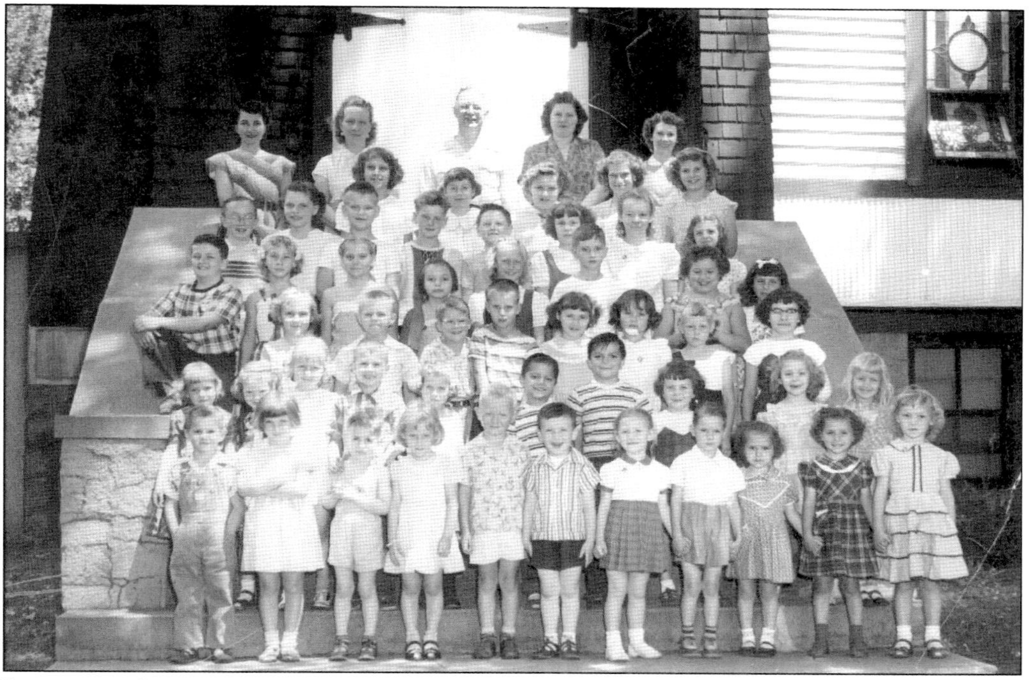

LUTHERAN CHURCH VACATION BIBLE SCHOOL. Another tradition in Perry congregations, as in churches everywhere, is vacation Bible school. Held in the summer, Bible school often comprises a weeklong program of instruction and activities. Here the 1952 Bible school participants at Trinity Lutheran Church pose for a picture.

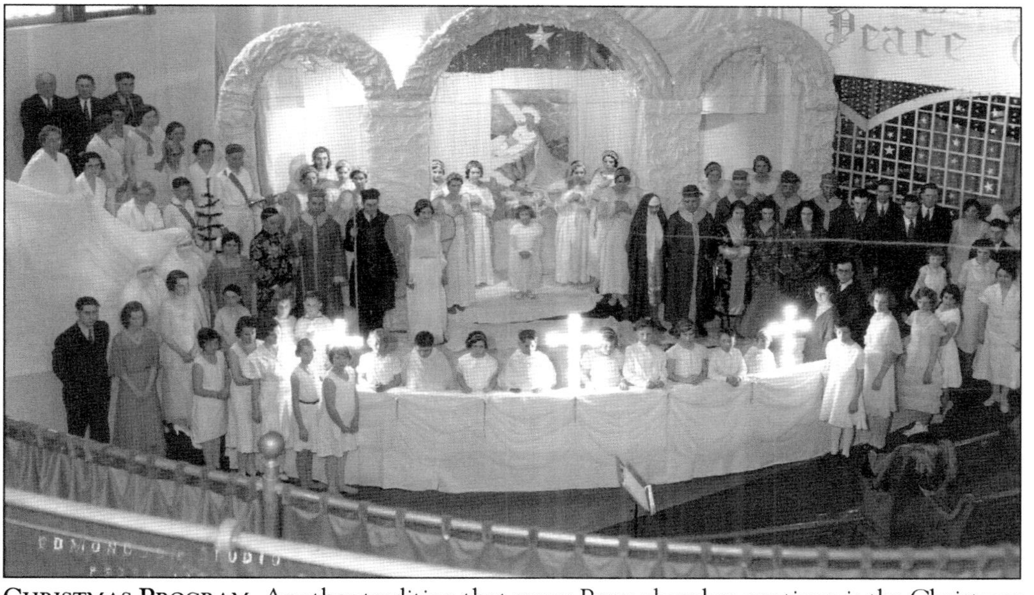

CHRISTMAS PROGRAM. Another tradition that many Perry churches continue is the Christmas program, often a dramatic presentation of the Christmas story put on by Sunday school students. This 1950 program, *White Gifts of the King*, took place at the Methodist church in Perry.

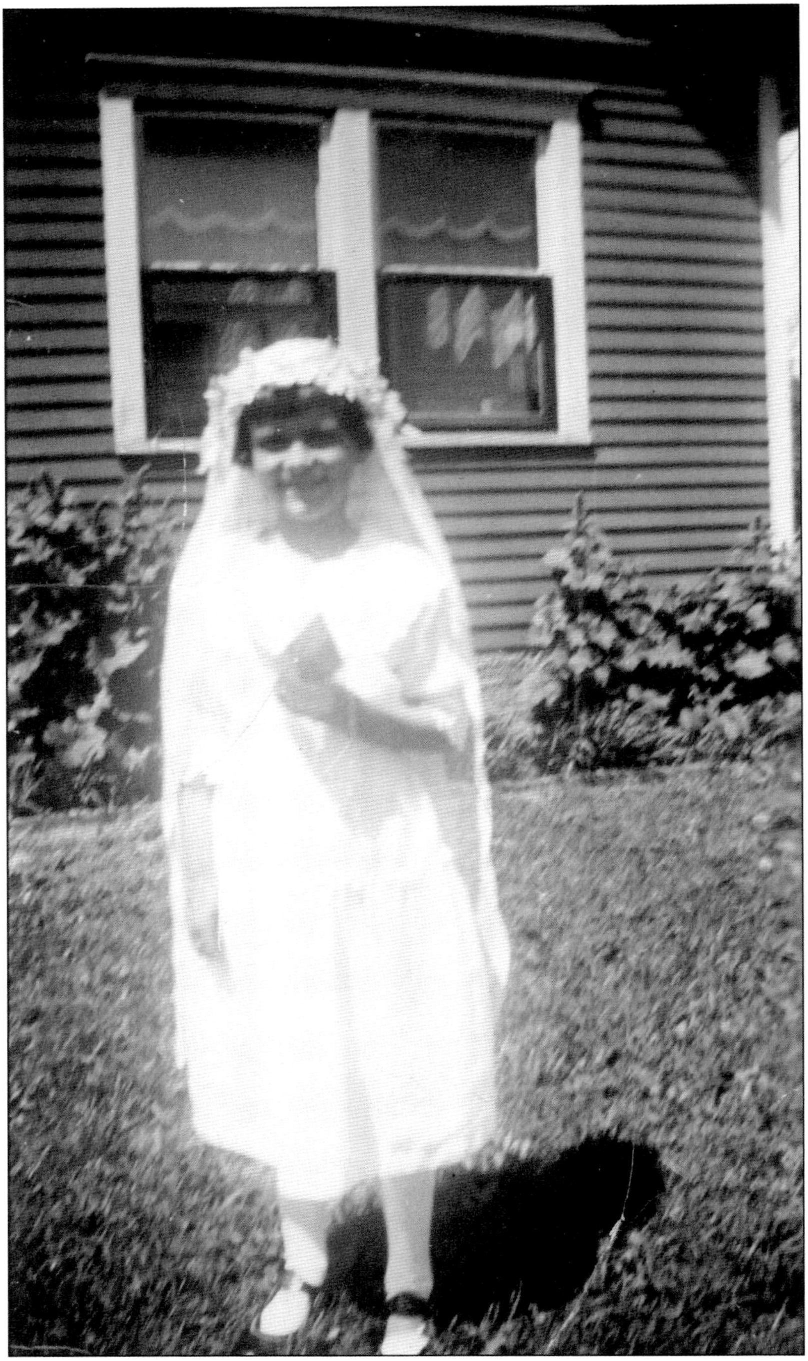

RITA RIPPERGER'S FIRST COMMUNION. As in churches everywhere, first communion is an important rite of passage for children in Perry's churches. Rita Ripperger Smithson grew up on a farm near Lacona and attended Rosemount School, a Catholic country school with eight grades. Her family moved to Perry when she was in high school. This photograph of her dressed in white for first communion in 1936 echoes many photographs from Catholic families in Perry.

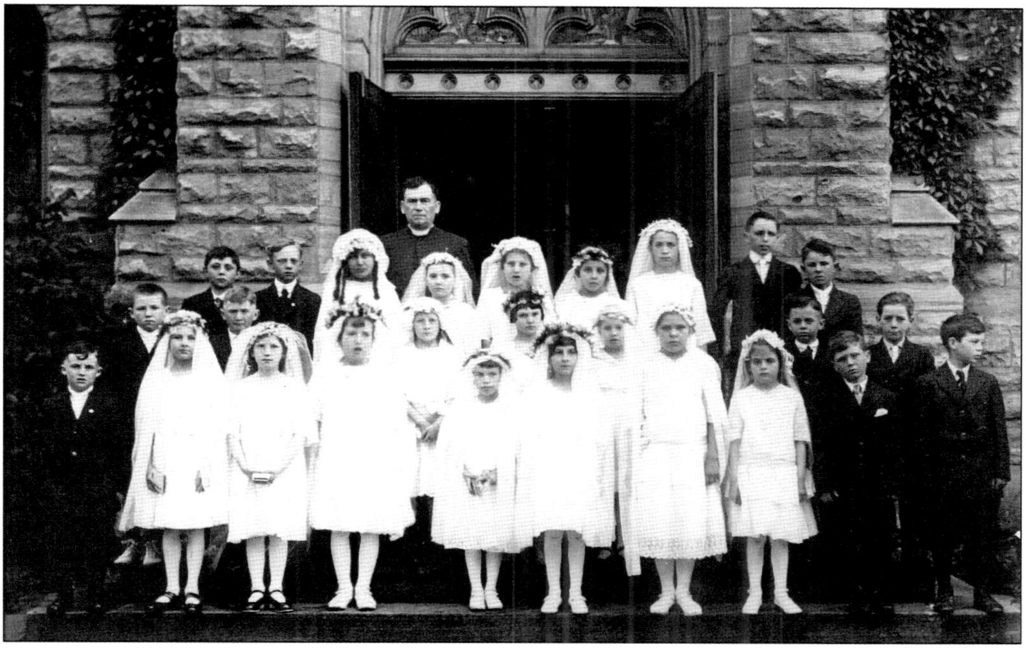

St. Patrick's Catholic School First Communion. Religious education was part of the curriculum at St. Patrick's, founded in 1920. Here students celebrate the school's initial first communion.

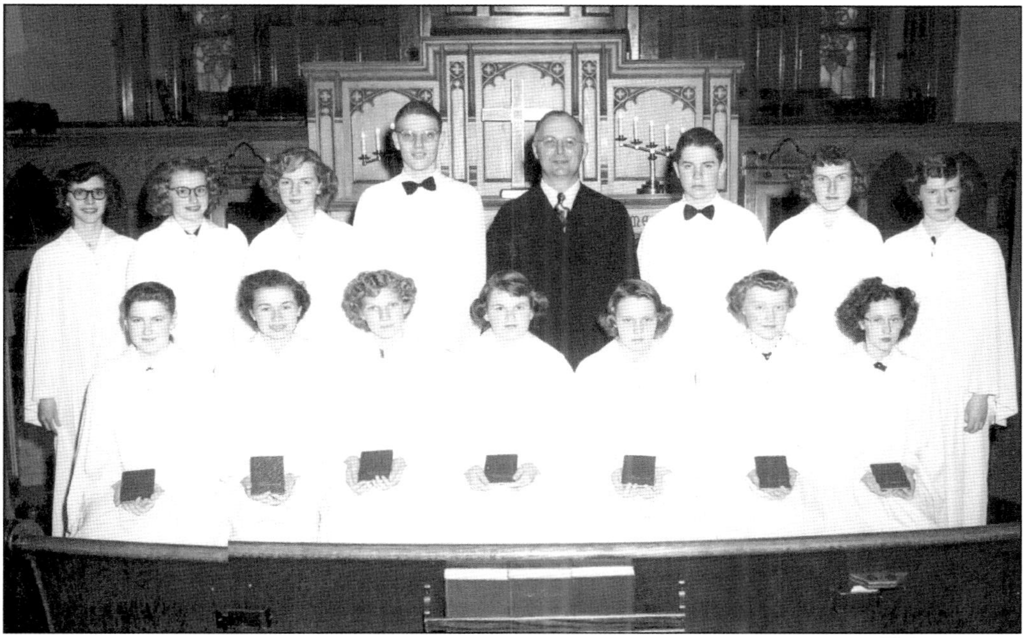

Lutheran Church Confirmation. Another important rite of passage for members of Perry churches is confirmation, a reaffirmation of baptism usually undertaken around age 14, following a year or more of classroom instruction. Here the 1940 confirmation class poses at Trinity Lutheran Church.

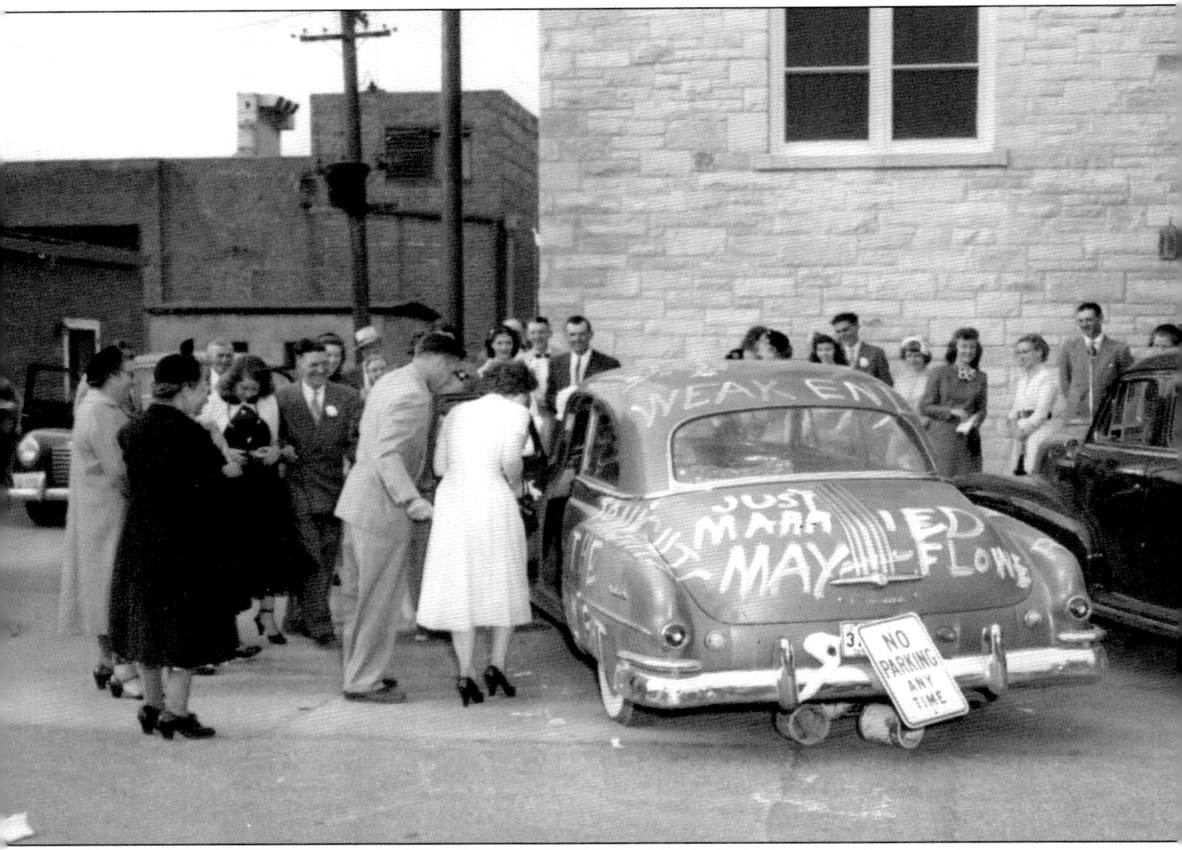

MARVIN AND ROSE MENZ WEDDING DAY. For many, churches are the site of important rites of passage, from baptism through confirmation to weddings and funerals. Marvin and Rose Menz farmed near Perry after marrying in 1953. Prior to the wedding, Marvin was part of the construction crew that built the Christian church in 1951.

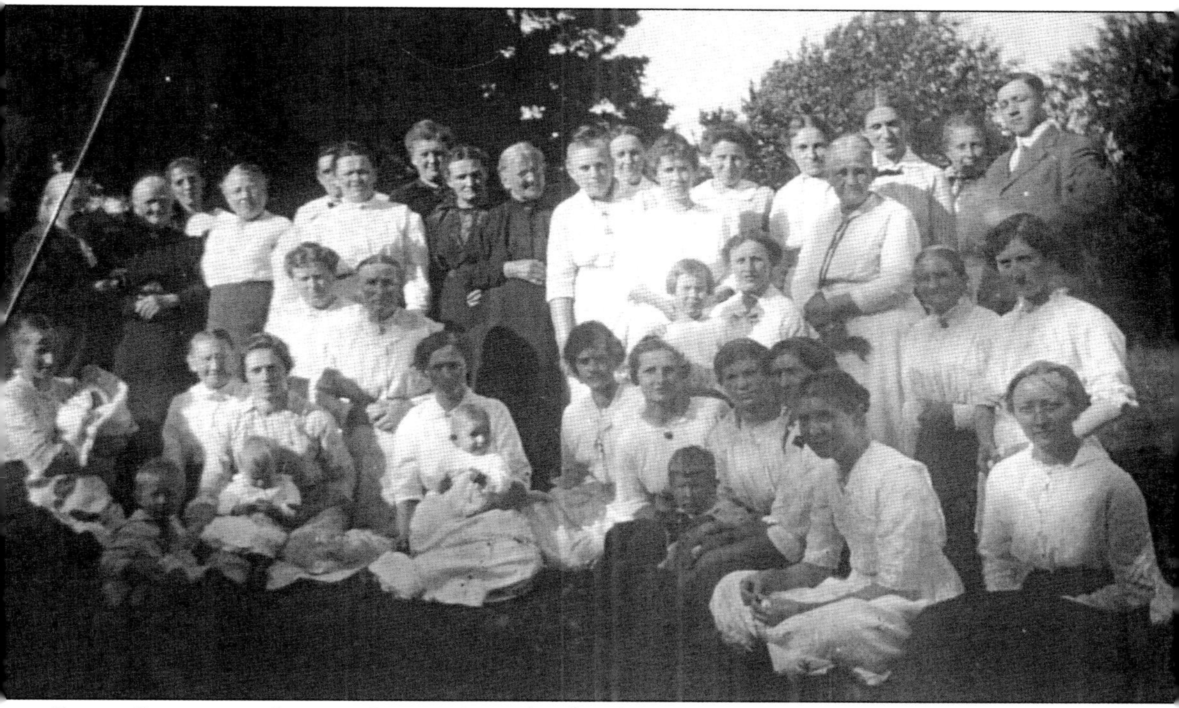

Christ Lutheran Church Ladies Aid. The church has long been a social hub for residents of Perry and other small towns. The ladies aid group pictured here was part of the Christ Lutheran Church congregation in Bouton, a small town five miles east of Perry. A German Lutheran (Missouri Synod) congregation, the church began holding services as early as 1890.

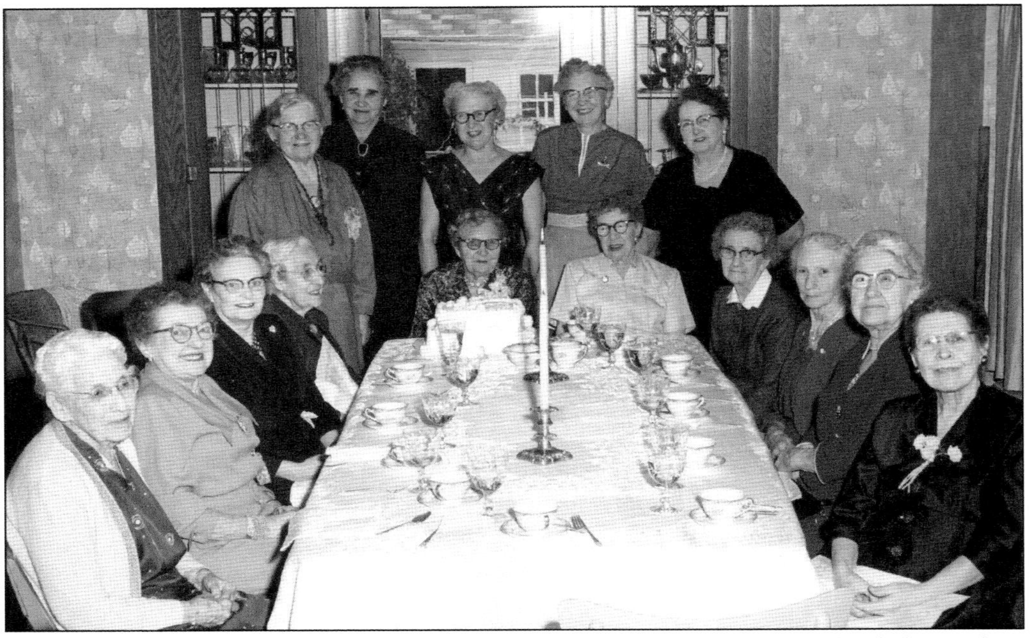

FIRST PRESBYTERIAN CHURCH SUNDAY SCHOOL. Here in 1957, a Sunday school class gathers at the home of one of its members, Grace McDonald, demonstrating again how important churches have been in maintaining the social fabric of small towns. Grace McDonald was also instrumental in forming the Soroptimist Club sorority in Perry. Grace and her husband, Fred, ran McDonald Drug in Perry.

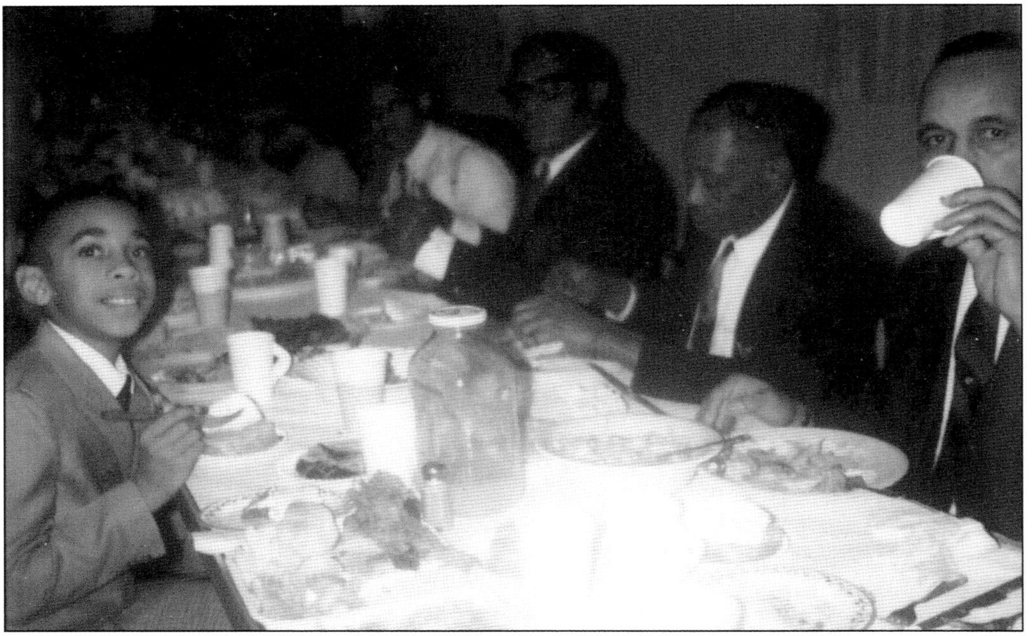

POTLUCK. Most churches thrive because of the close community ties that develop not only through worship but also through other activities shared by their members. A potluck is another occasion for this type of fellowship. Here Phillip Tindrell, Jr. attends a church potluck in 1970.

Five

LOSS

Every community suffers loss. Sometimes loss is catastrophic when it happens all at once and destroys a whole community. Other times, loss for a community is gradual and happens so slowly that it takes awhile before the community notices.

In a small community in the Midwest, much of the loss is accidental—someone might be in a car or farm accident. These losses often have tragic consequences for the family and the neighborhood. Often people remember exactly where they were years later when someone close to them died.

Because Perry was a railroad town, train accidents were always a worry. Over the years of the railroad, local men lost their lives in train wrecks. Even today, residents recount when someone from Perry was killed in a train wreck.

In a community this size, loss is also connected to national and international events. Local people lost their lives in World War I, the 1918 flu epidemic, World War II, and the conflicts in Korea and Vietnam.

Another kind of loss happens when economic forces play out at a local level. During the Depression, farms were lost. Railroad work slowed down, and people were laid off or worked much less. The ups and downs of the economic picture led to the farm crisis of the 1980s. Finally after many years of struggle, the last Milwaukee Road train went through Perry in 1980. This economy turndown altered the lives of the whole community.

Yet the residents of Perry remain hopeful. When the newest immigrants are asked about why they are in Perry, they say, "Because it is safe and the schools are good." These same traits have in been in Perry since its beginning. Perry is an exemplar of the continued resilience of small towns.

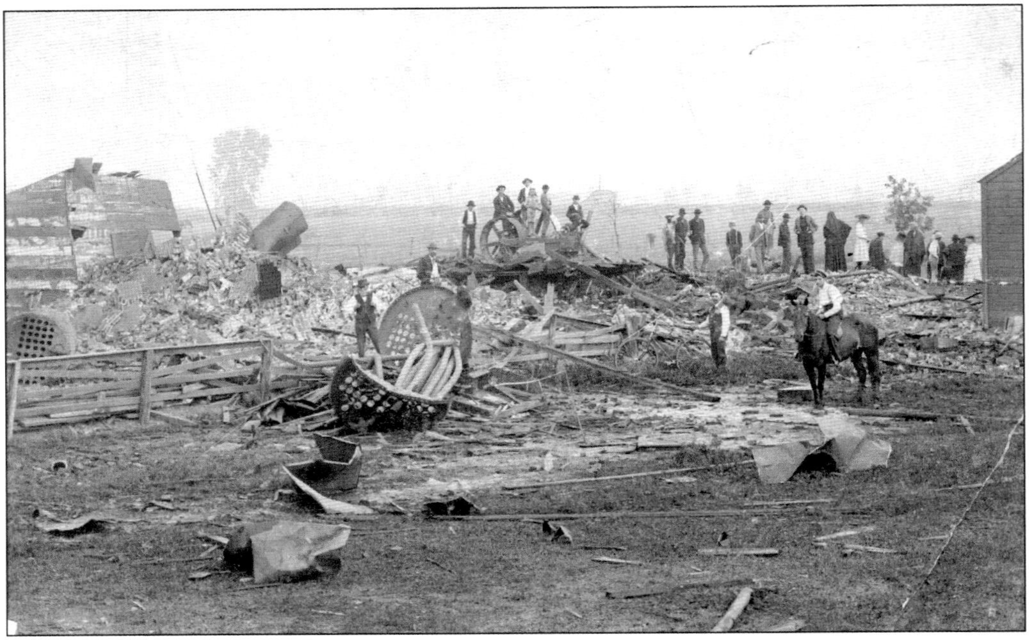

Light and Water Plant Explosion. In July 1894, the light and waterworks plant exploded. The demand for hot water had been particularly heavy that day, and the water in the boiler was very low. It was not long before the boiler was below the safety point. Superintendent Henry Hock was killed in the explosion.

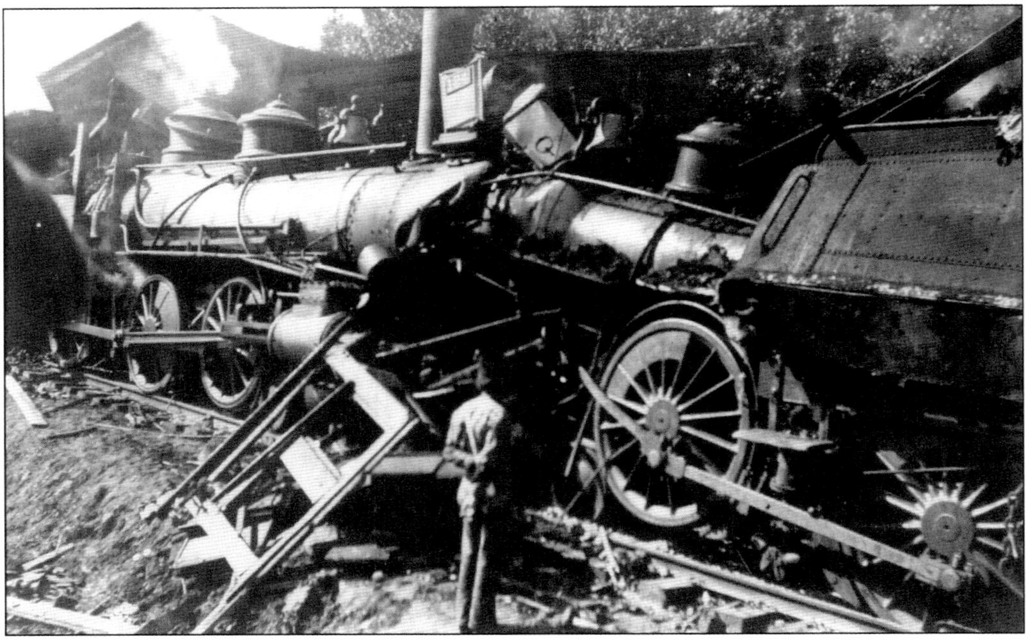

Train Wreck. Perry was a busy railroad community, and train wrecks were always a worry. In this wreck on the Chicago, Milwaukee and St. Paul Railroad line between Collins and Rhodes, Milwaukee Road train No. 92 crashed into a work train. Engineer Samuel Marckres of Perry and 10 others died in the crash.

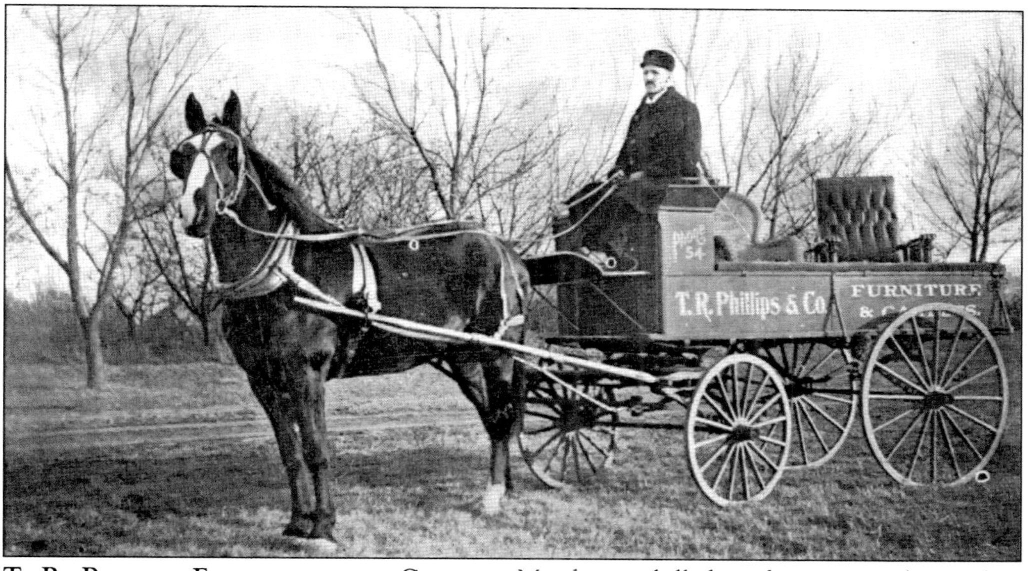

T. R. PHILLIPS FURNITURE AND CASKETS. Merchants skilled in furniture making often expanded their business to include making caskets. Furniture makers sometimes even served as funeral directors. T. R. Phillips came to Perry on February 1, 1894, to begin working with Gamble Furniture Store. He was in charge of its undertaking department for eight years when he decided to go into business for himself in 1902.

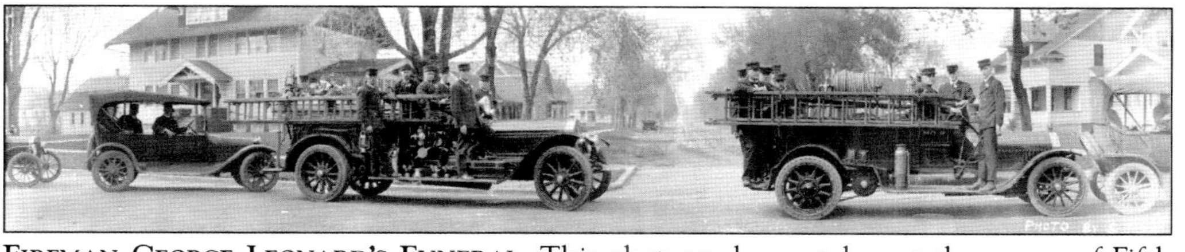

FIREMAN GEORGE LEONARD'S FUNERAL. This photograph was taken at the corner of Fifth and Warford Streets. George Leonard was a community leader who owned a building in the 1200 block of Second Street and volunteered with the fire department. His funeral was held at the Methodist church on May 13, 1917. Per his wishes, a fire truck carried his casket to Violet Hill Cemetery with volunteer firefighters as escorts.

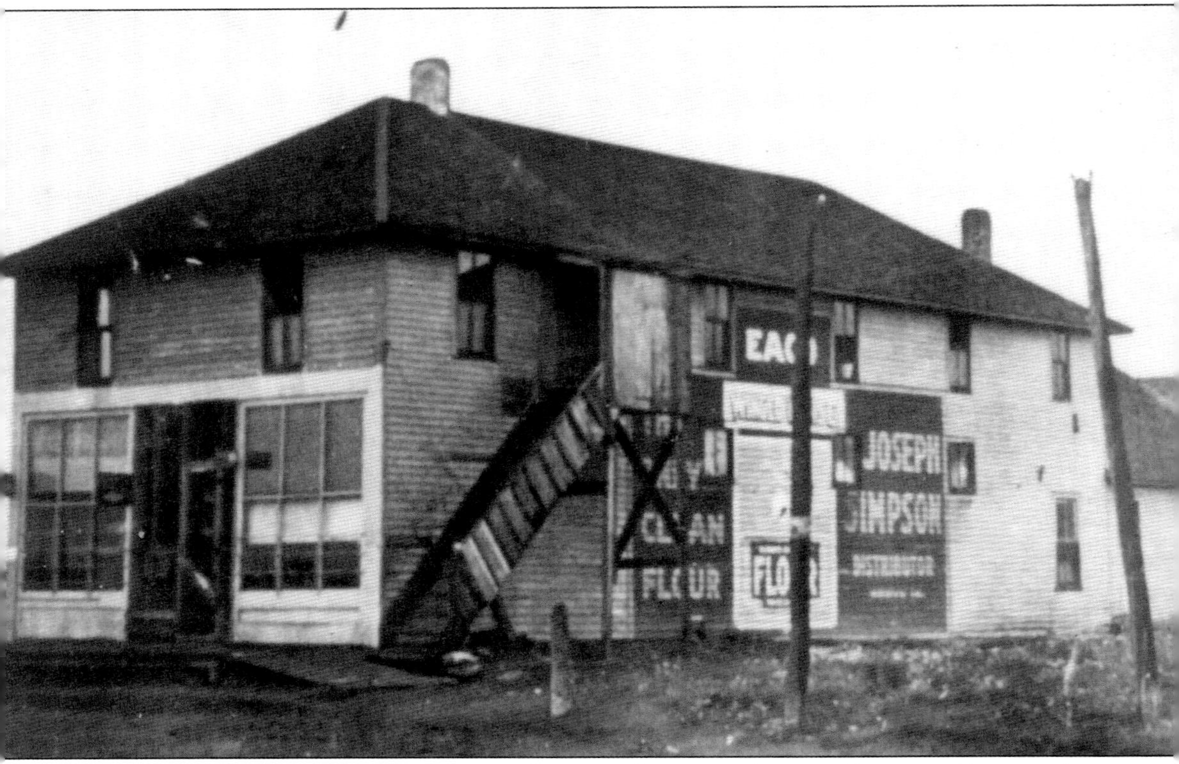

Thomas Hall Opera House and Simpson Store in Angus. Some small towns thrive, but not forever. Angus was such a town. It was a coal-mining town about four miles northwest of Perry but also served as a terminal for the Minneapolis and St. Louis Railroad. Although it thrived in the late 1800s, it died out by the early 1920s as the mines closed. Many of the houses there were moved to Perry. When its building was torn down in 1925, the Simpson Store was relocated to the north part of Angus.

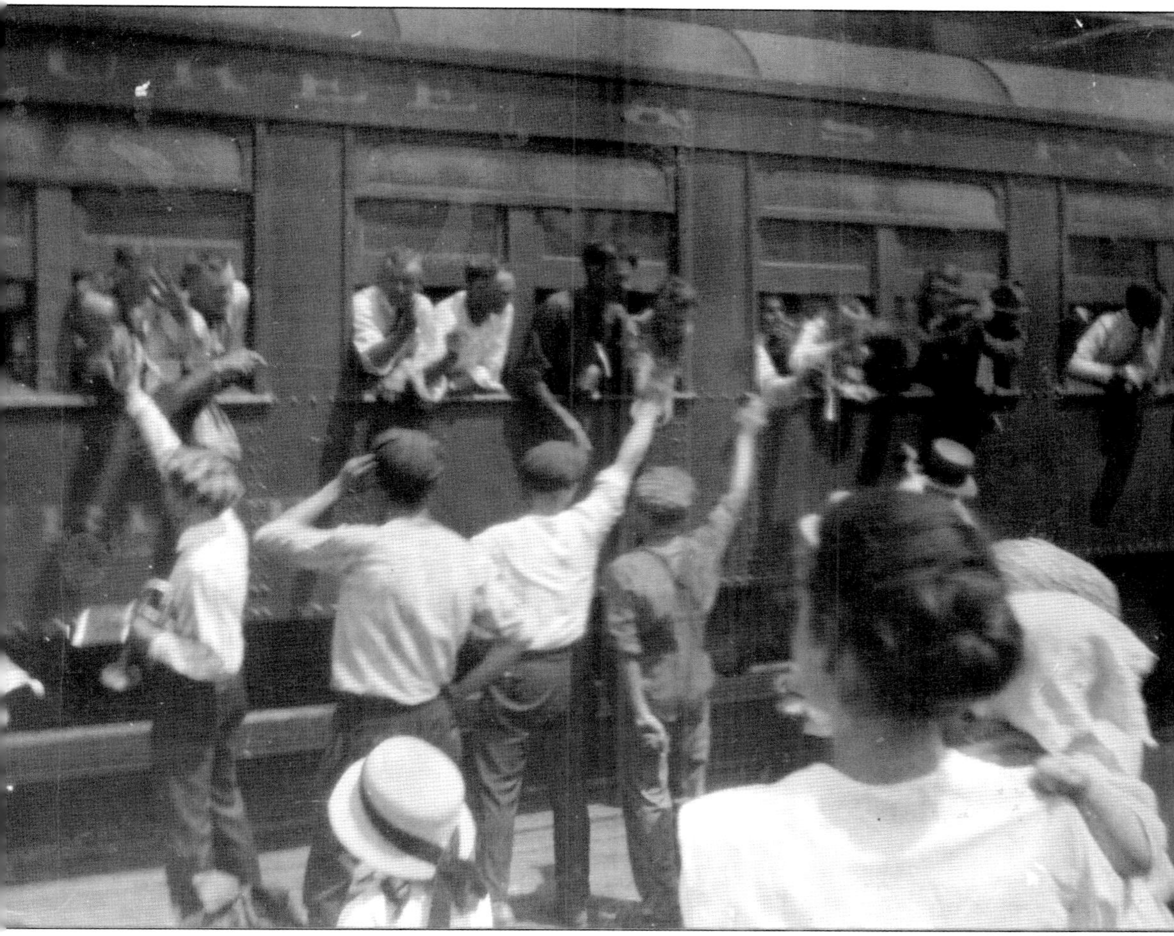

ARMY CONTINGENT LEAVING. Throughout the history of Perry, many residents served in the armed forces. Here an army contingent is leaving Perry around 1915.

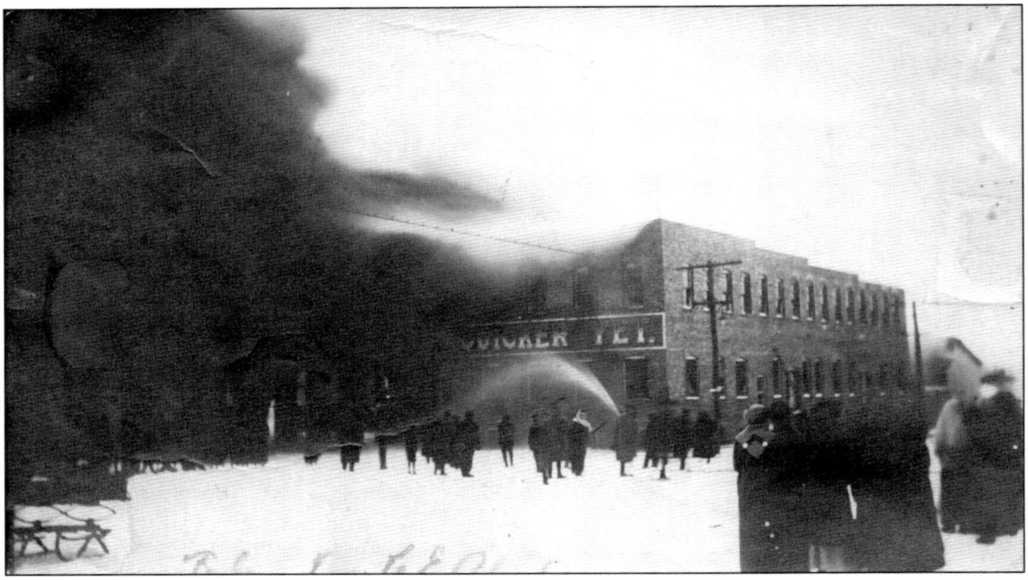

GLOBE MANUFACTURING COMPANY FIRE. Over time, fire has taken many buildings and businesses in Perry. It posed a particular threat when more buildings were built of wood and there was less equipment and manpower to fight the flames. Originally Perry had a bucket brigade to fight fires. A fire department was organized in 1879, and by 1880, Perry had a fire engine and engine house. In January 1915, fire destroyed the Globe Manufacturing Company building on West Second Street.

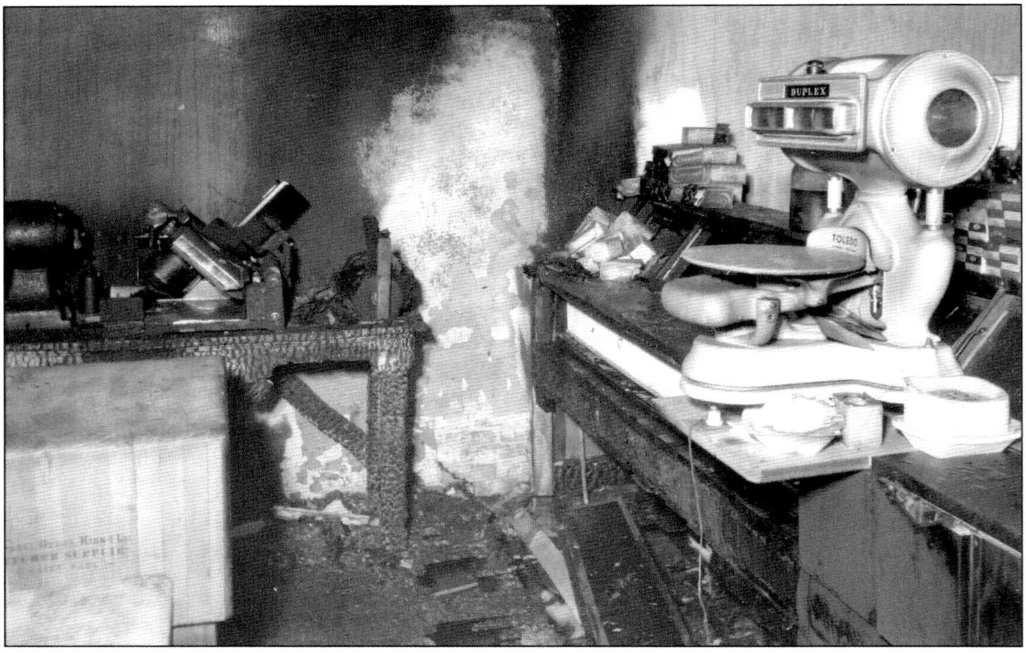

IGA STORE AFTER FIRE. Paul Seaton purchased this grocery, originally called Woods Food Store, in 1934. Located at 1217 Second Street, Seaton's store was affiliated with the Independent Grocers Association (IGA). In 1936, a fire greatly damaged the building.

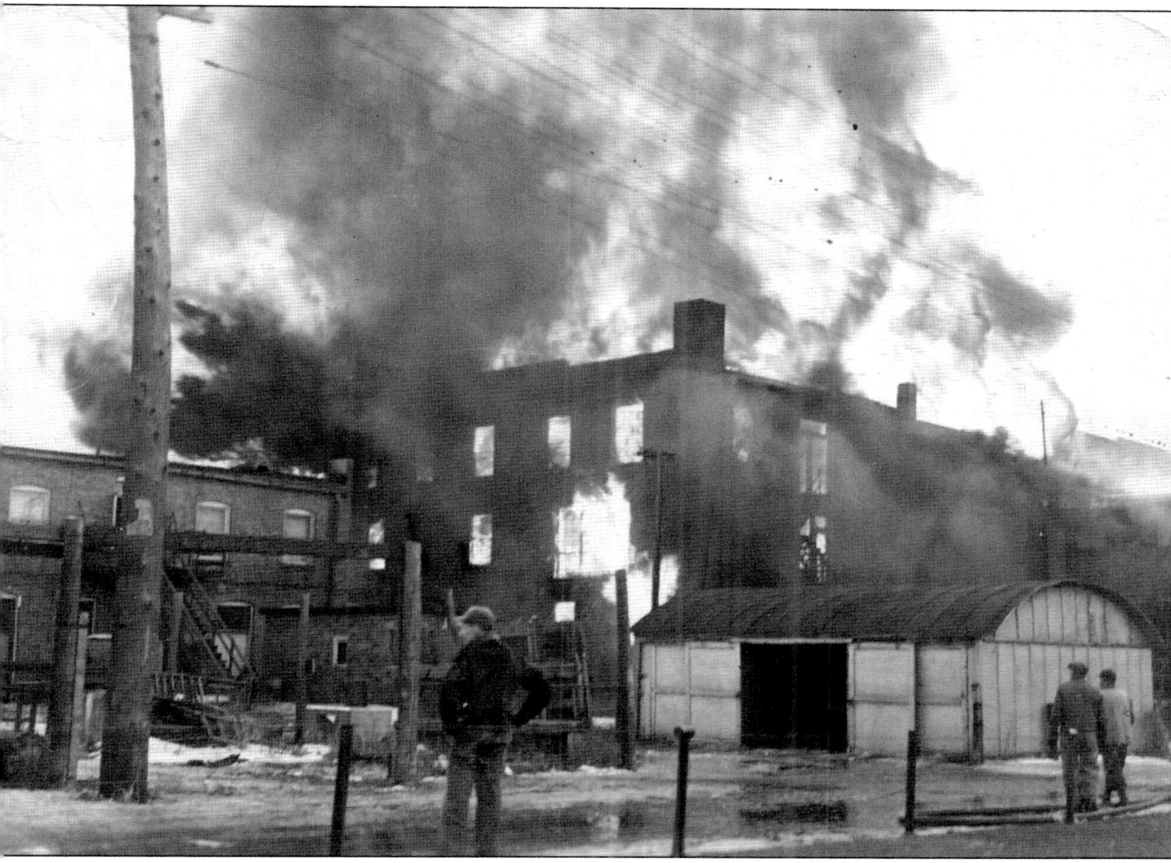

WOOLWORTH STORE FIRE. The F. W. Woolworth store and all its contents were destroyed by fire on February 12, 1945. The entire Carter Block at the corner of Second Street and Willis Avenue burned, for a loss estimated at between $150,000 and $200,000.

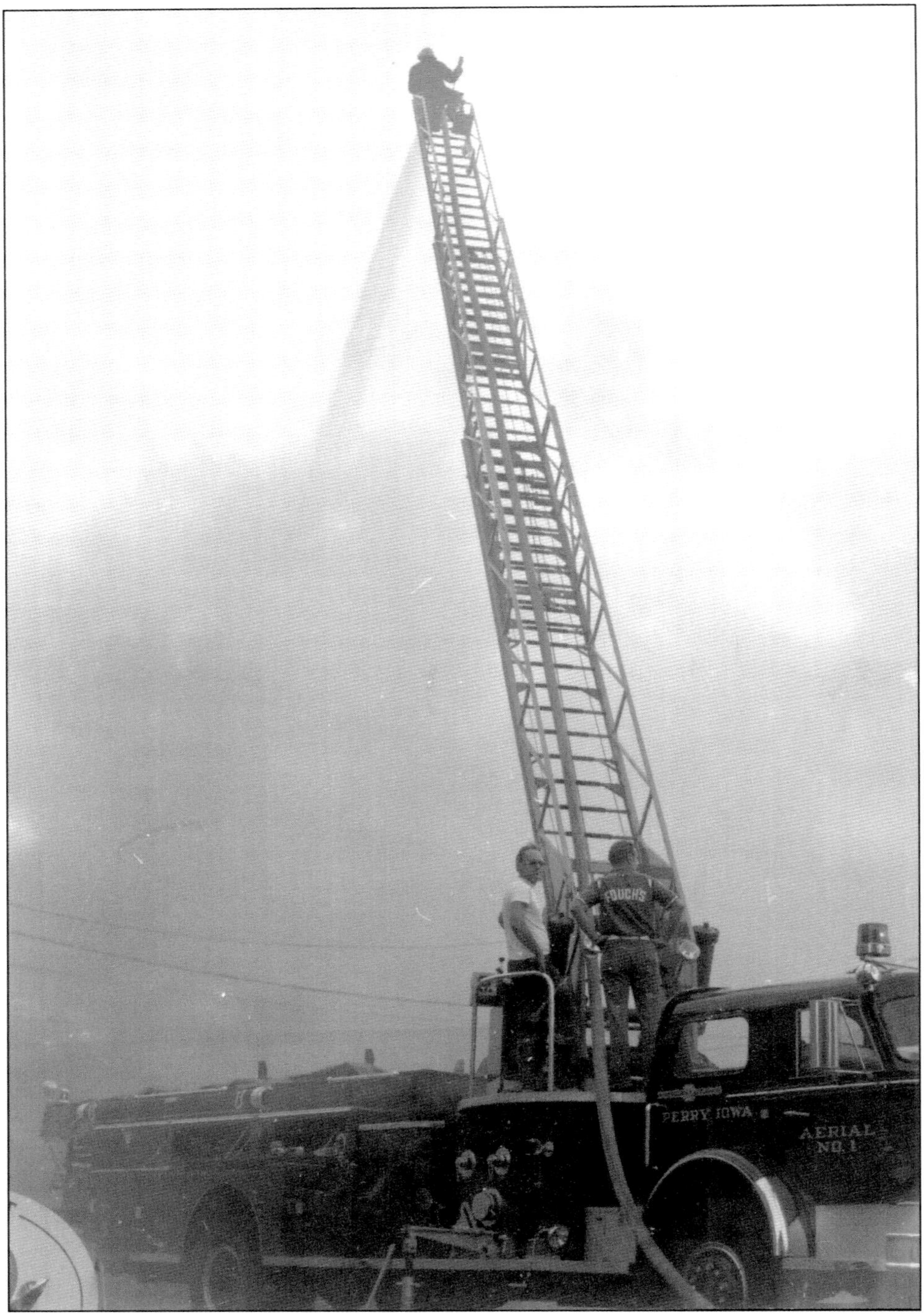

Perry Lockers Fire. The Perry Refrigerated Locker Company at 1114 First Avenue offered refrigerated space for freshly butchered beef, hogs, and other foods. Most people rented a locker to keep frozen meats after butchering or buying beef from a farmer. Some may have used their lockers for fruits and vegetables. The building caught fire on September 18, 1977, while workers were re-tarring the roof.

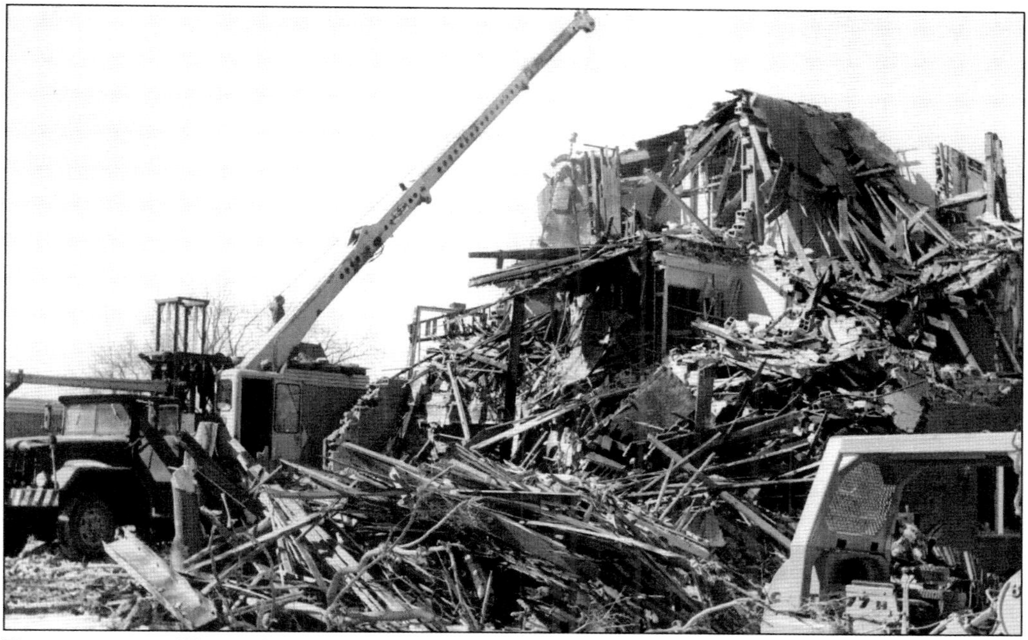

DEMOLITION OF KING'S DAUGHTERS HOSPITAL. As a town grows and changes, buildings change purpose and are often demolished. The former King's Daughters Hospital in Perry was torn down in 1978. It served the community as a hospital from 1914 to 1956 before it was converted to Perry Lutheran Home.

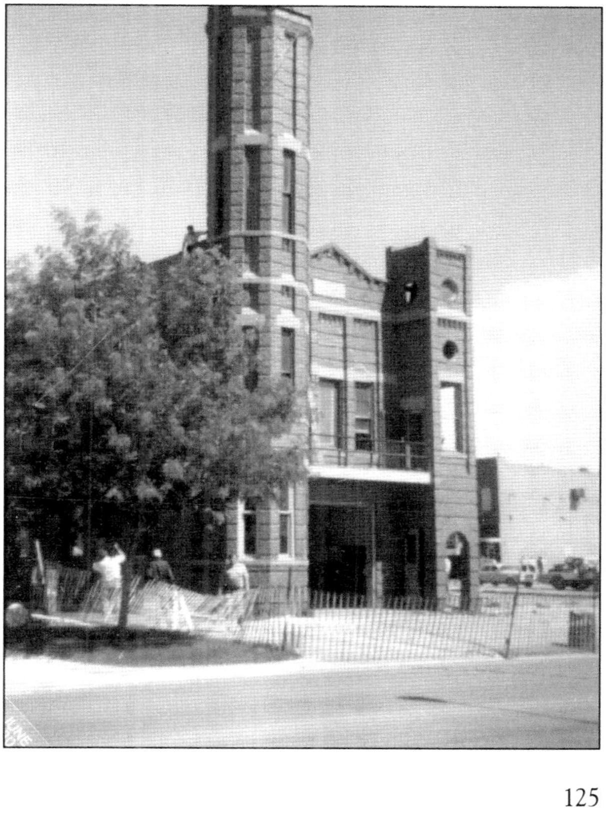

OLD PERRY FIRE STATION. This fire station, built in 1905, was named to the National Register of Historic Places in 1978. The Perry Fire Department was organized in 1879 with 15 members as a volunteer department. The building itself was demolished in 1979.

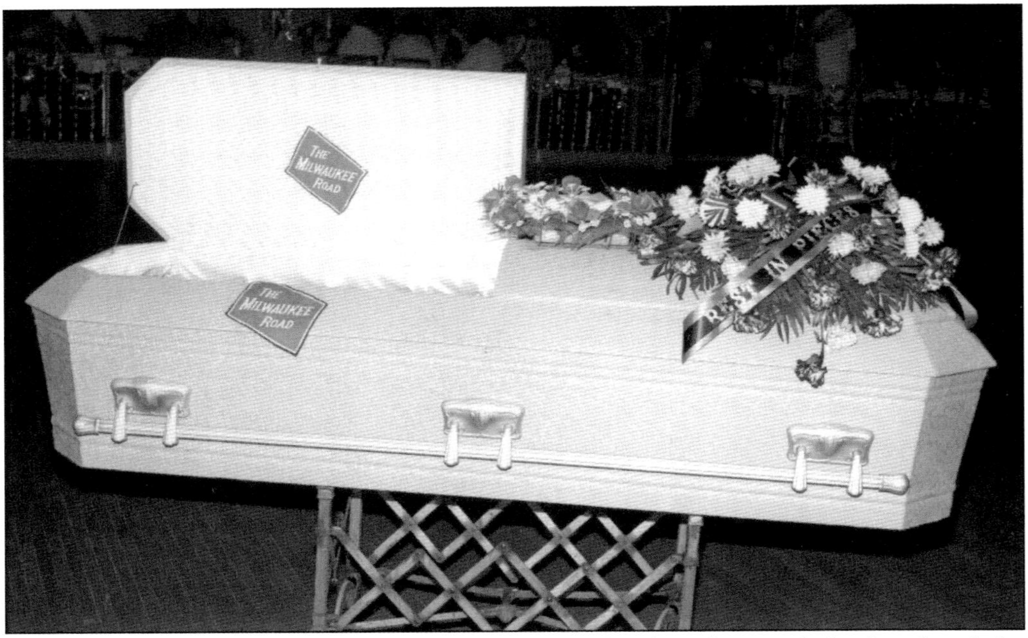

IOWA DIVISION, MILWAUKEE ROAD. Bringing the railroad to the area helped to found the town. The railroad existed in some format for more than 100 years. However, as the industry declined, the Milwaukee Road shut down its operation in 1980. This picture by Bill Ohde Photo in Manning commemorates the end of the Milwaukee Road line.

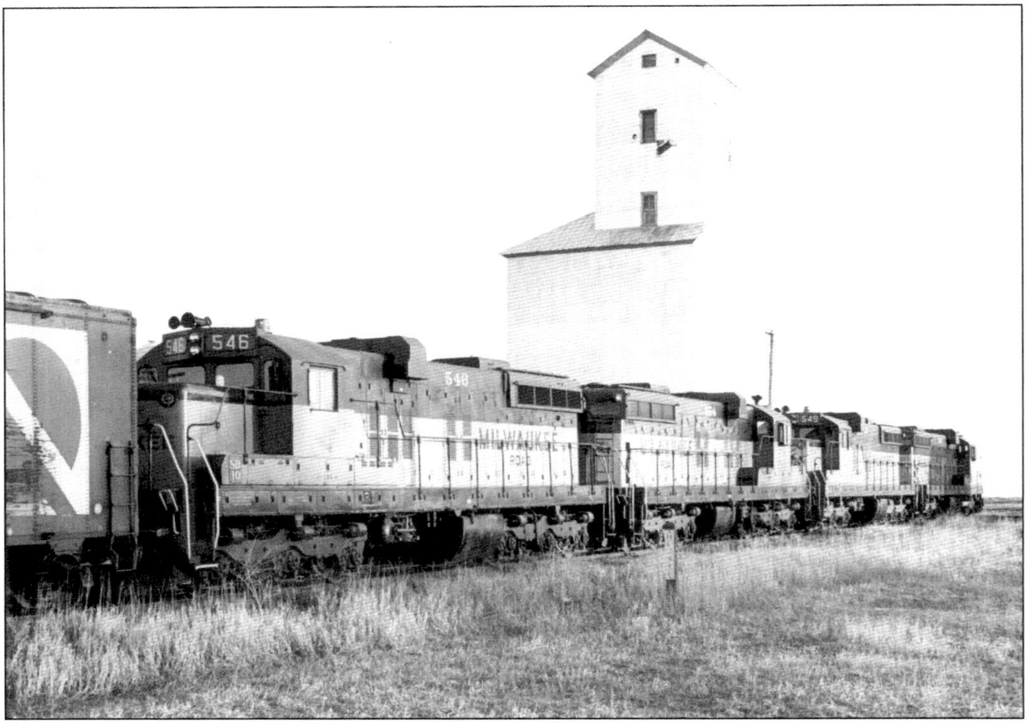

LAST MILWAUKEE GRAIN TRAIN. The last Milwaukee grain train went through Perry in 1980.

BIBLIOGRAPHY

Atherton, Lewis. *Main Street on the Middle Border.* Bloomington: Indiana University Press, 1984.

Comstock, Gary. "Grandma's Backbone, Dougie's Ankles." In *A Place of Sense: Essays in Search of the Midwest*, edited by Michael Martone. Iowa City: University of Iowa Press, 1988.

Morain, Thomas. *Prairie Grass Roots: An Iowa Small Town in the Early Twentieth Century.* Ames: Iowa State University Press, 1988.

Schwieder, Dorothy. *Iowa: The Middle Land.* Ames: Iowa State University Press, 1996.

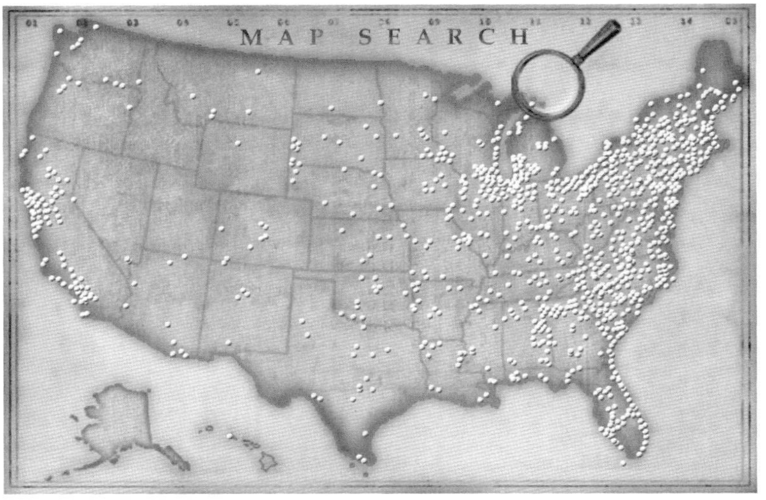
MAP SEARCH